Kristian Jebsens Rederi AS
Bergen

A Group History

By
W. J. Harvey

http://worldshipsociety.org

Other titles by the same author:

GLEN AND SHIRE LINE   In association with Malcolm Cooper and the late William Laxon.
The history of two companies, one of Scottish origin, the other Welsh, both trading along similar paths before being united in the downfall of the Royal Mail Group, to become part of the Liverpool based Alfred Holt & Company (Blue Funnel Line).
(Published by Ships in Focus Publications, Longton, 2005 - ISBN 1-901703-65-7)

BP: A Group Fleet History.   In association with Dr. Ray Solly.
A profusely illustrated history of this multi-faceted fleet of over 1,000 vessels be they owned outright, or through subsidiary and associate companies. The work also details the development of the tanker in parallel with the growth of the group since inception as the Anglo-Persian Oil Company.
(Published by Chatham Publishing Ltd., London, 2005 - ISBN 1-86176-251-6)

ARKLOW SHIPPING
A profusely colour-illustrated fleet history of the ever-expanding, Arklow based shipping group, from 1966, including their formative companies and now including a Netherlands based subsidiary.
(Published by Bernard McCall, Portishead, 2004 - ISBN 1-902953-15-0)

SHAMROCK SHIPPING – Including the David Dorman Group.
The history of two Irish based companies from 1888 and 1881 respectively, through unification to today's much diminished shipping activity.   (Published by The World Ship Society Ltd., Windsor, 2004 - ISBN 0 9543310 -3-6)

SAFMARINE - The South African Marine Corporation Ltd – A Group History.
In association with C. R. Mackenzie.
The history of the Cape Town based company from 1946 until its 1999 dismantling and sale.
(Published by The World Ship Society, Gravesend, 2002 - ISBN 0 905617-98-3)

THE CLYDE SHIPPING COMPANY   In association with P. J. Telford.
The history of the Glasgow based company from 1815 until its 2000 acquisition by Cory Towage Ltd.
(Published by P. J. Telford, Canterbury, 2002 - ISBN 0 9542527-0-5)

CORY TOWAGE LTD – A Group History
The history of the company and their owned, managed, and chartered vessels, together with the fleets of their subsidiary and associated companies.
(Published by The World Ship Society, Gravesend, 2000 - ISBN 0 905617-93-2)

SHIPS IN FOCUS – BLUE FUNNEL LINE   In association with John Clarkson and Roy Fenton.
A pictorial fleet history of the Liverpool based shipping group.
(Published by Ships in Focus Publications, Longton, 1998 - ISBN 1 901703-00-2)

HADLEY
The history of the Hadley Shipping Company Ltd., and their associate companies.
(Published by The World Ship Society, Gravesend, 1997 - ISBN 0 905617-83-5)

HEAD LINE (G. Heyn & Sons Ltd.)
The history of the Ulster Steamship Company Ltd. and their associate companies.
(Published by The World Ship Society, Kendal, 1990 - ISBN 0 905617-53-3)

STENA (1939 – 1989)
The first fifty years of the Swedish controlled multi-national shipping and trading group.
(Published by Stena Ab, Gothenburg, 1990 - ISBN 91 85786-411)

EMPIRE TUGS   In association with Ken Turrell.
The history of the EMPIRE prefixed, British Government tugs, introduced during WW 2
(Published by The World Ship Society, Kendal, 1988 - ISBN 0 905617-47-9)

Contents

Acknowledgements 4
Foreword By Atle Jebsen 5
The Company 6
    The Formative Years 6
    A Change of Direction 9
    Cultivated Growth 14
    Rough Weather Ahead 22
    Riding The Storm 27
    Restructuring 31
The Fleet 36
    Notes On The Individual Ship Histories 36
    Kristian Jebsens Rederi AS 37
    Jebsen – Hartmann Carriers 178
    Time- Charters 186
A Selection Of General Arrangement Plans 207
Bibliography 218
Key to Funnels On Back Cover 218
Ship Index 219

Published in the United Kingdom

by

The World Ship Society Ltd.,

Mayes House, Vansittart Estate, Arthur Road, Windsor SL4 1SE.

© 2005 W. J. Harvey and The World Ship Society Ltd.

All rights reserved. No part of this work may be reproduced, stored in a retrieval system or transmitted in any form or by means, electronic, mechanical, photocopying, recording or otherwise, without the written permission of the publisher.

The right of W. J. Harvey to be identified as the author of this work has been asserted by him in accordance with the Copyright, Design and Patent Act 1998.

ISBN 0 – 9543310-6-0

Typeset by The Highlight Type Bureau Ltd., 2, Clifton Villas, Bradford, BD8 7BY.
Printed by The Amadeus Press, Ezra House, West 26 Business Park, Cleckheaton, BD19 4TQ.

Acknowledgements

During my 24-years of intermittent research into this company, I have been greatly assisted by many people and organisations. It is therefore only fitting that I offer my sincere thanks to them. If anyone has been overlooked then please also accept my thanks.

LLOYDS REGISTER OF SHIPPING, 71, Fenchurch Street, London.

Information Department

Barbara Jones and **Anne Cowne**
The information department at Lloyds Register is a gold mine of information for the researcher, especially if they visit and undertake their own research. It is open, office hours, Monday to Friday, and apart from other publications they boast a complete run of Lloyds Register books, many posted and all laid out on shelving rather than in a basement archive, as in so many other establishments, where it is necessary to order in batches. The aforementioned staff are extremely knowledgeable in their business and more than willing to advise of supplementary sources of information.

Maritime Information Publishing Group,

Leslie Spurling, Richard Pryde, Peter Brazier and **Chris Cheetham** for permitting my reference to the confidential shipbuilding records data to confirm or in a few cases, correct my own researched shipbuilding information. No less helpful than the information department, although their information is always subjected to confidentiality constraints. The activities undertaken by this department of Lloyds Register have recently been merged with those of Fairplay and as such have moved south of the Thames to Redhill are now restyled as Lloyds Register Fairplay Ltd.

WORLD SHIP SOCIETY

The late **Rowan Hackman** for his unstinting help with launch dates and other snippets of information from his personal archives. A real gentleman, now sadly missed. The relevant period custodians of the Members Questions team, and especially **Tony Smith** of the Photograph Library.

JEBSEN GROUP.

Atle Jebsen, and **Johs Sletheug,** Bergen, for taking time out from their busy schedule to willingly read and corroborate the manuscript, **Ole Stene**, Bergen, for answering my numerous queries and his supply of additional information, photographs and group literature and also **John Small**, of Jebsens (UK) Ltd., for likewise taking time out to meet with me at an early stage, supplying me with much information and putting me in touch with the Bergen Headquarters.

PHOTOGRAPHS

Photographs used for illustrations are credited to their source, where known. If unknown it is quoted as Author's Collection.

FOTOFLITE

A recognised source of extremely good quality, aerial photographs. Their unstinting help with checking their catalogue against my shopping list and providing one off prints to the size I requested, rather than their standard sizes, was of extreme benefit. Fortunately for them and myself they have since gone electronic, so enabling the buyer to peruse their library at leisure.

Foreword By Atle Jebsen

Kristian Jebsens Rederi AS (KJR) has over the 76 years of its existence owned, leased and chartered many ships. Bill Harvey has, in an excellent way, managed to list and comment on all the vessels that have been under control of KJR all these years.

I am very impressed with Bill's dedication and enthusiasm for exploring the history of the KJR Group. The book gives very practical and exact information about the fleet of KJR.

I would like to thank Bill Harvey for his dedication to this work, and for such an outstanding result of his efforts.

This book will no doubt be a very interesting and useful source of information, both for the Jebsen family, for Jebsens employees – past and present – as well as for all our customers and associates, and all others with an interest in the KJR Group.

Sincerely yours,

Atle Jebsen

Bergen
July 2005.

The Company
The Formative Years

When the name Jebsen is mentioned in the bulk carrier fraternity minds automatically think of Bergen and the Norwegian based Jebsen companies. One cannot fault that train of thought but, when the Jebsen family tree is consulted the picture is not quite so clear cut.

The story begins further south, in fact in Holstein in Denmark. It was there that the Jebsen family originated and remained until 1842 when Peter Jebsen ventured north to Norway. Shortly after his arrival he became aware of the potential for water-power and wasted little time in setting up a textile factory at Arna, north of Bergen. Following upon his success with his venture he persuaded two of his brothers to join him in Norway and soon a second textile factory was opened near Bergen. The factories remained Norway's two largest textile businesses for a considerable time. Peter Jebsen meanwhile had developed his business interests, investing in building and shipowning activities.

Amongst Peter Jebsens descendants was his Grandson Kristian S. Jebsen, born in 1901. Kristian had been educated in Norway and by the late 1920's had also become well educated, both in England and Norway, in the many aspects of shipping.

Despite a dramatic slump in World trade forcing many shipowners to place their ships into lay-up to await a possible upturn in the market place, Kristian Jebsen set about the task of persuading potential investors that there were still profits to be made even during a recession.

It was an uphill struggle as Kristian had little capital resources of his own. Being held in high regard, in part through Family reputation but in the main, through his strength of character, he by the age of 28, had succeeded in raising, 800,000 Kroner (then, about £40,000). Using that raised capital during 1929, he founded Kristian Jebsens Rederi AS, with their Headquarters in Bergen.

Kristian S. Jebsen – Founder of the Jebsens Group of companies. (Courtesy of Atle Jebsen)

That new company placed orders for two 2,500 dwt single-deck ships for operation in the North Sea trades. Named **VIGSNES** and **GARNES** they were reasonably cheap to construct due to the recession in World trade and entered service during 1930. As would be expected at the time, freight rates were also at an all-time low but the reputation and knowledge of Kristian enabled the company to pick up and combine enough cargoes to minimise ballast voyages. Operating within slender margins the ships sailed both outward and homeward at near full capacity enabling the enterprise to make ends meet and survive, if only just. The funnel markings were black with a broad white band approximately two-thirds up from the base, on which was a broad black wavy band.

DS AS NOR (founded 1915) in 1935, was taken into partnership / management and as trade began a slow recovery two further vessels were constructed in 1936. Completed as **KORSNES** and **TELNES**, they were jointly owned by Kristian Jebsens Rederi AS and DS AS NOR. Kristian however was not a person to speculate and moved only when all risks had been carefully calculated. His philosophy was one of proceeding logically, step by step, not putting himself into the position of winning or losing everything in one throw, and moreover, never being clever at the expense of his clients and thus jeopardising future relationships.

The company continued to develop steadily, operating from offices located at Torvalmenning 8, Bergen, but war was just around the corner and when it arrived it was to totally disrupt the fleet.

VIGSNES (Jebsens)

In January 1940, **TELNES** departed from New York bound to Antwerp and Rotterdam but failed to arrive and, believed to have succumbed to the elements, she was subsequently posted as "Missing presumed lost". Two vessels **VIGSNES** and **GARNES**, escaped capture when Germany invaded Norway in April 1940. **KORSNES** was not so fortunate, being taken by the invading forces and operated by them until late in 1944 when she was sunk by Allied aircraft bombing at Narvik. She was however raised in 1945 and towed to Bergen for repairs but never re-entered company service. She was sold whilst under repair during 1946, with the agreed delivery being upon completion of repairs in 1947.

Meanwhile, with a two-vessel fleet the company strove for survival, and a partnership / management agreement with AS Finn Johnsens, another Norwegian company, saw their vessel **AUN** enter the fleet during 1941. **VIGSNES** was taken on charter by the British Government's Ministry of War Transport during 1943 and was placed under management of J. A. Bilmeir & Company, of Cardiff. That arrangement lasted until January 1945 when shortly after returning to Kristian Jebsens control she was lost to a German submarine in the Irish Sea so that, at armistice, a fleet of only

GARNES as owned, and the managed **AUN** was being operated but that too was to alter as **GARNES** also became an indirect war loss when she exploded a loose mine and sank off Terschelling in March 1946.

Such was the reputation of Kristian Jebsen, coupled with the financial strength of company, they were able to start rebuilding the fleet from within their own resources, something not many small companies could do. Initially, **VIGSNES** was ordered from J. Crown & Sons Ltd., Sunderland, for delivery during 1948, whilst the managed **AUN** was sold for further trading the same year. A contract at an Italian shipyard for another Norwegian owner was purchased for completion as **GARNES** in 1948.

Having studied market trends carefully Kristian foresaw the increase of oil as a major commodity requiring sea transport and the decision was taken to digress into the tanker trade. Orders for two "larger than standard" vessels were placed in Britain for delivery by the Clyde yard of Lithgows during 1949 and 1951. September 1949 saw **ALTNES**, a traditional three-island type vessel with machinery and accommodation aft and navigation-bridge forward, delivered by Lithgows. She was delivered with a grey hull that was subsequently changed to black with the new funnel markings of yellow with a broad, black edged, white band approximately two-thirds up from the base, on which was a broad black wavy band. As stated earlier **ALTNES** was somewhat larger than the traditional tanker of the day giving her an edge in securing cargoes. She was followed into service by **TELNES** a slightly larger vessel delivered by Lithgows in November 1951. With that vessel the pattern was set for the use of "T" names for the tankers henceforth entering the fleet. A replacement **AUN** was ordered by AS Finn Johnsens for delivery during 1952 and when delivered Kristian Jebsens Rederi AS were appointed as Technical Managers. With the new fleet of two cargo vessels and two tankers the company slowly regained business whilst their reputation also continued to grow in parallel. An opportunity for controlled expansion arose during 1954, wherein a second-hand cargo vessel was purchased from other Norwegian owners and renamed **KORSNES**.

Keeping a watchful-eye on World affairs during 1955, Kristian foresaw the disruption in the Middle East causing problems with the Suez Canal and immediately fixed **TELNES** with a long-term charter at a minimum freight rate, that being adjustable upwards according to market fixtures. He also placed orders in Norway and Japan for new, slightly larger tankers for delivery in 1957. Those moves proved visionary as tanker rates began to rise rapidly. Whilst under construction Kristian fixed both new tankers with long-term charters, commencing upon their delivery. His other charters were reported, at the time as being profitable but not at excessive levels.

Toward the end of the 1950's Kristian was looking at the aspects of transporting commodities such as coal, grain, fertilisers, sugar etc, in bulk, utilising purpose built vessels. Once again, seen in a pioneering role, he placed orders, initially for two such vessels for delivery during 1962. Those vessels were designed to lift larger than normal cargoes on a shallow draft thus enabling them to enter smaller ports otherwise prohibitive for such large cargoes. His philosophy had led him to believe that the shipowner was only one link in the production chain and ought to look further than his own interests. The shipowner was of course running his own business but when carrying cargo he had become part of someone elses business as well. The other party in turn, would regard the transportation of raw materials as a stage in their production line and as such want it to be managed efficiently and predictably. Such a person would favour ships that carry their goods as cheaply as possible and would also favour long term contracts. Although the price of such an arrangement may be higher than desired, it would enable them to plan well ahead with the knowledge of what their costs would be. Such arrangements were well suited to Kristian's developing style of operation.

A Change of Direction

In 1959 offices were relocated to Bradbenken 1, Postboks 413 – 415 Bergen, and in 1960 a sister to the Italian built **KORSNES** was purchased, again from other Norwegian owners, being renamed **RAKNES**.

Two bulk carriers were ordered from Lithgows Ltd., on the Clyde, that being the catalyst for a major undertaking between the company and the Clyde shipyards over the next decade. These orders were placed during a period of depression in the world market, and as such the company was able to negotiate a "favourable price" as shipyards clamoured for all available work. Whilst under construction Kristian set about arranging either long or short term Contract of Affreightments for their employment, and such was his success that a third vessel was ordered.

British Titan Products Ltd., was a company with which Jebsens had a long standing association since the 1930's. Kristian had spelled out the details of his new vessels, and had successfully agreed charter-terms with them. They required titan ore transporting from eastern and western Australia, where ports were shallow and cargoes normally around 10,000 tons maximum, and also from Canada. The new vessels were ideally suited as they could load half as much again, thereby reducing costs. Two cargoes would equate to three in normal vessels. The new vessels, and their successors, were able to enter many small inlets and ports to gather-up several small batches of this rare and expensive cargo before departing for the U.K. That arrangement also suited the customer as the expensive commodity now being transported in regular size shipments, arriving just before requirement also reduced capital being tied up in stockpiles.

BERNES   (Author's collection)

The initial two vessels were delivered to the Norwegian parent company as **BRUNES** and **BERNES**, on schedule, in 1962. Those names commenced a long line of bulk vessels with names starting with the letter "B", reportedly B = bulk. The third was delivered as **BRIMNES**, in 1963. She however was placed in the ownership of the British subsidiary Tenax Steam Ship Company Ltd., which was located at 9, Basinghall Street, London. That company had been owned by Norwegian interests Odfjell Rederi, Bergen and was taken over by Kristian Jebsens Rederi AS, as the majority shareholder, in partnership with AS Investa.

Speaking at the hand-over ceremony on 6 April 1962, aboard **BERNES**, Sir James Lithgow BT, Chairman of Lithgows Ltd., extolled her virtues. He predicted her type as being the tramp of the future, stating "These are the message boys of the future and the vessels their bicycle 'jack of all trades' and British tramp ship owners would do well to consider it seriously." Whilst urging British tramp owners to begin replacing their out of date 'tween deck vessels having accommodation amidship and build similar vessels he praised the Norwegians for having his foresight and ordering the vessels and modernising their fleet at bargain prices. Also aboard was Kristian Jebsen who stated that his first vessel of the type **BRUNES** was in service and that he believed her 15,000 tons deadweight carrying capacity would become the popular size to replace the ageing "Liberty" type ship. He went on to say that ships of that economical type, he thought, would create their own trade being that they were extremely flexible. Her design enabled varied cargoes to be transported. Grain could be carried in self trimming, hopper-type holds, without a need for shifting boards, whilst she could carry a wide variety of other bulk commodities in the holds and packaged timber on deck. To generate such a generous carrying capacity her side tanks were angled upward at 30 degrees with corrugated sides thus providing the hopper effect for the holds. These tanks, used for ballast, were accessible through hatches on the main deck when carrying grain. No.1 hold deep tank also provided for water ballast whilst her double bottom tanks provided oil fuel storage and further water ballast areas. That design resulted in a minimal space requirement for the engine-room and accommodation that was placed well aft. Her generators were mounted on rubber pads to reduce the associated vibration leading to a quieter crew accommodation.

Younger son Atle Jebsen, meanwhile, had entered the family business during 1962. Born at Bergen on 10 November 1935, he was educated in Norway before attending Queen's College, Cambridge, where he successfully attained his degree in economics. Thereafter, he spent 5-years training in ship broking offices in Oslo, Hamburg and New York before joining the company, shortly after which AS Finn Johnsens Rederi ceased trading in 1963. Their one ship **AUN** was purchased by Kristian Jebsens Rederi AS, and renamed **LEKNES** to bring her into line with the Jebsen style of names ending in NES. Also in this year Kristian Gerhard Jebsen chose to split away from the family business to forge his own path in the shipping fraternity.

Gearbulk

In 1963 elder son, Kristian Gerhard Jebsen established his own company - Kristian Gerhard Jebsen Skipsrederi AS, operating from Markevei 2A, Postboks 387, Bergen. This new company initially speciallised in cement transportation and subsequently ordered a liquified gas carrier. In the early 1970's he joined forces with Louis Dreyfus et Cie, Paris; Buries Markes Ltd, London; and Mowinckels of Norway, to build and operate a fleet of varying sizes of bulk carriers under the auspices of GEARBULK. That company was then operated in similar markets as the original Jebsen organisation. The GEARBULK consortium lasted until 1991 when it was dissolved with the majority of the vessels being purchased by Kristian Gerhard Jebsen under the auspices of individual owning companies, the ships all having ARROW as a suffix to their names - **PUFFIN ARROW, RAVEN ARROW** etc. However the GEARBULK trading name continued to be used for the K.G. Jebsen operation.

H. Clarkson & Company Ltd., a well-known London based ship owner / broker were increasingly becoming involved in the business of ship leasing and financing for other operators. At the end of 1964 they agreed to finance a series of "handysize" bulk carriers to be part-owned by or leased to Kristian Jebsens Rederi AS, but in whichever case to be operated within the Jebsen Bulk Pool. Due to the success of the earlier bulk trio within the fleet, the company returned without hesitation to the Clyde for this series of improved-design vessels.

ALTNES (World Ship Society Photograph Library)

Also ordered around this time were the first of a series of small cargo vessels to be built by Fr. Lürssen at Bremen, Germany. These were for delivery over a prolonged period, each being an improvement of the earlier units. The first of these small vessels – **ALTNES** of 3,450 dwt – replaced the first tanker of the same name, that having been deemed obsolescent was sold due to the rapid increase in tanker size on the World market. Two sistervessels, **GARNES** and **KORSNES**, were delivered at the end of 1965 and early 1966, whilst **BINSNES**, a larger 16,900 dwt bulk carrier was ordered from Scott's on the Clyde by Clarksons together with an option for a sister. That option however was not taken, having been replaced with another firm order for **BOLNES**, a still larger vessel of 19,800 dwt, that being followed by two orders, both for a pair of 19,710 dwt sisters.

The Investment Grant Scheme

In January 1966 the then British Labour Government, wanting to increase industrial investment generally, introduced a scheme offering companies Investment Grants in cash. The initial rate was 20%, but that was jacked up to 25% the following year. Those grants applied as much to ships as other plant and machinery. Loosely speaking, that meant in the case of a ship, with a 75% bank loan and a cash grant of 25% little capital was required for an established company and it was hardly surprising therefore that a tempting proposition like this attracted many takers.

A considerable number of British shipowners took advantage of the scheme. It was not even a requirement to build in a U. K. shipyard and inventive minds overseas, particularly in Scandinavia, were soon jumping on the band wagon and forming British companies to join in the bonanza.

In all between January 1966, when they were introduced, and September 1969 the total of investment grants paid or due to be paid amounted to some £285 million, which translated into newbuilding orders totalled around £800 million, a lot of money in those days.

That was equivilent to replacing no less than 40% of the national fleet. But of the £285 million paid in grants no less than £91 million was in respect of ships ordered by U.K. companies controlled by non-residents.

Although the rate was reduced back to 20% in 1969, it took the publication of Lord Rochdale's 1970 Report on the Shipping Industry and a White Paper by the newly elected Conservative Government under Edward Heath to conclude that Investments Grants were "too expensive and inefficient". They were abolished forthwith.

The sale of tankers **TELNES** and **TORNES** during 1965 was once again, due to their being outsized in the marketplace. Their sale was closely followed by the delivery of **BOLNES**, the first of the second series of five Clyde built bulkers that had been ordered under the British Government's "Investment Grant Scheme", both by the company and their associates. Although **BOLNES** had been ordered jointly by the Tenax Steam Ship Company Ltd., and H. Clarkson & Company, she was launched and completed for the shipbuilders own account and placed under Tenax Steam Ship Company Ltd, management. That transaction came about when the shipbuilder decided to finance one of the ships for operation within the Jebsen Pool as a potential source of additional profits in the longer term.

Faced with the dilemma of the tanker fleet continually being outmoded by the unrelenting increase in size of new vessels, the company decided to order a new large 80,000 dwt vessel, with the intention of placing themselves slightly ahead in size and get longevity service from her. The name **TELNES** was revived for the new tanker, which had her size quickly increased so that when she joined the fleet in 1966, she entered the annals of company history. Firstly at just shy of 90,000 dwt, she took, and has to this day held the record of being the largest ship ever owned. Secondly she was the last tanker to be built for, and operated by the company.

Tragedy struck both the Jebsen Family and company in 1967, when Kristian S. Jebsen was killed in a train crash in Upper State of New York. The Jebsen company henceforth became controlled by his younger son Atle Jebsen who, as the newly appointed Chief Executive Officer, set about consolidating the business. The Tenax Steam Ship Company Ltd. moved their offices to Bloomfield House, 85 London Wall, London, whilst the parent company entered a new aspect of the business when they began also taking suitable vessels on long-term charter, to supplement their own fleet. One such W. German trio were designated the "Fiducia class". Within a short period their owners were acquired by Jebsens thus creating a W. German base.

FIDUCIA   April 1974 with blue funnel – outward from Rotterdam.   (J. K. Byass)

Jebsens meanwhile had commenced trading with coal from Longyearbyen, Svalbard in 1965 and in 1968, took over the business and continue to be the sole coal-trader on Svalbard. A new coal-mine was opened at Svea in 2001 and Jebsens signed a 15-year shipping and logistics contract with the coal company Store Norske Spitsbergen Grubecompani AS. Hitherto this time the largest ship trading coal was 20,000 dwt, but the contract is currently being serviced with ships from 6,000 up to 80,000 dwt, exclusively by Jebsens. Of the annual production of around 3 million tons, about 80% is being transported in Panamax size vessels, being so named because they are of the maximum size able to transit the Panama Canal. Also in 1968 Jebsens acquired Erling Mortensen AS of Oslo. This concern operated successfully as brokers and henceforth would also act on behalf of its new owners, whilst retaining a position of competition in the open marketplace. Acquisitions are usually balanced by disposals and **TINNES** was sold upon completion of her charter in 1968 followed somewhat surprisingly by **TELNES** a year later, after only three years service with the company. The decision to dispose of tanker operations was taken as a result of the Suez War which had blocked the canal, the very situation which had been used to company benefit during the mid 1950's. The problem this time was that such was the world demand for oil, that to maintain the supply routes "Very Large Crude Carriers" (VLCC's) were planned by the oil companies to combat the closure of the Suez Canal. Each of the planned new giants could replace up to three vessels of the **TELNES** size or ten of the **TINNES** size. Having hitherto maintained a small tanker operation, Jebsens basically could not afford the capital investment to build and operate the size of tanker proposed and as such decided to concentrate on the dry bulk market. A new livery was also being gradually introduced for the fleet wherein hulls were repainted in a slate grey colour instead of the light grey or black older style. Coupled with the withdrawal from tanker trades came the decision to revert to the original black and white funnel marking that lasted until 1974 when black and white gave way to blue and white in similar proportions.

RAKNES approaching Eastham Locks on the Mersey (W. J. Harvey)

Meanwhile, the first unit of a modified "Altnes" class vessel was introduced following assessment in service. This slightly larger 4,330 dwt, type were designated the "**RAKNES** class". The basic changes were to the forecastle, poop and quarterdeck areas removing much of the rake. Another single 4,440 dwt unit was built as **TELNES** but although designated an "Altnes class" she looked more like the "Raknes class". She was also unique in having a bulbous bow.

Cultivated Growth

Being totally satisfied with past performance wherein all vessels delivered to Jebsens by the Scottish shipyards since 1961 were either on time or ahead of schedule, Jebsens, in a rare display of confidence took the bold decision not to opt for competitive tender, but to go straight to the shipbuilder in question. Orders were therefore placed with Lithgows by the Jebsen / Clarkson consortium for the "Baugnes class", an updated and modified version of the second generation of Clyde bulkers. Some of those orders were sub-contracted by Lithgows to the Scott Shipbuilding yard at Greenock.

BAUGNES (W. J. Harvey)

Initially the series was for six vessels costing around £10.5m. It was however increased to eight vessels with options for a further three of a larger type worth £7m. One of the eight was subsequently transferred to the joint-account of pool-partners Anatina AS and Alfa AS, Norway, to be completed as their **AQUILA**. That latter company later sold the vessel back to Jebsens and she was renamed **BRISKNES**. As this third generation series, built on Clydeside, and the smaller Vegesak second generation series were under construction Jebsens were constantly negotiating finances to achieve what they considered to be the best all round package possible. Those negotiations produced many new facets to their operations. Vessels were delivered under lease, as partnerships or wholly owned, but all operated under Jebsens management within the pooled fleet. That policy also caused several ownership changes, either during or after construction, such as the group of W. German operators. Atle Jebsen bought the shipping company Reederei J. Jost of Flensburg, controllers of the chartered "Fiducia class" trio, and from this base Kristian Jebsens Rederi AS increased their fleet under W. German registry by buying up limited partnerships (Kommandittgesellschaft). These ships were then managed by:

>Brinknes Schiffahrtsgesellschaft Frank Lange.

>Langra Schiffahrtsgesellschaft GmbH & Company KG,

>Nordsee Frachtschiffahrtsgesellschaft GmbH & Company KG.

As the first units of the larger of the German built vessels came into service, as **JENNES** and **BRINKNES**, under W. German ownership it heralded a new concept of cargo handling for the company. They, together with the third generation Clyde vessels and numerous subsequent vessels were fitted out with Velle derrick-cranes. This equipment enabled bulk cargo to be self-discharged by the vessel, utilising grabs that were carried aboard. The derrick had more rigging than the standard cargo derrick for operating the grab.

The versatile "Velle" derrick with grab (Jebsens)

Jebsens Amman offices (Jebsens)

The operations of "Jebsens Bulk Carriers", the generalistic trading name, were steadily expanding and being consolidated. This was being achieved through the establishment of growth-markets and thereby offices around the world. This process became a solid foundation for the success of the company so that by the 1980's, Jebsens had established a network of offices in Fremantle, Melbourne, Auckland, Tokyo, Singapore, Manila, Hong Kong, Philadelphia, Montreal, Mexico City, Alexandria, Madras, Amman, Glasgow, London, Hamburg, Flensburg, Johannesburg, Paris and Oslo, without which the expansion of the group would have dwindled.

During 1972, Tenax Steam Ship Company Ltd., London, was restyled as Biovale Ltd., only to be restyled again in 1973 as Jebsens (UK) Ltd., London. They had begun to receive new vessels such as **FURUNES**, the initial unit from the "Furunes class" a modified version of the "Jennes Class" Even then the Furunes design was being altered. The final vessel of the trio **FALKNES** appeared with a totally different superstructure on the same hull format. This was to be the first of the "Falknes class" but remained a lone vessel, as Jebsens ship designers as we have witnessed, are continually on the move as new designs are planned to meet an ever-changing customer requirement. In this instance a new "R class" was already on the drawing board.

With the older Clyde-built bulkers due to be replaced, the company began to dispose of them as the new Japanese built 21,000 dwt, "S" type were delivered. The "Swiftnes class" of six vessels had been ordered from Nippon Kokan – four for the account of Tenax and two for Clarksons, and were of a type well suited to the many small ports served by the Jebsen fleet, being specifically designed with a shallow draft, enabling greater quantities of cargo to be loaded thus providing greater economies for the shipper. As with earlier name styles the initial letter signified the type of vessel. In this case "S" = shallow draft. The "Swiftnes class" subsequently redesignated "Saltnes class" started a Contract of Affreightment with salt from Port Dampier to smaller ports in Japan. The ships were self-discharging the salt, which was a new concept in Japan.

It was becoming more apparent that the company was operating a policy wherein they had a continual renewal programme for the fleet with vessels remaining in their service for an average maximum of ten years, although some vessels were disposed of after a much shorter period. To finance that never-ending programme of modernisation, further outside finances were necessary and often resulted in some complicated deals being struck with some unlikely partners.

SWIFTNES in South African waters. (Author's collection)

One such partnership entered into was with the Nile Steamship Company Ltd., London, a British Government controlled finance company that later was restyled as Investors In Industry Ltd. and later still as 3I plc. Their involvement was with one of the new "Brimnes class", assuming financial responsibility from Harrisons (Clyde) Ltd.

BRIMNES in the New Waterway, outward from the Botlek (W. J. Harvey)

A second-hand vessel was purchased from other Norwegian owners and renamed **FRINES**, to supplement the **ALTNES** and **RAKNES** classes. She was a product of the same shipyard having originally been ordered and sold by Jebsens, so was to all intents and purposes a sistership.

The three 3,000 dwt, "Tornes class", short-sea traders / mini-bulkers that had been delivered by the Norwegian Batservice Verft AS, at Mandal, one to the Norwegian and two to the British registered fleet during 1971 – 72. After a relatively short period they were sold, in 1974, to the Scottish based Gault and Denholm groups of companies, the latter of which had, in the interim also become involved in the management of **BAKNES, SWIFTNES** and **SEALNES**. **MORNES** was renamed **MONACH** for operation within their own fleet. The other pair **FONNES** and **TORNES**, were renamed **GALLIC STREAM** and **GALLIC MINCH**, and were owned by Gallic Estates, later Gallic Shipping Ltd. (Gault Group). The latter pair initiated a new concept of operation for

Jebsens as an agreement within their sale contract was that they would be chartered back to Jebsens. The **GALLIC STREAM** was however lost after only a short time on back-charter.

TORNES became GALLIC MINCH for back-charter to Jebsens. (Author's collection)

H. Clarkson & Company Ltd., meanwhile, had merged with Dene Shipping Ltd, a subsidiary of the Silver Line Group, as a means to developing their own bulker business. As a result, by the end of 1973, early 1974 they had sold their investment in the "S" class vessels to Jebsens whilst purchasing Jebsens investment in the "B" class and transferred them out of the Jebsen pool to the fleet of Silver Line Ltd, wherein they were given Scottish river names prefixed by silver. At that juncture Silver Line Ltd., who were also expanding their own bulker operations negotiated the acquisition of the larger **BRAVENES**, she becoming their **SILVERDON** upon completion of trials.

BINSNES **as SILVERTWEED** in Australian waters. (M. R. Dippy)

As one door closes however, another opens. On 1 January 1974, a joint venture was established 50:50 between Kristian Jebsens Rederi AS and the Dillingham Corporation, an Hawaiian based conglomerate, listed on the NYSE. Dillingham invested US$32 million and Kristian Jebsens Rederi AS contributed eight bulk carriers, one bare-boat charter and two new ships on order. With the additional financing Jebsens were able to expand their fleet quite quickly (eight vessels between 1975 and early 1976). Dillingham had become a partner in a thriving business that was able to provide earnings on their investment almost immediately. The ships were formally owned by two new companies:

❏ Dillingham Jebsen Shipping Corp., Liberia.

❏ Jebsen Dillingham Shipping Ltd., London.

With the new partnership came the introduction of the blue to replace the black on the funnel, in the same proportions.

The Dillingham-Jebsen partnership, in conjunction with Kristian Jebsens Rederi AS, placed orders in Japan for a series of two classes of bulk carriers all to have "B" names, for delivery over a four-year period. The first, the "Birknes-class" was to be built by Nippon Kokan, and **BIRKNES**, the class-name vessel was delivered during 1974. **BERGNES** – second in the series, was contracted to be sold when nearing completion. She undertook her trials and was completed as **BERGNES**, but was almost immediately renamed **IRON CAPRICORN** for her new owners the Australian Broken Hill Propriety organisation.

BERGNES **as IRON CAPRICORN** (M. R. Dippy)

Suntana Shipping Ltd., was meanwhile, formed to own **BULKNES** during her long period of charter to Comalc Propriety, Melbourne, and for which period she was operated with Australian crew.

Having hitherto concentrated on the deep-sea bulker fleet, the management now turned attention to developing their short sea fleet operations, having gained considerable experience through their own small vessels and those small chartered vessels. A substantial volume of orders were placed in the U.K., Germany and Norway.

CLYDENES outward from the Manchester Ship Canal. (J. K. Byass)

A series of four newly designed "Clydenes class" mini-bulkers were ordered by Jebsens and H. Clarkson & Company, from Ferguson Shipbuilders on the Clyde. The series, all fitted with cargo handling equipment, were to have "C" names, whilst in parallel, the first units of the slightly larger 4,400 dwt, fully ice-strengthened "Fonnes class", were ordered from Lürssens, a Bremen yard, long associated with the Jebsen group. Initially there were to be four vessels in this series also, they carrying "F" names.

FONNES returning from builders sea trials. (Author's collection / Fr. Lürrsen Werft)

The most prolific series to enter service however was the nine 6,300 dwt, "Rossnes class" gearless mini-bulkers that were ordered with twin Normo type engines, from three Norwegian shipyards for the Norwegian register and the further seven similar vessels ordered with single Pielstick type engines, from Appledore Shipbuilders in North Devon, as the "Ringnes class", for the British register. The Appledore series however, included three optional contracts Yard No's. 109; 110 and 111 that were quickly sold to other British shipowners urgently requiring vessels of that type and size, leaving only four to enter Jebsens British fleet. When completed, the three that were sold had been fitted with a slightly modified superstructure, different propulsion machinery and were additionally fitted with gantry cranes. The "Rossnes class" had an in-built design option that would enable the installation of a deck crane amidship, if so desired in later life. This can readily be seen when comparing both the Norwegian and British R type general arrangement illustrations on page 211.

RISNES outward from Rotterdam, passing Maassluis (W. J. Harvey)

Engine-room plan of the 4 500 bhp "Risnes".

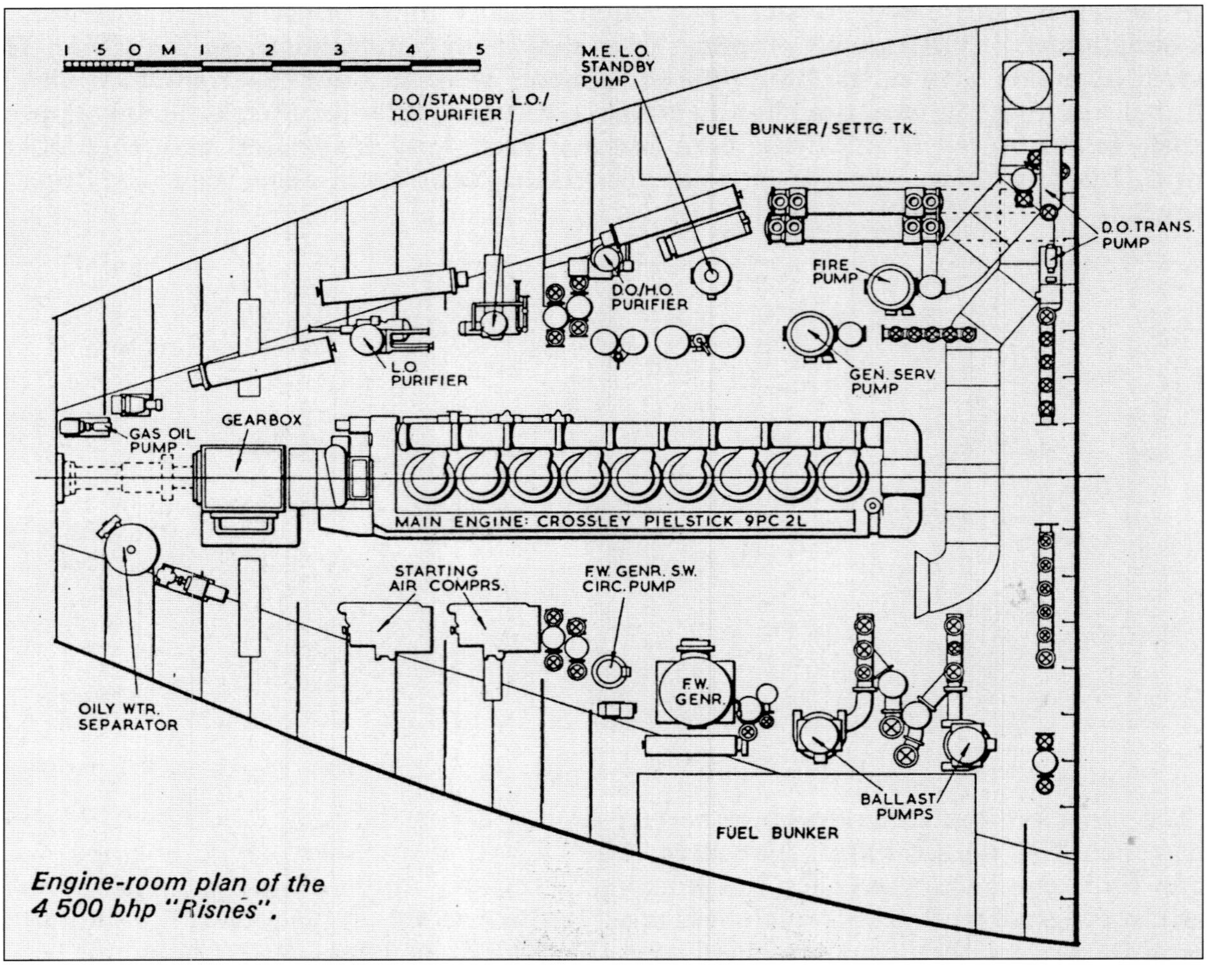

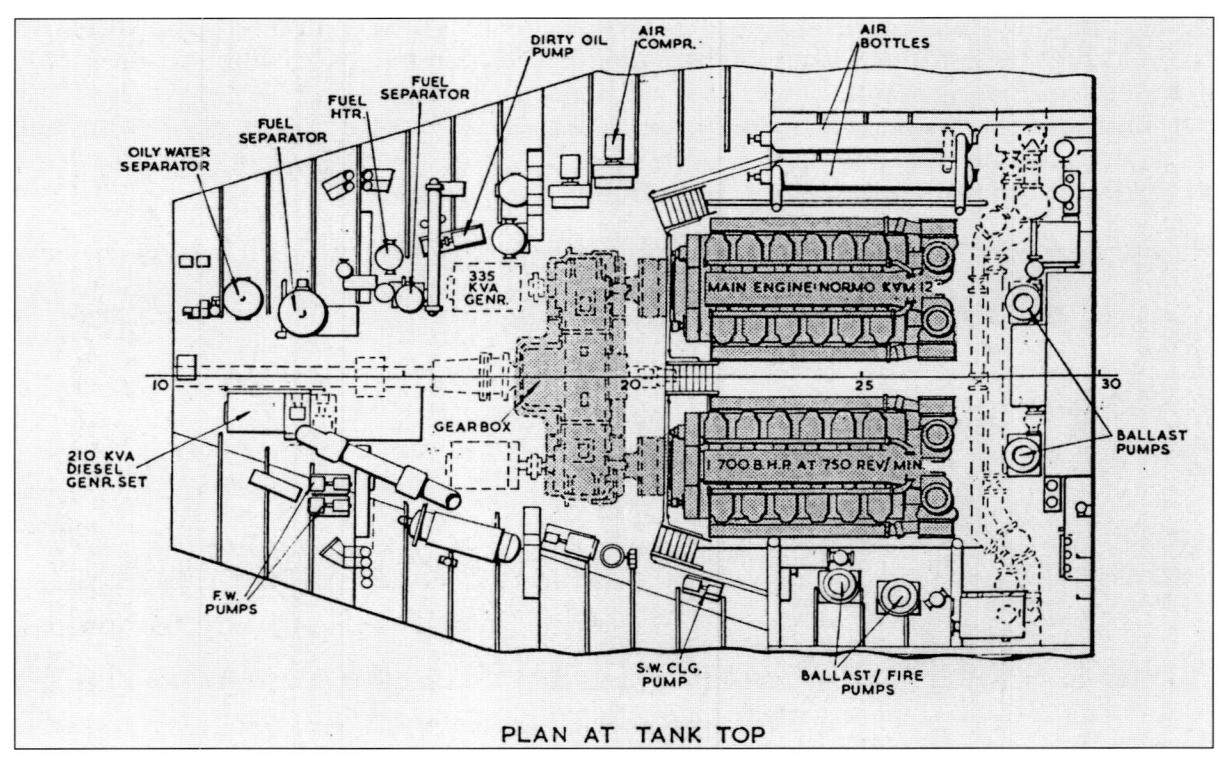

A comparison of the British built "R" class engine room layout above and the Norwegian version below
(Jebsens)

PLAN AT TANK TOP

ROSSNES with charterer's funnel. (W. J. Harvey))

Seen in later life as **ARKLOW BEACH,** this was one of the three optional contracts at Appledore that were sold to British buyers, and completed with deck cranes and different main machinery. (Terry O'Conallain)

BAYNES (M. R. Dippy)

Sumitomo Heavy Industries Ltd., delivered **BAYNES** at Uraga in 1976, as the lead vessel of the 34,540 dwt, "Baynes-class", they being the second series of "B" vessels ordered from Japan in 1974.

Rough Weather Ahead

The growth-bubble however, was about to burst as financial difficulties began emerging from different directions late in 1976 and early in 1977. The primary reason was a sudden and drastic downturn in the bulk market, pre-empting a serious depression in World trade. Following on tradition, meanwhile, Jebsens had been keeping apace of what may lay ahead and the potential of the offshore oil support industry had been studied in detail by the directorship over several years. Seen at the time as a market with growth potential, it was to become a major diversification for the group. Through the support of Hambros Bank, Kristian Jebsens Rederi AS, had in 1976, at very favourable terms, taken over two Levingstone type drilling rigs (**ALADDIN** and **SINBAD**) from KS Waage Drilling AS.

Later, Jebsens Drilling Ltd. was founded in 1979 and became the owner of the two former Waage rigs. Bouyant earnings from the drilling operation were utilised to help finance the bulk fleet replacement programme. The company was later listed as Jebsens Drilling plc, at the AIM London Stock Exchange. Subsequently an H3 rig (**ALI BABA**) was acquired by the company. In an attempt to offset the shortfall in earnings from the dwindling bulker market, Pacnorse Drilling Corporation was founded by the Dillingham, Jebsen partnership and Santa Fe International Corp, a World leading drilling contractor. The new organisation would take over the contracts for two purpose built self-propelled and dynamically positioned drilling ships early in 1977. They had, as part of a trio, been ordered by the Santa Fe International Corp. in 1976 from Scott's Shipbuilders as Yard No. 746 and 747, and had been scheduled for delivery during 1977 and 1978 to their subsidiaries Ocean Drilling Corp. 1 and Ocean Drilling Corp. 2. Yard No. 745 had already been delivered as **BEN-OCEAN LANCER** to another operator. When Jebsens took over the contracts for the remaining pair, they had them re-scheduled for delivery in 1979 and 1980, and subsequently allocated the names **PACNORSE I** and **PACNORSE II** having created Pacnorse Drilling Corporation I and II as the owning companies for the drillships. Having further studied the market for this type of vessel in greater detail however, and so as not to financially overstretch themselves, yard No. 747 was cancelled during September 1977.

Elsewhere, in the face of adversity, many operators for reasons of survival were attempting to re-negotiate their building-programme debt repayments. Jebsens were no exception and had to urgently re-finance some of the tonnage still outstanding. Further response to the crisis saw several orders and optional orders for new bulk vessels being cancelled:

Four "Birknes class" vessels from Nippon Kokan
- Yard No. 353 (proposed as **BULKNES**) cancelled 3.1976.
- Yard No. 356 (proposed as **BARNES**) cancelled 3.1977.
- Yard No. 357 (proposed as **BRINKNES**) cancelled 3.1977.
- Yard No. 358 (proposed as **BAUGNES**) cancelled 3.1977.

Two "Baynes class" vessels from Sumitomo
- Yard No. 985 (proposed as **BLIDNES**) cancelled 9.1976.
- Yard No. 990 (proposed as **BOLDNES**) cancelled 9.1976.

Two "Framnes class" options from Lürssen Werft.
- Yard No. 13456 (proposed as **FAIRNES**) cancelled 6.1977.
- Yard No. 13457 (proposed as **FULLNES**) cancelled 6.1977.

Two "Clydenes class" options from Ferguson Shipbuilder .
- Yard No. 476 (proposed as **CHARTNES**) cancelled 6.1977.
- Yard No. 477 (proposed as **CLEARNES**) cancelled 6.1977.

Early in 1977, other external changes were being undertaken that were to also effect the company. The Ferguson shipyard on the River Clyde, had been taken over as part of the British Government's programme of nationalising shipyards. That action had seen the creation of British Shipbuilders. Ferguson's yard had the "Clydenes class" of two mini-bulkers on order by the company plus the two now-cancelled options. Of the remaining pair, one was re-allocated to a neighbouring yard by British Shipbuilders, and allocated a new yard No.

Although Jebsens were cancelling orders for larger and smaller size vessels they had, on the other hand, been negotiating a financial package with the Saudi Arabian based Abdul Lateef Jameel Establishment. Those negotiations concluded during 1977 and under the agreement they would purchase some of the existing Jebsen vessels and furthermore would part-fund the construction of a series of new design of medium sized bulk carrier to be operated within the Jebsens Pool. As part of that package, ownership of the new vessels varied between the two parties depending on which had the larger investment. Jebsen-Jameel Carriers Ltd., was created as the controlling company, (owned 50:50 by Jebsen & Jameel), but several new companies appeared under that umbrella over the subsequent years, as delivery of those vessels commenced and as finances were continually restructured. The following subsidiaries were controlled by one or other partner, as stated earlier, dependent on who had the greater financial investment, all three under the Liberian register:

Renfrew Shipping Ltd;

Rothway Shipping Ltd;

Roxborough Shipping Ltd;

The series of three classes of 12,000 dwt, vessels, within a year of the agreement, began entering service with "F" names – said to define their suitability to also transport forestry products.

Ships operating within this agreement carried a slight variation to the funnel markings. On the blue base of the traditional Jebsen funnel was placed two letters "j" in lower case, back to back but with only one dot in a central position above them. This was also carried as a bow crest in lieu of the traditional Jebsen "KJR" crest.

FRINES (Author's collection / Fotoflite)

FARNES on the River Medway. Her two 25-ton, forward cranes are on a single rotatable column. In the photograph they are servicing one hatch apiece. They can also, if so required, be used in tandem side by side to lift 50-tons. (see FULLNES on page 144 with cranes stowed in tandem position. (Chriss Reynolds collection)

As finances were further restructured the owning companies were later restyled as :

        Bedouin Birknes Shipping Ltd., (late Roxborough Shipping Ltd.);

        Bedouin Brunes Shipping Ltd., (late Renfrew Shipping Ltd.);

        J. J. Shipping Ltd., (late Rothway Shipping Ltd.).

        J. J. Chartering Ltd., (bareboat owners of **FIRMNES** and **FARNES**).

FJELLNES (World Ship Society Photograph Library)

There was also a flurry of activity with other new companies entering the group portfolio as many new financial packages were thrashed out, resulting either in being wholly owned, or by further partnerships being undertaken as other shipowners became aware of the advantages of belonging to a specialist shipping pool:

Jebsens Hamburg GmbH & Company KG,

Brema Reederei GmbH & Company KG (J. Jost, Flensburg, manager).

Isskip h/f., Iceland.

Nesskip h/f., Iceland.

In contrast to the deep-sea fleet, the short-sea fleet was seeing orders placed for both geared and gearless versions of the same hull profile. These were to be delivered by Norwegian builders over the next few years as the "Altnes class" and "Korsnes class". In general terms, the short-sea was performing better than the deep-sea operation, although the latter was beginning to show signs of steady recovery.

The "Altnes class" and later "Korsnes class" that were loosely based on the German built "Fonnes class", were quickly found to be lacking in capacity and were sent for lengthening, as indeed were the "Fonnes class". Even at the planning stage their hatch arrangements had been altered. When the vessels were lengthened a new hold was added between the number two crane and the accommodation block aft, as seen in the photograph of **ALTNES** above. In the case of the "Korsnes class" they had no cranes.

Dillingham, Jebsen Shipping Corp Ltd., was in 1979, restyled as Pacnorse Shipping International Ltd., and Jebsen, Dillingham Shipping Ltd., restyled as Pacnorse Shipping (UK) Ltd. Pacnorse was an abbreviation of Pacific and Norse, signifying the areas of co-operation, and during 1980 an unusual 50:50 partnership was entered with the Egyptian owned, Misr Bank for the formation of the Misr Edco Shipping Company S. A. E., under the Egyptian flag. This company would build two RoRo ferries for their own services and initially one bulk carrier for operation within the Jebsen fleet. This bulk carrier would be supplemented by others at a later date if favourable conditions were to prevail. All three vessels were ordered through Jebsens from Norwegian shipyards.

The Jebsen Group, despite adverse trading conditions, continued to strengthen the services being offered to their customers, that being instrumental in the lengthy development of the self-unloading bulk carrier during the late 1970's. Loosely based on the Canadian "Great Lakers" the unusual aspect of this type of vessel is that the cargo is carried in silo-bottomed type holds. When the ship discharges the hatch covers remain closed as the cargo drops to the bottom of the hold and is carried away on a conveyor belt system and is projected through a slewing boom onto the quayside. Having satisfied themselves with the advantages and disadvantages of the concept before placing orders the company, in 1982 took delivery of **TELNES**, the prototype of what was to become a long series of nine such vessels, each being an improvement of the previous, based on experience and customer feed-back. The initial system was capable of discharging 1,800 tons per hour regardless of weather, that figure having since been much improved upon and indeed the vessels themselves have grown with each new construction.

TELNES (Author's collection / Fotoflite)

Riding The Storm

Being a diverse organisation, not just confined to shipping, the Jebsen Group and Atle Jebsen personally were participating in the take-over by Elkem AS, of Union Carbide's ferro-alloys division, which included plants in USA, Canada and Norway. At one time Jebsens owned about 35% of these plants. Being a very large customer of Jebsens, Elkem needed a Joint Venture partner to be able to take over this business, and in 1981 found Jebsens willing to participate. By the late 1980's both the Jebsen Group and Atle Jebsen had sold their shareholding to Elkem AS.

Also in the summer of 1981, Jebsens entered into yet another marine partnership, one that unfortunately was, through the course of time, to prove disastrous. On that occasion it was with the Hong Kong based Wheelock Maritime International – a company itself jointly owned by Wheelock, Marden & Company Ltd., and World Wide Carriers. Central to the joint venture agreement was the fleet of eight vessels, **BARKNES**, **BAYNES**, **BELLNES**, **BESSNES**, **BINSNES**, **BOLNES**, **BRAVENES** and **BRISKNES**. These were sold on a lease-back basis to the Carrian controlled Grand Marine Holdings, to finance two new classes of ships that had been ordered by Wheelock for operation within the Jebsen pool. These were to be three geared-Panamax type and three 18,000 grt, geared crane and grab type.

LIMELOCK (V. H. Young)

Elsewhere in the Far East, another agreement of co-operation was in late 1981, ratified with Botelho Bulk Transport Corp., Philippines, originally formed in 1946. Their fleet of vessels mainly carried names of Philippino Generals. The company was in 1982, renamed Aboitiz, Jebsen Bulk Transport Corp., (ABOJEB), after the Aboitiz Group bought 60% of the shares in the company. ABOJEB has since expanded into ship management, crewing and owning, as well as in commercial pool-participation with the Jebsen Group in Pacific and South-East Asia. Although a substantial fleet of vessels, mainly ferries, have been or are under the management of ABOJEB they have been deemed as being outside the scope of this publication.

All was not well over the horizon however, and in 1982, Carrian (Grand Marine Holdings) ran into financial difficulties and Wheelock initially did not want to, and later, was unable to invest further funds to fulfil their obligations under the joint-venture. The Wheelock debacle unfortunately, was at a time of high investment in modernisation of the Jebsens fleet, coupled with a falling $US. Orders had been placed for a two newly designed series of vessels. One order by Jebsens (UK) Ltd., with Govan Shipbuilders on the Clyde, was for four 45,000 dwt, "Lakenes class". The order by Pacnorse Shipping International was placed with the Japanese Namura Shipbuilding Company, for six 48,000 dwt, "Locknes class". All ten vessels were for delivery during 1984 / 1985. Fearing an imminent Wheelock collapse, Jebsens hurriedly set about damage limitation by formulating an interim survival package which during 1983 saw many transactions undertaken. Due primarily to the Carrian crisis, and also because of the number of new vessels scheduled to enter service, the fleet was becoming cumbersome to control financially. To offset that burden an approach on feasibility, led to agreement being reached wherein Compagnie Generale Maritime (C.G.M.), France, would acquire a holding in two of the Norwegian "R" class minibulker series whilst two others would be sold to Jebsens France – all four sailing in Jebsens North Sea Pool. The four units were transferred to French flag and given "saint" names. That transaction provided an expansion of Jebsens trading in Europe, as well as a considerable cash profit. Another such deal was worked out with the Swiss Acomarit / Massoel company for the **CLARKNES**, **CLYDENES**, **SPRAYNES** and **SALTNES**. The sale of two further "Saltnes class" to Jordan National Shipping Lines was coupled with a contract to manage the vessels on behalf of their new owners. The most drastic measure however, came on the 23 August 1984 when three of the Namura contracts, proposed as Yard No. 863 (**LURNES**), 864 (**LYNGNES** or **LINKNES**) and 866 (**LAUNES**), were cancelled, together with two at Govan proposed as Yard No. 262 (**LEKNES**) and 263 (**LIFTNES**).

The Wheelock Demise.

In 1982 the Carrian Group collapsed and the Wheelock organisation were unable to recover the purchase price of their Pacnorse investment and also found themselves in difficulties due to the shortfall of return in other investment. This was resultant of the declining state of the dry bulk market wherein they had ordered their new tonnage at the height of the market and it was now being delivered into a dead market. To survive, a massive injection of cash would be required but the continual losses being incurred by the shipping arm where a millstone around their neck. Several of the fleet were transferred to Philippine flag and renamed with a MANILA prefix whilst Wheelock Marden International approached their property arm parent - Realty Development, for a capital injection of $12 million over three years until the expected upturn in the market. Although financially strong (estimated reserves of HK$ 2 billion) from Hong Kong property dealings, Reality Development refused to sanction any such transfer. However a $ 4 million standby facility was made available, but only if the fleet was drastically reduced. Wheelock Chartering meanwhile had successfully arranged a barter deal with Iran, wherein eleven ships were to be exchanged for $100 million of crude oil. Together with some other ship sales, that reduced the Wheelock debt by around $70 million. Even so, with that transaction cash-flow problems were worsening, as vessels were found to be extremely difficult to dispose of in a depressed market. Realty Development moved swiftly and took over Wheelock, Marden & Stewart - the insurance arm. In October 1984, however, they dealt the death blow, by declaring their refusal to support the shipping operation any further. Therefore, on 7 March 1985 share dealings were suspended. Restructuring plans proposed by accountants Ernst & Whinney were declined by company creditors. The Directorship decided in July 1985, to voluntary liquidate the company, that being approved at an extraordinary general meeting on 2 August 1985. Wheelock Maritime International was henceforth wound up with HK$ 704 million liabilities against HK$ 10.4 million assets. The banks then took control of the remaining fleet, including vessels awaiting delivery or under construction, selling them for the best price obtainable in what was at the time, a depressed and volatile marketplace.

However, even with all the protectionate measures that had been hurriedly put in place, when the Wheelock demise finally came, it still left Jebsens with an estimated loss of Norwegian Kroner 80-million, forcing an approach to their creditors for a more lenient restructuring of their finances. The Wheelock joint venture had been undertaken at a time when the bulk markets, as stated earlier, were entering yet another and more devastating slump, having rallied somewhat following the late 1970's market depression. This time around though, the outcome was much more dramatic with many well-known operators disappearing. Some decided to withdraw from shipowning to invest in other activities, whilst many others collapsed financially having overstretched themselves. The Wheelock organisation was no exception to that plight as to a lesser extent were Jebsens, both falling victim to a third-party collapse. To assist the Jebsens recovery programme the greater part of the fleet was transferred into single ship companies mainly under the Philippine flag. Initially they took **PHILIPPINE** or **MANILA** prefixed names before changing to **GENERAL** as the normal, falling into line with units of the Aboitiz, Jebsen fleet.

From the remnants of the Wheelock fleet the Iranian National Shipping Company was able, in 1984, to acquire amongst others, several good quality, young vessels. Some had been destined for operation within the Jebsen Bulk Pool.

    PRIMELOCK launched as, but completed as **MANILA FAITH** became **IRAN AFZAL**.
    PHILIPPINE SUCCESS launched as, but completed as **IRAN AKHAVAN**.
    WORLD FRATERNITY became **IRAN ADL**.
    MANILA PRIDE became **IRAN AMANAT**.
    ODINLOCK became **IRAN DEYANAT**.
    THORLOCK became **IRAN SHARIAT**.

In 1985 from the aftermath, Wheelock Marine Chartering Ltd, was restyled as Fenwick Marine Services Ltd., and became involved with some company vessels.

From within the black cloud, however, a ray of light appeared. A joint venture that primarily evolved from the uniqueness and versatility of Jebsens beltship concept, was that of Jebsens-ACZ. This was formed in conjunction with Van Oord ACZ, Holland, a specialist dredging and subsea operator, and subsequently two "T" class beltships were converted to unload aggregates at sea via an overside pipe to enable sea-bed pipelines to be covered. That partnership continues and has witnessed a growth in size of vessel now being employed. (see explanatory illustration on next page)

Partnership and re-negotiation were methods of generating stability. However, when opportunity arises one acts quickly. One such opportunity saw two of the "B" class sold to the U.S.S.R., which was at the time picking up numerous modern, high-technology bulkers at rock-bottom prices as their Western owners willingly divested themselves in an attempt to survive financially. In the face of a deepening depression, further cut-backs were deemed necessary within the fleet and sales resumed with one of Jameel's vessels following her sisters into the Soviet fleet in 1985, followed by another in 1986. The three Wheelock **KRISLOCK /LIMELOCK** Panamax ships either directly or indirectly passed to the Danish A. P. Moller group for further service under Singapore flag. By late 1986, the Jebsen Group was beginning to stabilise again, having successfully re-negotiated much of their finances. A new holding company was established – Dreggen Invest AS – with Atle Jebsen as majority shareholder, and the other shareholders being Jebsens Executives and close business partners. Despite the returning stability however, the Jameel Organisation, having been shaken by the effects of the crisis, began a phased withdrawal of their investment during 1987 when four vessels were renamed into their normal style of having "JAY" as a suffix whilst Jameel's investment of 50% in four 12,000 tonners was bought at favourable terms by Dreggen Invest AS. A dramatic slump in oil prices also prompted Jebsens to progressively withdraw from the offshore market by the end of the 1980's, selling the three conventional drilling rigs, although they did retain their holding in **PACNORSE 1** for a few years thereafter.

(London) Ltd.) as a management company to continue the operation of the three colliers on behalf of Jebsens / Bishopgate. Those vessels eventually passed into the direct ownership of the Powergen Plc, in 1995.

The Jebsen Group meanwhile had, in the late 1980's, commenced a trading co-operation with Swedish, Erik Thun Ab, Lidkoping, for their North Sea fleet of self-unloading vessels. In furtherance of that co-operation, in 1989, Erik Thun Ab and Dreggen Invest AS established Jebsens-Thun, Luxembourg, to operate only the belt-unloading vessels of both partners, whereupon funnels were amended to white with black top with blue JTB above the Jebsen blue wave device.

EOS one of the Thun owned beltships with the JTB funnel markings. (World Ship Society Photograph Library)

The Beltship Concept.

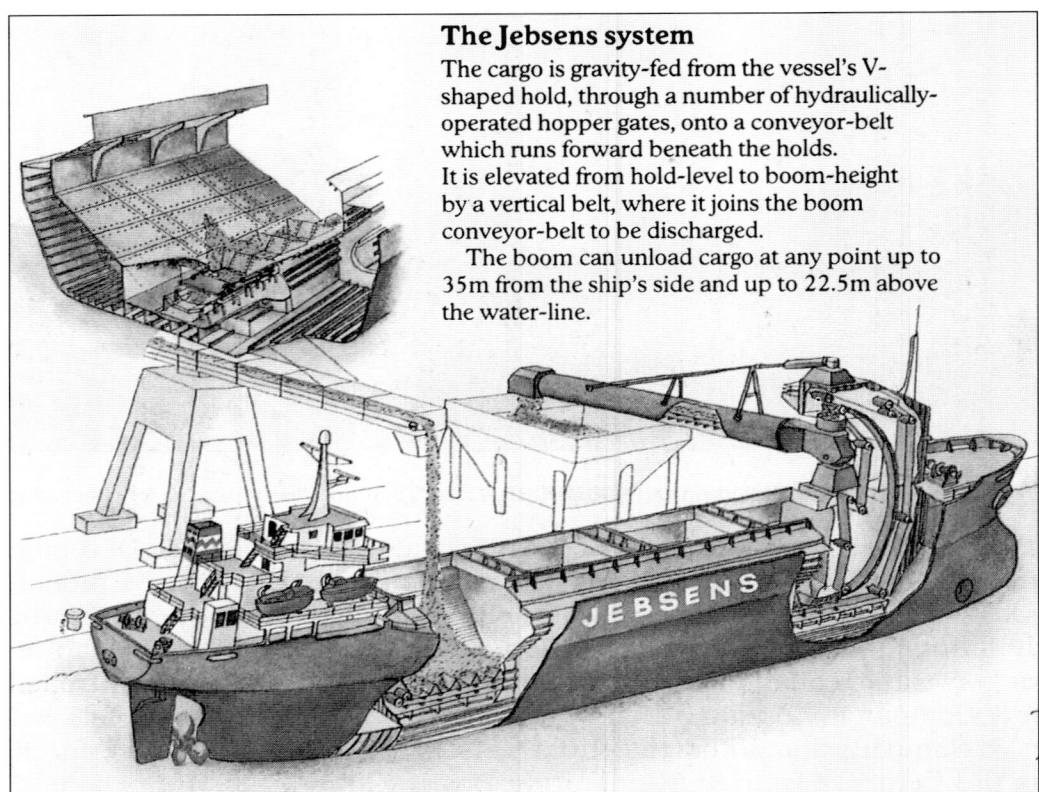

The Jebsens system

The cargo is gravity-fed from the vessel's V-shaped hold, through a number of hydraulically-operated hopper gates, onto a conveyor-belt which runs forward beneath the holds. It is elevated from hold-level to boom-height by a vertical belt, where it joins the boom conveyor-belt to be discharged.

The boom can unload cargo at any point up to 35m from the ship's side and up to 22.5m above the water-line.

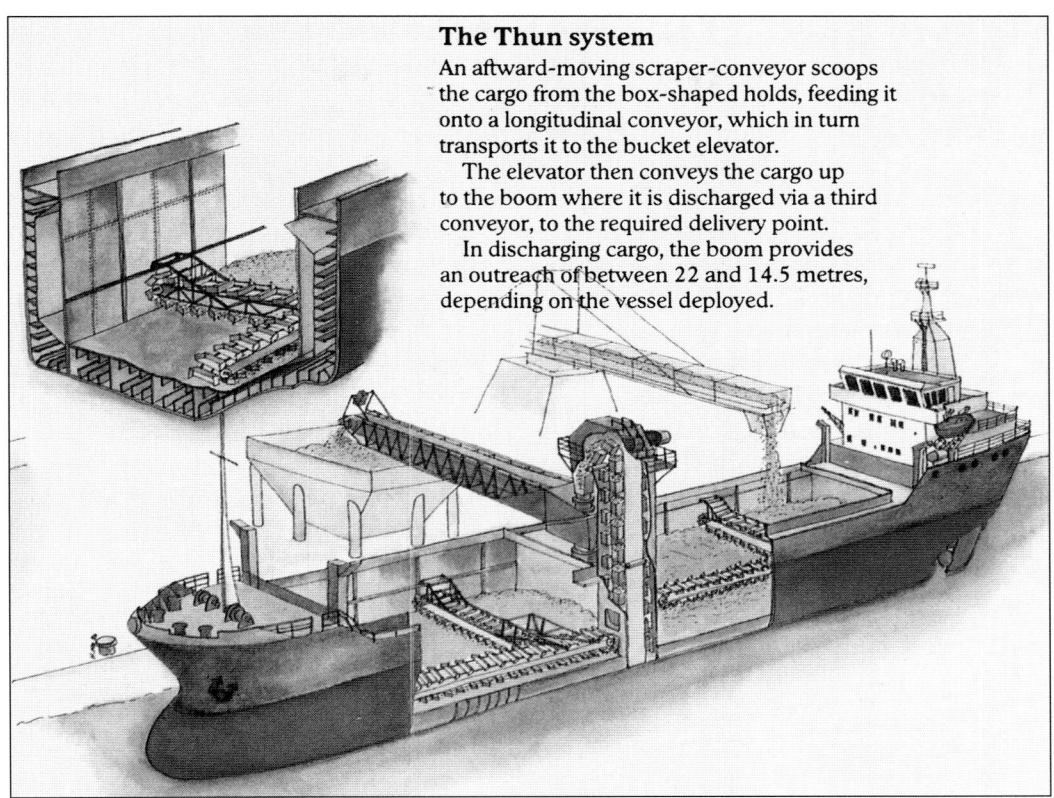

The Thun system
An aftward-moving scraper-conveyor scoops the cargo from the box-shaped holds, feeding it onto a longitudinal conveyor, which in turn transports it to the bucket elevator.

The elevator then conveys the cargo up to the boom where it is discharged via a third conveyor, to the required delivery point.

In discharging cargo, the boom provides an outreach of between 22 and 14.5 metres, depending on the vessel deployed.

It was not a particularly happy relationship and after only a short period, Erik Thun Ab decided that they wanted to continue as a wholly-owned family company. Jebsens bought Thun's share of the company and original Thun self-unloaders were phased out, together with some Contracts of Affreightments, although Jebsens retained a diminishing financial interest in the new vessels through Norwegian Partners Ltd. As a result of the de-merger, the last in the series of new ships was cancelled. IMO No. 9048665, planned as **MUSTNES**, was from Ferus Smits BV., Foxhol (Yd. No. 291).

ODRANES one of the numerous Polish controlled vessels operated by Jebsens.

(Internet source)

In an ever-changing marketplace being independent does not necessarily prove to be the best for prosperity. Such was the reputation of Jebsens operation many other major shipowning concerns were only too happy to form alliances. An association with the Polish Steamship Company was commenced in 1992, one which resulted in one long-term bare-boat charter and two time-charters of newly built vessels, being designed for Jebsens trade, together with four other vessels being long-term chartered.

Within months the most prolific alliance was entered into, when during 1993 the Norwegian Paal Wilson & Company AS, merged their business 50:50 with Jebsens, to operate their combined fleets, under the auspices of Jebsen Wilson Eurocarriers AS (JWEC). Both partners continued to own their respective fleets separately, but marketing and operation was undertaken by the new concern which had, as a result of the merger, become Europe's largest short sea operator with a combined fleet of over eighty vessels, either owned or chartered. (Fairplay 24 and 31 December 1992). Excluded as being outside the scope of this work, the Wilson vessels retained their own livery and were of 500 – 2,000 dwt operating on liner services usually carrying names of five letters ending in O. Jebsens vessels of 4,000 – 6,000 dwt operated on distribution of bulk materials. The operation became a major market factor in the North Sea, with many long-term Contract of Affreightment being developed as "alliance contracts", and as such was to subsequently attract the financial entrepreneurs.

HAUGO, seen on the River Trent, typifies the modern Wilson-fleet. (World Ship Society Photograph Library)

With the short-sea operation successfully merged the deep sea operations came under scrutiny. A decision was taken that saw the name and trading rights of Jebsens Bulk Pool (JBP) sold to Western Bulk Shipping, during 1994, including the employment of ships and the rights to time-charter agreements, but did not include the ships involved, although several were renamed to WBL style whilst completing existing contracts. Satisfied with the outcome of their endeavours thus far, Jebsens were in the market for further avenues of expansion by 1995. A 50:50 joint venture was agreed with Hartmann Reederei of Leer, Germany to operate some of the original fleet and construct a series of new bulk carriers under the auspices of Jebsen, Hartmann Carriers. All the new vessels would be managed by Athena Marine Ltd., of Cyprus. Hulls colours were changed from the slate grey to brick red with J. H. C. amidship instead of Jebsens, whilst the white band on the funnel changed to pale yellow, that being the only change to the funnel markings.

The Aboitiz, Jebsens partnership was not affected by any of the foregoing, although when Jebsens, together with Joint Stock Northern Shipping Company, of Archangel, agreed to further extend their co-operation and build up to ten 3,500 dwt mini-bulkers at Komarno, Slovakia, for Jebsen operation, both Aboitiz and Jebsen placed orders for a group of four new 7,400 dwt vessels with the Ukranian, Kherson shipyard. Three would emerge with Aboitiz family names and one with a traditional Jebsen name.

Elsewhere meanwhile, a chain of events began to unfurl in June 1996, one that was destined to have a significant bearing on the Jebsen group. Paal Wilson & Company AS, in partnership with Mosvold Farsund Invest, acquired 50.2% of Actinor Shipping AS. (Until May 1992 Actinor Shipping AS had been Hafslund Transport AS until restyled when demerged from Hafslund Nycomed). Actinor ASA, in December 1997, purchased a 75% stake in both Jebsen SA Group and Jebsens Management AS, for $20m, through Actinor Short Sea, (at the time reported as operators of over 70 bulkers). Following the acquisition of Jebsens Eurocarriers AS and Jebsens Ship Management (Bergen) AS by Actinor, the Jebsen Group was drastically re-organised. The Jebsens SA company that had been sold to Actinor ASA comprised only of the conventional North Sea mini-bulk carriers, including the related organisation and staff, and from that acquisition came Wilson Eurocarriers AS and Wilson Ship Management AS. Atle Jebsen remained Chairman for a period following the sale, and until subsequent events overtook the business, traditional Jebsens ship names remained, although hull colours changed to the Wilson blue. The Wilson funnel markings were added, albeit changed from being pale blue with black top, to blue with black top, under which was placed a red-edged white band with a black "W" incorporated in the middle of a dark blue band, looking not unlike the Jebsen wave. Wilsons henceforth replaced Jebsens on ship sides. The remaining Jebsens vessels, operations thereof and related staff continued under Atle Jebsen management. Beltship Management AS was established during 1997 as a 50:50 partnership between Jebsens and Heidelberger Zement Group of Germany. This joint-venture comprised of the whole of the belt-unloader business, including the leasing and ownership of 9 vessels.

Big however, is not always beautiful in the modern financial world. A large successful business can attract speculators. Only 3-years after the Actinor / Wilson Group acquired control of Jebsens North Sea fleet to enlarge, Actinor sold the whole operation during 2000, to In Ship AS, Haugesund, with Kristian Eidesvik and Ole Henrik Nesheim as majority shareholders. From that juncture all evidence of any Jebsens involvement was swept aside as traditional Jebsens names were replaced with place or river names prefixed with WILSON. (e.g.**WILSON TYNE**), Despite these changes Wilson Ship Management AS, remain responsible for some of Jebsens vessels.

Another part of Jebsens operations was to change hands in late 2000 when the Alfred Hartmann Group began negotiations to buy Jebsens' 50% in Jebsen, Hartmann Carriers. They wished to change direction and form another joint venture elsewhere. Subsequent to acquisition, the company was on 1 April 2001, restyled as United Bulk Carriers. The funnel was changed to blue with a red band in place of Jebsens blue wave on pale yellow band, and JHC on the hull was replaced with UBC. The "B" and "S" class bulkers hitherto operated with Jebsens style "B" and "S" names were all renamed with the UBC prefix to new names starting with "B" or "S" to signify their class. E.g. **SPRAYNES** became **UBC SYDNEY**. The separate "A" class vessels were not renamed, they mainly being operated on charter-work. However, the overall association between Hartmann and Jebsens continued in the Pacific trade under Trans Pacific Parcel Service (TRANSPAC). In June 2001, **SWIFTNES** loaded the first cargo of package timber to inaugurate the TRANSPAC service between Australasia and the W. Coast of America and Canada. Hans Jurgen Hartmann also remains involved with Jebsens through the operation of "S" beltships **SPLITTNES, STONES** and **SANDNES**.

Now in his seventieth-year, Atle Jebsen has through the passage of time, overcome the many challenges encountered by the Jebsens Group which, with a now radically different business portfolio, have a seventy-six year proven track record and today continue in many facets of shipping around the World, primarily with their self-unloading beltships.

The Fleet.

The following chronological fleet listing contains all vessels known to have been owned, managed or chartered, whether registered under the parent company and Norwegian flag or subsidiary, offshore companies with external flag. Part One contains all the vessels, of which the Company was deemed as "Beneficial Owner". Part two contains an inconclusive list of vessels known to have been chartered.

Notes On The Individual Ship Histories

The first line gives:-

The relevant chronological number of the ship in the history; ship name(s); the first (1) second (2) etc. to carry the name, period in the fleet. Additionally, I have, from the mid 1950s, quoted the LR/IMO number above the chronology number / ship name. This number remains constant throughout the ships life, unlike the Official Number that regularly changes when sold or re-registered to another country. IMO numbers must now be displayed externally on the vessel, more usually on the hull at the stern.

The second line gives:-

Tonnages (g.= gross, n.= net, d.= deadweight), followed by the dimensions. Up to 1956 vessels were measured in feet and tenths, length x breadth x depth, between perpendiculars. That is indicated by "feet" at the end of the dimension quoted. In 1956, Lloyd's Register of Shipping commenced listing dimensions differently. The new system introduced quoted the overall length x extreme breadth x summer draught, as opposed to the earlier measurement between perpendiculars. That gave a more realistic dimension with the vessel appearing longer than before. The dimensions quoted from 1956 were in feet and inches and, from 1975, in metres. In the histories, where the new system is being quoted 'oa' has been placed at the end of the relevant dimension. In later vessels (BB) after the first dimension figure signifies a bulbous bow. Occasionally vessels are re-measured on acquisition or sale and those new measurements, including those in the case of vessels being lengthened are listed below the original measurements. (e.g. Post 1989: 12,345g. 7,654n. etc. etc.).

*The inclusion of any additional measurement details also effects the machinery details listed below.

(*normally – see above) The third line commences the machinery details:-

Number of engines, steam turbine or triple expansion etc., followed by the number of cylinders (bore and stroke where known) in the case of steam powered vessels, or, in the case of motor vessels, the number of cylinders, followed by the number of S.C.= stroke cycle and S.A.= single acting D.A. = double acting, (bore and stroke where known). In both cases, that is followed by the machinery type (where known), manufacturers thereof, propeller details, total (n = nominal; b = brake; s = shaft; i = indicated) horse power produced, and speed of vessel (where known). If a vessel is, at any time, re-engined during its career then the relevant details are given below the original machinery. (e.g. Post 1975: 6-cyl. 2 S.C.S.A. etc. etc.)

The subsequent lines detail the ship history.

The type of vessel, (geared / gearless refers to cargo handling equipment; TEU = **T**wenty-foot or **E**quivalent **U**nit container).

Keel laying, launch and completion dates (where known), shipbuilder, including yard number (where known), followed by the career details.

In all cases, the existing ship histories have been corrected to the end of <u>May 2005.</u>

Official Numbers.

With this group owning multi-national companies and operating a multi-national fleet, the task of listing Official Numbers was difficult. Some O. N's were not listed in the usual sources of reference, so the vessel would appear not to have one. However as vessels changed ownership or flag, and I have been successful in locating an O.N., that has been added in brackets, immediately after the relevant entry of change in the ship history section. The reason behind that is to try and identify the O. N. to the relevant country.

THE FLEET OPERATED BY

Kristian Jebsens Rederi AS
and
their derivative, subsidiary and associate companies.

1. VIGSNES (1) (1930 – 1945)
1,599g. 937n.   244.8 x 37.7 x 15.7 feet.
T.3-cyl. (17¼", 29" & 49" x 33") steam engine made by the shipbuilder. 138 nhp. 9 kts.
1930: Completed by Bergens Mekaniske Verksteder AS, Bergen (Yard No. 213), for Kristian Jebsens Rederi AS, (Kristian Jebsen junior, manager), Norway. 1943: Chartered to The Ministry of War Transport, London, (J. A. Bilmeir & Company, Cardiff, appointed as managers). 1.1945: Kristian Jebsen junior resumed management. 22.1.1945: Sailed from Cardiff bound for the Mersey Estuary, in convoy MH.1. 23.1.1945: Sunk by the German submarine U 1172, (commanded by Kuhlmann), in a position 53.33 N., 4.17 W. 24.1.1945: Two of her ships lifeboats washed ashore near Amlwych, N. Wales.

2. GARNES (1) (1930 – 1946)
1,559g. 888n.   250.6 x 39.3 x 17.4 feet.
T.3-cyl. (17¼", 29" & 49" x 33") steam engine made by the shipbuilder. 138 nhp. 9 kts.
1930: Completed by Bergens Mekaniske Verksteder AS, Bergen (Yard No. 214), for Kristian Jebsens Rederi AS, (Kristian Jebsen junior, manager), Norway. 24.3.1946: Exploded a mine whilst off Terschelling and sank. (Some sources quote 24.3.1947)

3. KORSNES (1) (1936 – 1947)
1,726g. 992n. 2,550d. 260.8 x 41.2 x 17.4 feet.
C.2-cyl. (15¾" & 31½" x 31½") steam engine with a low-pressure steam turbine made by Bergens Mekaniske Verksteder AS, Bergen, double reduction geared to screw shaft. 145 nhp. 10 kts.
3.3.1936: Launched by Rosenberg Mekaniske Verksteder AS, Stavanger (Yard No. 145), for AS DS Nor, (Kristian Jebsen junior, manager), Norway. 1936: Completed. 27.11.1944: Damaged by aircraft whilst at Narvik, and sank. 8.1945: Refloated and subsequently towed to Bergen for repair. 10.1946: Sold to O. Skjelbred Knudsen, Denmark, to be taken over when all repairs were completed. 1947: Delivered to Dampskslsk. Patria AS, (O. Skjelbred Knudsen, manager), Norway, and renamed PATRIA. 1957: Sold to A. Zedler, W. Germany, and renamed KAHLBERG. 25.2.1965: Arrived at Hamburg for demolition by Eisen und Metal AG.

4. TELNES (1) (1936 – 1940)
1,694g. 992n. 2,550d. 260.8 x 41.2 x 17.4 feet.
C.2-cyl. (15¾" & 31½" x 31½") steam engine with a low-pressure steam turbine made by Bergens Mekaniske Verksteder AS, Bergen, double reduction geared to screw shaft. 145 nhp. 10 kts.
27.8.1936: Launched by Rosenberg Mekaniske Verksteder AS, Stavanger (Yard No. 146), for AS DS Nor, (Kristian Jebsen junior, manager), Norway. 1936: Completed. 9.1.1940: Departed from New York, bound to Antwerp and Rotterdam but did not arrive. 3.1940: Posted as "missing, presumed lost".

AUN

(Author's Collection)

5. AUN (1) (1941 – 1948)
1,908g. 1,137n. 270.6 x 43.0 x 18.6 feet.
T.3-cyl. (19", 31" & 52" x 36") steam engine made by the shipbuilder. 162 nhp. 10 kts.
1930: Completed by Smiths Dock Company Ltd., Middlesbrough (Yard No. 916), for Finn Johnsens Rederi AS, (Finn Johnsen, manager), Norway. (O.N. 9042). 1941: Following a merger, Kristian Jebsen Junior, appointed as manager. 1948: Sold to Rederi Ab Lerberget, (Joel Fange, manager), Norway, and renamed LIANA. 1950: Jan Erik Fange appointed as manager. 1962: Sold to Rederiet for s.s.Liana, (L. E. Pahlsson manager), Norway. 1963: Sold to Anchamar SA, Panama, and renamed MARGHERITA. 19.9.1970: Arrived at Split for demolition by Brodospas.

VIGSNES

(Author's collection)

6. VIGSNES (2) (1947 – 1967)
1,931g. 1,043n. 2,840d. 278.6 x 41.5 x 17.7 feet.
T.3-cyl. (16½", 26" & 47" x 33") steam engine made by North Eastern Marine Engineering Company Ltd., Newcastle. 780 ihp. 10 kts.

1.10.1947: Launched by J. Crown & Sons Ltd., Sunderland (Yard No. 222), for Kristian Jebsens Rederi AS, (Kristian Jebsen junior, manager), Norway. 1947: Completed. 1967: Sold to AS Live and Arne Ostensjo AS, Norway, and renamed PAX. 1970: Sold to Karapoul Shipping Company Ltd., Cyprus, and renamed CARPO. 5.1.1972: Grounded off Wicklow whilst inward bound from Casablanca. 11.1.1972: Refloated, discharged then taken to Liverpool for dry docked inspection. 24.2.1972: Delivered to Haulbowline Industries Ltd., at Passage West, Ireland, for demolition.

GARNES

(Author's collection)

5126354

7. GARNES (2) (1948 – 1966)

2,401g. 1,363n. 3,125d. 305.8 x 43.2 x 18.6 feet.
6-cyl. 2 S.C.S.A. (450 x 740mm) Fiat type oil engine made by S. A. Ansaldo, Genoa. 1,350 bhp. 12 kts. Subsequently fitted with a thwartship thrust propeller forward.
General cargo vessel with eight 5-ton derricks.
1948: Completed by Societa Odero-Terni Orlando, Spezia (Yard No. 316) for Kristian Jebsens Rederi AS, (Kristian Jebsen junior, manager), Norway. 1966: Sold to Reederei "Nord" (Klaus E. Oldendorff), W. Germany, and renamed NORDHEIDE. 1973: Sold to Karterado Compania Naviera SA, Greece, and renamed KARTERADO. 1976: Sold to Nomsar Compania Naviera SA, (Karterado Compania Naviera SA, managers), Greece, and renamed VOUNITSO. 1978: Sold to Butterfly Compania Maritime SA, Panama, and renamed LUCKY STAR II. 1981: Sold to Athens Breeze Compania Naviera SA, Panama, (O.N. 8561-PEXT 4). 1986: Reported as having been demolished.

8. ALTNES (1) (1949 – 1963)

9,025g. 5,193n. 13,580d. 505.6 x 62.2 x 28.8 feet.
4-cyl. 2 S.C.S.A. (670 x 2,320mm) Doxford type oil engine made by D. Rowan & Company Ltd., Glasgow. 4,500 bhp. 13 kts.
Motor tanker.
18.4.1949: Launched by Lithgows Ltd., Port Glasgow, (Yard No.1045), for Kristian Jebsens Rederi AS, (Kristian Jebsen junior, manager), Norway. 9.1949: Completed. 1963: Sold to Theo Papadimitriou, Greece, and renamed MYRRINELLA. 19.2.1969:

Laid up at Piraeus. 14.6.1974: Arrived, in tow from Piraeus, at Burriana for demolition.

ALTNES (Author's collection)

TELNES at Swansea. (Author's collection)

9. TELNES (2) (1951 – 1965)
11,006g. 6,146n. 16,100d. 505.7 x 68.4 x 37.4 feet.
5-cyl. 2 S.C.S.A. (750 x 1,500mm) B&W type oil engine made by J. G. Kincaid & Company Ltd., Greenock. 4,850 bhp. 12 kts.
Motor tanker.
24.5.1951: Launched by Lithgows Ltd., Port Glasgow (Yard No. 1062), for Kristian Jebsens Rederi AS, (Kristian Jebsen junior, manager), Norway. 10.1951: Completed.
5.4.1965: Delivered at Bilbao for demolition.

5406584
10. AUN (2) (1952 – 1963)
1,900g. 1,011n. 2,700d. 265.0 x 41.3 x 17.8 feet.
C.2-cyl. (16¾" & 33-7/16" x 33-7/16") steam engine with low-pressure steam turbine made by the shipbuilder, double reduction geared to screw shaft. 1,200 ihp. 11.5 kts.
General cargo vessel with eight 5-ton derricks.
5.4.1952: Launched by Nylands Verksteder AS, Oslo (Yard No. 369), for Finn Johnsens Rederi AS, (Kristian Jebsen, manager), Norway. 1952: Completed. 1963: Purchased by Kristian Jebsens Rederi AS, (Kristian Jebsen, manager), Norway, and

renamed LEKNES. 1967: Sold to AS Live, Norway, and renamed VELOX. 1970: Sold to Companhia Maritima Weston SA, Panama, and renamed WESTON. 1976: Sold to Portaitisa Shipping Company Ltd., Cyprus, and renamed NICOLAOS G. 1977: Sold to Yakub Nseir, Syria, and renamed SYRIA STAR. 1981: Sold for demolition.

AUN (Author's collection)

KORSNES (World Ship Society Photograph Library)

11. KORSNES (2) (1954 – 1966)
2,474g. 1,324n. 3,130d. 308.8 x 43.2 x 18.6 feet.
6-cyl. 2 S.C.S.A. (450 x 740mm) Fiat type oil engine made by SA Ansaldo, Genoa. 1,350 bhp. 12 kts.
General cargo vessel with eight 5-ton derricks.
23.5.1948: Launched as MAURANGER by Societa Odero Terni Orlando, La Spezia (Yard No. 314), for Skibs Hosanger AS, (Westfal-Larsen & Company AS, managers), Norway. 1948: Completed. 1954: Purchased by Kristian Jebsens Rederi AS, (Kristian

7.9.1966: Completed. 1978: Sold to Trasporti Minerali Trieste SpA (T.M.T.), Italy, and renamed VISPY. (O.N. 730). 1984: Sold to Veneta Mineraria SpA, Naples, Italy. (O.N. 1489). 1986: Sold to Comemar SrL., Italy. 20.10.1991: Arrived at Piraeus under tow of the Greek tug KAPPA POWER (339g. / 59), for repairs. 1991: Sold to La Palma Marine Corp., Honduras, and renamed FORTUNE. 10.1993: Sold to Grafity Shipping Ltd., Cyprus buyers, and renamed SOTIRIS. 12.1993: Sold to P. P. Winds Shipping Company Ltd., Cyprus, and renamed MAVROUDIS. 6.1994: Sold to Prestige Shipping Overseas Inc., (P. P. Winds Shipping Company Ltd., Cyprus, managers), Belize, and renamed DAKIS 1. 1995: Vessel arrested at Vassiliko Bay in relation to registration anomalies. 1999: Sold to Belvento Trading Company, Bolivia, and renamed RED SKY BOLIVIA. (O.N. 005-31). 1999: Renamed RED SKY. 2001: Sold to Almonjo Shipping SA, and renamed GOLD I. Under Tonga flag. (O.N. 1089). 8.4.2002: Whilst at Port Said, fully laden, suffered leakage through a propeller gland that caused serious engine problems. Assistance was provided and the vessel was moved to a safe position and placed under arrest. 2004: Sold to unspecified Comoros flag buyers.

GARNES on the River Ouse at Goole (Author's collection / J. K. Byass)

6618249
24. BOLNES (1) (1966 –1972) Binsnes class
11,144g. 6,665n. 20,147d.   520' 0" (BB) x 71' 5" x 29' 6" oa.
6-cyl. 2 S.C.S.A. (680 x 1,250mm) Sulzer 6RD68 type oil engine made by the shipbuilder. 7,100 bhp. 13 kts.
Bulk carrier with five 7-ton derricks.
1.4.1965: Ordered from Scotts Shipbuilding & Engineering Company Ltd., Greenock (Yard No. 706), jointly by Tenax Steamship Company Ltd., and H. Clarkson & Company Ltd., London. 29.11.1965: Keel laid. 30.8.1966: Launched for the shipbuilder's own account, (Tenax Steamship Company Ltd., managers), London. (O.N. 306975). 28.10.1966: Completed, at a cost of £1,406,077. 1972: Owners restyled as Scotts of Greenock (Est.1710) Ltd. 1972: Sold to Tenax Steamship Company Ltd., London. 1972: Owners restyled as Biovale Ltd., (Kristian Jebsens Rederi AS, managers). 1972: Sold to Compania Ultramarine SA, Greece, and renamed OCEAN SOVEREIGN, under Liberia flag. (O.N. 4347). 1978: Transferred to Greek flag. 1983:

Sold to Lincoln Maritime SA, Panama, and renamed INGAPIRCA. 1983: Sold to Maritima Andina SA, Ecquador. 1985: Sold to Naviera del Pacifico C. A. (NAPACA), (Irgens Larsen AS, managers), Ecquador, and renamed MARIA JOSE. 23.8.1986: Arrived at Ulsan for discharge followed by sale for demolition. 27.8.1986: Moved out to an anchorage and subsequently during the passage of Typhoon "Vera", dragged her anchor and grounded at a position 35.28 N., 129.33 E., in a severely damaged condition. 1.11.1986: Delivered "as lay" to Hyundai Precision Industry Company Ltd., Ulsan. 5.11.1986: Demolition commenced in situ.

BOLNES 26 June 1969, with dark hull. Evidence of the old pale grey hull shows through.
(World Ship Society Photograph Library)

BIRKNES at Leith

(Author's collection)

6713142
25. BIRKNES (1) (1967 – 1973) Birknes class
12,456g. 6,297n. 19,710d. 521' 10" (BB) x 71' 4" x 31' 1½" oa.
6-cyl. 2 S.C.S.A. (620 x 1,400mm) B&W 6-62VT2BF-140 type oil engine made by J. G. Kincaid & Company Ltd., Greenock. 6,550 bhp. 14.5 kts.
Bulk carrier with five 7-ton derricks. Fitted for 2 passengers.
11.4.1967: Launched by Lithgows Ltd., Port Glasgow (Yard No. 1162), for Kristian Jebsens Rederi AS, (Kristian Jebsen, manager), Norway. 6.7.1967: Completed. 1973: Sold to Panlyras Shipping Corp., Greece, and renamed CAPTAIN PANDELIS S. LYRAS.

6-cyl. 2 S.C.S.A. (620 x 1,400mm) B&W 6-62VT2BF-140 type oil engine made by J. G. Kincaid & Company Ltd., Greenock. 7,200 bhp. 14 kts.

Bulk carrier with five 11½-ton derricks.

25.7.1968: Launched by Lithgows Ltd., Port Glasgow (Yard No. 1170), for Tenax Steamship Company Ltd., (Kristian Jebsens Rederi AS, managers), London. 23.10.1968: Arrived in tow at Bergen for completion by Bergens Mekaniske Verksteder AS. 13.12.1968: Completed. (O.N. 336992). 1972: Owners restyled as Biovale Ltd., (same managers). 1973: Owners restyled as Jebsens (UK) Ltd. 1973: Sold to Seven Seas Transportation Ltd., India, and renamed SATYA PADAM. (O.N. 1561). 1988: Sold for demolition.

BELLNES on the New Waterway in June 1970, showing signs of the old pale grey hull.

(W. J. Harvey)

6829020

30. BELLNES (1) (1969 – 1974) Birknes class

12,404g. 6,368n. 19,710d. 521' 10" (BB) x 71' 4" x 31' 1¼" oa.

6-cyl. 2 S.C.S.A. (620 x 1,400mm) B&W 6-62VT2BF-140 type oil engine made by J. G. Kincaid & Company Ltd., Greenock. 7,200 bhp. 14 kts.

Bulk carrier with five 7-ton derricks.

22.10.1968: Launched by Lithgows Ltd., Port Glasgow (Yard No. 1171), for Tenax Steamship Company Ltd., (Kristian Jebsens Rederi AS, managers), London. 19.3.1969: Completed for H. Clarkson & Company Ltd., (Tenax Steamship Company Ltd., managers), London. (O.N. 337096). 1972: Managers restyled as Biovale Ltd. 1973: Managers restyled as Jebsens (UK) Ltd. 1974: Renamed SILVERFORTH, and removed from management. 1975: Sold to Silver Bulk Carriers Ltd., London. 1978: Sold to Cordoba Shipping Company Ltd., Greece, and renamed ALBAFORTH. 1982: Sold to Yusuf Kalkavan Ogullari Denizcilik Yatirium Sanaya ve Ticaret AS, Turkey, and renamed KAPTAN YUSUF KALKAVAN. (O.N. 5067). 15.2.1986: Suffered main engine failure and grounded at a position 15.13 N., 42.32 E., 7 miles off Saleef, and was abandoned by her crew. 26.4.1986: Refloated by Selco Singapore (Pte) Ltd., Singapore. 24.5.1986: Arrived at Suez in tow of SALVICEROY (492g. /72). 11.12.1986: Beached in Suez Bay, having developed leaks. 2.3.1987: Sold by auction to Said Abdul Fadeel and Ali Abdul Hafez. 3.6.1987: Arrived at Gadani Beach having been resold for demolition.

6904416

31. VIGSNES (3) (1969 – 1978) Raknes class

As built;   2,806g. 1,733n. 4,380d. 314' 4" x 45' 8" x 20' 10" oa.
Post 1994:   2,672g. 1,575n. 4,380d.
Post 1997:   2,672g. 1,575n. 4,450d.
Two, 8-cyl. 4 S.C.S.A. (250 x 300mm) Normo LSMC8 type oil engines made by Bergens Mekaniske Verksteder AS, Bergen, geared to a single screw shaft with a controllable pitch propeller. 2,080 bhp. 12.25 kts.
Ice strengthened general cargo vessel with four 5-ton derricks.
3.12.1968: Launched by Fr. Lürssen Werft GmbH & Company, Bremen-Vegesak (Yard No. 13390), for Kristian Jebsens Rederi AS, (Kristian Jebsen, manager), Norway. 15.4.1969: Completed. 1978: Sold to Slobodna Plovidba, Yugoslavia, and renamed ROGOZNICA. 1991: Transferred to S. P. Shipping Ltd., (Slobodna Plovidba, managers), St Vincent and The Grenadines flag. (O.N. 3377). 1993: Transferred to Croatia flag. 1994: Sold to Libertas Development Corp, Dubrovnik, and renamed AMALIJA. 2000: Sold to Globex Ltd, Durres, Albania, and renamed DARIL.

VIGSNES returning from builders sea trials   (Author's collection / Fr. Lürrsen Werft)

BRUNES leaving the New Waterway. (W. J. Harvey)

6910013
32. BRUNES (2) (1969 – 1975) Baugnes class
13,124g. 8,265n. 21,206d. 520'4" (BB) x 75' 0" x 31' 3½" oa.
Two, 8-cyl. 4 S.C.S.A. (450 x 540mm), B&W 8S45HU type oil engines made by Helsingor Skibsvaerft og Maskinfabrik AS, Helsingor, geared to a single screw shaft with a controllable pitch propeller. 8,800 bhp. 14.5 kts.
Bulk carrier with six 12-ton Velle type derricks capable of operating grabs carried aboard.

18.2.1969: Launched by Lithgows Ltd., Port Glasgow (Yard No. 1172), for Kristian Jebsens Rederi AS, (Kristian Jebsen, manager), Norway. 2.9.1969: Completed. 1975: Sold to Antar Shipping Ltd., Greece, and renamed KATHY C. 1978: Sold to Viva Maritime Inc., Greece, and renamed BRENDA. 1980: Renamed MINORIES LUCK. 1981: Sold to D. Kosmos, C. Karafotias and E. Karaelias, Greece, and renamed DIMITRIOS. 1982: Sold to White Water Bay Shipping Company, Greece. 1.2.1983: Whilst on a voyage from Rotterdam to Bombay, wrecked on Cabezos Reef, five miles from Tarifa Light, in a position 36.00 N., 05.42 W.

TINNES (Author's collection)

6915922
33. TINNES (2) (1969 – 1978) Raknes class
As built;   2,806g. 1,733n. 4,450d. 314' 4" x 45' 8" x 20' 10" oa.
Post 1994: 2,718g. 1,575n. 4,428d.
Two, 8-cyl. 4 S.C.S.A. (250 x 300mm) Normo LSMC8 type oil engines made by Bergens Mekaniske Verksteder AS, Bergen, geared to a single screw shaft with a controllable pitch propeller. 2,080 bhp. 13.5 kts.
Ice strengthened general cargo vessel with four 5-ton derricks.
16.4.1969: Launched by Fr. Lürssen Werft GmbH & Company, Bremen-Vegesak (Yard No. 13396), for Kristian Jebsens Rederi AS, (Kristian Jebsen, manager), Norway. 22.9.1969: Completed. 1978: Sold to Obalna Plovidba, Split, Yugoslavia, and renamed CIKOLA. 1982: Sold to Splitska Plovidba, Yugoslavia. 1991: Sold to Cement Transport and Shipping Company Ltd., (Splitska Plovidba managers), St Vincent and The Grenadines flag. 1992: Transferred to Splitska Plovidba dd, Split, Croatia, and to Croatia flag.

6917499
34. BAUGNES (1969 – 1979) Baugnes class
13,124g. 8,265n. 21,546d. 520' 4" (BB) x 75' 0" x 31' 3½" oa.
Two, 8-cyl. 4 S.C.S.A. (450 x 540mm) B&W 8S45HU type oil engines made by Burmeister & Wains Maskin-og-Skipsbyggeri, Copenhagen, geared to a single screw shaft with a controllable pitch propeller. 8,800 bhp. 14.75 kts.
Post 1978: 12-cyl. 4 S.C.S.A. (400 x 460mm) Pielstick 12PC2V-400 vee type oil engine made by Aktibolaget Lindholmen Motor, Gothenburg. 7,800 bhp. 14.75 kts.
Bulk carrier with six 12-ton Velle type derricks capable of operating grabs carried aboard.
19.5.1969: Launched by Lithgows (1969) Ltd., East Yard, Port Glasgow (Yard No. 1173), for Kristian Jebsens Rederi AS, Norway. 17.11.1969: Completed. 1978: Re-engined. 1979: Sold to Jin Yang Shipping Company Ltd., South Korea, and renamed WESTBON. 1982: Sold to KS Line Corp., S. Korea. (O.N. BSR-695582). 1984: Sold to

Korea Shipping Corp., South Korea. 21.11.1986: Arrived at Ulsan for demolition. 22.11.1986: Hyundai Precision Industry Company Ltd., commenced work.

35. FIDUCIA (1)   **(1969 – 1975)** see ship No. C.2. in part two.

36. GRATIA   **(1969 – 1977)** see ship No. C.3. in part two.

37. LAETITIA   **(1969 – 1975)** see ship No. C.4. in part two.

BAKNES in Canadian waters. (Author's collection)

6929856
38. BAKNES (1970 – 1974) Baugnes class
13,241g. 7,951n. 21,546d. 520' 0" (BB) x 75' 0" x 31' 3½" oa.
Two, 8-cyl. 4 S.C.S.A. (450 x 540mm) B&W 8S45HU type oil engines made by AS Burmeister & Wains Maskin-og-Skibsbyggeri, Copenhagen, geared to a single screw shaft with a controllable pitch propeller. 8,800 bhp. 14.75 kts.
Bulk carrier with six 12-ton Velle type derricks capable of operating grabs carried aboard.
1968: Ordered from Lithgows Ltd., Port Glasgow (Yard No. 1175), by H. Clarkson & Company Ltd., (Tenax Steamship Company Ltd., managers), London. Order subcontracted to Scotts Shipbuilding & Engineering Company Ltd., Greenock. 30.12.1968: Keel laid. 1.10.1969: Launched by, builder restyled, Scotts Shipbuilding Company (1969) Ltd., Greenock. 10.2.1970: Completed for the Industrial and Commercial Finance Corporation Ltd., (same managers), London. (O.N. 338972). 1970: Owners restyled as the Nile Steamship Company Ltd., (J. & J. Denholm (Management) Ltd., Glasgow, appointed as managers), London. 1972: Managers restyled as Denholm Ship Management Ltd. 1974: Removed from management and renamed SILVERCLYDE. 1978: Sold to Silver Shipping (Jersey) Ltd. 1979: Sold to Argo Shipping (Jersey) Ltd., and renamed ARGOCLYDE. 1979: Sold to Heiracon Shipping Corp., Greece, and renamed CHIOS PILOT. 1981: Sold to Topaz Navigation SA, Panama, and renamed TOPAZ. (O.N. 11067-81C). 1982: Sold to Higgins Steamship SA, Philippines, and renamed LAPIS. 1984: Sold to Star Shipping Company, (Northern Star Shipping Company Ltd., Panama, managers), Hong Kong, and renamed INDUSTRIAL TRADER. 1986: Sold to Higgins Steamship SA, Panama. 1988: Sold to Marine Trust Shipping Company Inc., Panama, and renamed FIDILITY TRUST. 1989: Sold to Tong Yee Navigation Company SA, Panama, and renamed TONG YEE. 1990: Owners restyled as

Tong Yee Marine Company Ltd., (Hung Muo Shipping Agency Company Ltd., managers). 1994: Sold for demolition.

JENNES (Xerox copy source unknown)

6930790
39. JENNES (1970 – 1974) Jennes class
As built: 4,179g. 2,926n. 6,500d. 364' 3" (BB) x 56' 1" x 22' 11" oa.
Post 1974: 4,594g. 3,559n. 7,511d. 123.22 (BB) x 17.10 x 6.986 metres oa.
Two, 12-cyl. 4 S.C.S.A. (250 x 300mm) Normo KVM-12 vee type oil engines made by Bergens Mekaniske Verksteder AS, Bergen, geared to a single screw shaft with a controllable pitch propeller. 3,600 bhp. 13.75 kts.
Post 1977: Two, 12-cyl. 4 S.C.S.A. (250 x 300mm) Normo KVGB-12 vee type oil engines made by Bergens Mekaniske Verksteder AS, Bergen. 3,800 bhp. 13.5 kts.
General cargo vessel with four 7½-ton Velle type derricks capable of handling grabs carried aboard.
23.9.1969: Launched by Fr. Lürssen Werft GmbH & Company, Bremen-Vegesak (Yard No. 13397), for Nordsee Frachtschiffahrt GmbH & Company KG, (Reederei J. Jost), Flensburg, W. Germany. 5.3.1970: Completed. 2.3.1974: Arrived on River Tyne to be lengthened, by Swan, Hunter Ship Repairers Ltd. 1974: Sold to Midigirl Shipping Corp, Liberia, and renamed MIDIGIRL. 1976: Sold to Reederei J. Jost, Flensburg, W. Germany, and renamed JENNES. 1977: Re-engined, and renamed FJELLNES. 1981: Transferred to General Shipping Company Ltd., Philippines, and renamed GENERAL LIM. (O.N. 11446-81). 1983: Transferred to Aboitiz, Jebsen Bulk Transport Corp., Philippines. 1984: Transferred to Serpens (Panama) SA, Panama, (Aboitiz, Jebsen Bulk Transport Corp., managers). 1985: Sold to Splitska Plovidba, Yugoslavia, and renamed VELI VAROS. 17.9.1987: Delivered to Gadani Beach for demolition.

7013757
40. BULKNES (1) (1970 – 1984) Baugnes class
13,235g. 7,952n. 21,200d. 520' 4" (BB) x 75' 0" x 31' 3½" oa.
Two, 8-cyl. 4 S.C.S.A. (450 x 540mm) B&W 8S45HU type oil engines made by Helsingor Skibsvaerft og Maskinbyggeri AS, Helsingor, geared to a single screw shaft with a controllable pitch propeller. 8,800 bhp. 14.75 kts.
Bulk carrier with six 12-ton Velle type derricks capable of operating grabs carried aboard. Cargo handling gear was subsequently removed.
1968: Ordered from Lithgows Ltd., Port Glasgow (Yard No. 1176), by H. Clarkson & Company Ltd., (Tenax Steamship Company Ltd., managers), London. Order subcontracted to Scotts Shipbuilding & Engineering Company Ltd., Greenock. 2.7.1969: Keel laid by, builders restyled, Scotts Shipbuilding Company (1969) Ltd., Greenock.

19.3.1970: Launched. 5.6.1970: Completed for Tenax Steamship Company Ltd., London. (O.N. 339171). 1972: Owners restyled as Biovale Ltd., London. 1973: Owners restyled as Jebsens (UK) Ltd. 1974: Transferred to Jebsen, Dillingham Shipping Ltd., London. 1975: Transferred to Suntana Shipping Ltd., (Jebsens (UK) Ltd., managers), London. 1978: Shipping Corporation of New Zealand Ltd., appointed as managers. 1983: Jebsens (UK) Ltd., appointed as managers. 1983: Transferred to Jebsens Bulknes Ltd., (Jebsen Ship Management Ltd, managers), London. 1984: Sold to Sougerka Maritime Company Ltd., Greece, and renamed KAPETAN ANTONIS, under Panama flag. (O.N. 13077-Li). 1985: Sold to Julianae Shipping Corp., Panama. 4.1987: Sold to Metropolitana Oriental SA, Panama, and renamed CAPTAIN FRANK. 1988: Sold to Lloyd Shipping Company Inc., Panama, and renamed VALDORA. 1989: Marimed Shipping Ltd., appointed as managers. 1991: Sold to Transbulk Shipping Ltd., (Ilyas Investments SA, Karachi, managers), and renamed ALDORA. 1992: Sold to Java SA, (Goldbeam International Ltd., Hong Kong, managers), and renamed EXCELLUS, under Panama flag. (.N. 13077-PEXT). 26.2.1993: Panama flag closed – vessel sold to non-trading buyers, for demolition. 1998: Reported to Lloyds Register as trading again as ZHONG HAI, under Vietnam register. 5.2005: Still listed, in Lloyd's Register without owner, or manager, or flag.

BULKNES (Author's collection)

7009988
41. BRINKNES (1) (1970 – 1973) Jennes class
As built: 4,279g. 2,926n. 6,777d. 364' 3" (BB) x 56' 1" x 22' 11"oa.
Post 1974: 4,594g. 3,559n. 7,511d. 123.22 (BB) x 17.10 x 6.986 metres oa.
Two, 12-cyl. 4 S.C.S.A. (250 x 300mm), Normo KVM-12 vee type oil engines made by Bergens Mekaniske Verksteder AS, Bergen, geared to a single screw shaft with a controllable pitch propeller. 3,600 bhp. 13.5 kts.
Post 1977: Two, 12-cyl. 4 S.C.S.A. (250 x 300mm), Normo KVGB-12 vee type oil engines made by Bergens Mekaniske Verksteder AS, Bergen. 3,800 bhp. 13.25 kts.
General cargo vessel with four 7½ -ton Velle type derricks capable of handling grabs carried aboard.
21.1.1970: Launched by Fr. Lürssen Werft GmbH & Company, Bremen-Vegesak (Yard No. 13398), for J. Jost See-Transport GmbH, Flensburg, W. Germany. 20.6.1970: Completed for Brinknes Schiffahrtsges Franz Lange GmbH & Company KG, W. Germany. 1973: Sold to Midiboy Shipping Corp, Liberia, and renamed MIDIBOY. (O.N. 4539). 1974: Lengthened by Swan, Hunter Shiprepairers Ltd., Newcastle. 1977: Sold to Brinknes Schiffahrtsges Franz Lange GmbH & Company KG, W. Germany, re-engined, and renamed FOSSNES. 1977: Transferred to Kristian Jebsens Rederi AS, Norway. 1981: Transferred to Isskip h/f., Iceland, and renamed AKRANES. (O.N. 1589). 1989: Sold to Unicoast Maritime Company Ltd., Cyprus, (O.N. 708848).

4.4.1991: Arrived at Ferrol in tow of M. C. THUNDER (496g. /75), for repair having lost her rudder. 1995: Sold to Villach Shipping Company Ltd., (Osterreichischer Lloyd Ship Management GmbH, managers), Cyprus, and renamed VILLACH. 2002: Sold to Viceli Shipping SA, (Derpina SA, managers), and renamed MELTEM, under the Georgia flag. 2002: Renamed MELTEM G. 10.2004: Sold to Gram Shipping SA., Panama, and renamed ELTEM, under Comoros flag.

BRINKNES (Xerox copy / source unknown)

7029598
42. BINSNES (2) (1970 – 1973) Baugnes class
13,240g. 7,950n. 21,546d.   520' 4" (BB) x 75' 0" x 31' 3½" oa.
Two, 8-cyl. 4 S.C.S.A. (450 x 540mm) B&W 8S45HU type oil engines made by Helsingor Skibsvaerft og Maskinbyggeri AS, Helsingor, geared to a single screw shaft with a controllable pitch propeller. 8,800 bhp. 14.5 kts.
Bulk carrier with six 12-ton Velle type derricks capable of operating grabs carried aboard.
1968: Ordered from Lithgows Ltd., Port Glasgow (Yard No. 1179), by H. Clarkson & Company Ltd., (Tenax Steamship Company Ltd., managers), London. Order sub-contracted to Scotts Shipbuilding & Engineering Company Ltd., Greenock. 30.1.1970: Keel laid by, builders restyled, Scotts Shipbuilding Company (1969) Ltd., Greenock. 16.9.1970: Launched. 21.10.1970: Fire in hold whilst fitting out. 25.11.1970: Completed for H. Clarkson & Company Ltd., (same managers), London. (O.N. 341155). 1972: Managers restyled as Biovale Ltd. 1973: Managers restyled as Jebsens (UK) Ltd. 1973: Removed from management. 1974: Renamed SILVERTWEED. 1975: Sold to Silver Bulk Carriers Ltd. 1978: Sold to Silver Shipping (Jersey) Ltd. 1979: Sold to Argo Shipping (Jersey) Ltd., and renamed ARGOTWEED. 1979: Sold to the Putnam Corp., Greece, and renamed CHIOS CAPTAIN. 9.7.1980: Whilst on a voyage from Aqaba to Singapore was beached off Bombay having developed leaks. 24.7.1980: Refloated taken to Bombay and subsequently repaired. 9.8.1981: Arrived at Mariveles in tow of the Dutch tug MISSISSIPPI (674g. /60), and laid up. 1982: Sold to St. Paul Shipping Inc., Panama, and renamed DENNIS CARRIER. 1983: Sold to Merry Rich Shipping Inc., Panama. 1984: Sold to Northern Star Shipping Company, Hong Kong. 21-22.6.1985: Whilst still in lay up at Mariveles, was driven ashore by Typhoon "Hal" and wrecked.

TELNES proceding on sea trials. Note the addition of a bulbous bow to this design, this being the only unit with one fitted.

(Author's collection / Fr. Lürrsen Werft)

TELNES in later life when fitted with deck cranes amidship

(W. J. Harvey)

7018422
43. TELNES (4) (1970 – 1979) Altnes class
As built: 2,810g. 1,734n. 4,470d. 314' 4" (BB) x 45' 8" x 20' 0" oa.
Post 1994: 3,263g. 1,957n. 4,470d.
Post 1996: 2,876g. 1,124n. 4,470d.
Two, 8-cyl. 4 S.C.S.A. (250 x 300mm), Normo LSMC8 type oil engines made by Bergens Mekaniske Verksteder AS, Bergen, geared to a single screw shaft with a controllable pitch propeller. 2,080 bhp. 13.5 kts.
Ice strengthened general cargo vessel with four 5-ton derricks. Later converted to twin 5-ton cranes amidship in lieu of those derricks.
13.4.1970: Launched by Fr. Lürssen Werft GmbH & Company, Bremen-Vegesak (Yard No. 13399), for Kristian Jebsens Rederi AS, Norway. 15.10.1970: Completed. 1979: Sold to Dubhe di Navigacione SpA, Italy, and renamed MARIA DORMIO. (O.N. 209). 1994: Sold to Bruzia di Navigazione S. r. l., Crotone, Italy, and renamed MAR GRANDE.

7028489
44. BROOKNES (1) (1970 – 1976) Baugnes class
As built: 13,098g. 8,326n. 12,392d. 520' 4" (BB) x 75' 0" x 31' 3½" oa.
Post 1976: 16,709g 11,860n. 24,481d. 195.94 (BB) x 22.94 x 9.538 metres oa.
Post 1994: 16,522g. 6,466n. 24,481d.

Two, 8-cyl. 4 S.C.S.A. (450 x 540mm) B&W 8S45HU type oil engines made by Helsingor Skibsvaerft og Maskinbyggeri AS, Helsingor, geared to a single screw shaft with a controllable pitch propeller. 8,800 bhp. 14.5 kts.

Post 1982: Two, 6-cyl. 4 S.C.S.A. (450 x 520mm) MaK 6M552AK type oil engines made by Krupp-MaK Maschinenbau GmbH, Kiel. 8,782 bhp. 13 kts. Also fitted with a thwartship thrust propeller forward.

Bulk carrier with six 12-ton Velle type derricks capable of operating grabs carried aboard.

2.9.1970: Launched by Lithgows (1969) Ltd., Port Glasgow (Yard No. 1177), for Kristian Jebsens Rederi AS, Norway. 18.12.1970: Completed. 1973: Sold to Langra Schiffahrtsges GmbH & Company KG, (See-Transport GmbH, managers), W. Germany. 1976: Sold to Algoma Steamship Ltd., (Algoma Central Railway, managers), Canada, lengthened, and renamed ALGOSEA. (O.N. 318427). 1977: Converted into a self-discharging bulk carrier. 6.1979: Transferred to Algoma Central Railway, Saint Catharines, Ontario. 5.1982: Re-engined, and renamed SAUNIERE. 1990: Algoma Central Marine Inc., appointed as managers. 1996: Transferred to Canada flag. 2000: Restriction on voyage areas and seasons imposed. 2004: Seaway Marine Transport Inc., Saint Catharines, appointed as managers.

BROOKNES (R. D. Scott, courtesy of M. R. Dippy)

7112228
45. TORNES (2) (1971 – 1974) Tornes class
1,589g. 1,119n. 3,085d. 262' 5" (BB) x 45' 4" x 17' 5¾" oa.

16-cyl. 4 S.C.S.A. (250 x 300mm) Normo KVM16 vee type oil engine made by Normo Gruppen AS, Bergen, geared to a controllable pitch propeller. 1,650 bhp. 13.5 kts.

Post 1979: Two, 12 cyl. 4 S.C.S.A. (250 x 300mm) Normo KVM-12 vee type oil engines made by Bergens Mekaniske Verksteder AS, Bergen. 2,250 bhp. 13 kts.

Ice strengthened general cargo vessel with four 5-ton Velle type derricks capable of operating grabs.

23.1.1971: Launched by Batservice Vaerft AS Mandal (Yard No. 571), for Kristian Jebsens Rederi AS, Norway. 27.5.1971: Completed. 1974: Sold to Gallic Estates Ltd., and Denholm Line Steamers Ltd., London, (Denholm Maclay Company Ltd., managers), and renamed GALLIC MINCH. (O.N. 363443). 1975: Transferred to Gallic Shipping Ltd., (same managers). 1979: Re-engined. 1981: Sold to West Bay Shipping Ltd., London, and renamed ARGO SPRAY, under Hong Kong flag. (Gallic Shipping group). 1983: Sold to Companhia Naviera Puerto Plata SA, (Lineas Maritimas de Santo Domingo SA, managers), Dominican Republic, and renamed PUERTO PLATA. (O.N. 016). 6.1989: Foundered.

BRISKNES (M.R. Dippy)

7002382
46. BRISKNES (1) (1971 – 1974) Baugnes class
13,124g. 8,253n. 21,546d.   520' 4" (BB) x 75' 0" x 31' 3½" oa.
Two, 8-cyl. 4 S.C.S.A. (450 x 540mm) B&W 8S45HU type oil engines made by Helsingor Skibsvaerft og Maskinbyggeri AS, Helsingor, geared to a single screw shaft with a controllable pitch propeller. 8,800 bhp. 14.5 kts.
Post 1977: 12-cyl. 4 S.C.S.A. (400 x 460mm) Pielstick 12PC2V-400 vee type oil engine made by Ishikawajima Harima Heavy Industries (IHI), Tokyo. 7,800 bhp. 14.75 kts.
Bulk carrier with six 12-ton Velle type derricks capable of operating grabs carried aboard.
1969: Keel laid as BRISKNES by Lithgows (1969) Ltd., Port Glasgow (Yard No. 1174), for Kristian Jebsens Rederi AS, Norway. 11.11.1969: Launched as AQUILA for Anatina AS and Alfa AS, Norway. 10.4.1970: Completed. 5.1971: Sold to Kristian Jebsens Rederi AS, Norway, and renamed BRISKNES. 1974: Sold to Arcadian Shipping Ltd., Greece, and renamed JANET C. 1.1977: Re-engined. 1978: Sold to Evia Maritime Inc., Greece, and renamed MANOS SAVE. 1979: Sold to Pinecrest Services Inc., Greece, and renamed EFTHALIA. 1980: Sold to Mar de Internacional SA, Panama, (Kuk Dong Merchant Shipping Company Ltd., S. Korea, managers), and renamed BROTHER STAR. (O.N. BSR-705812). 1982: Transferred to Kuk Je Shipping Company Ltd., S. Korea. Prior to 5.6.1987: Arrived at Busan for demolition.

BLIDNES (W. J. Harvey)

7046211
47. BLIDNES (1971 – 1979) Baugnes class
13,116g. 8,261n. 21,546d.   520' 4" (BB) x 75' 0" x 31' 3½" oa.
Two, 8-cyl. 4 S.C.S.A. (450 x 540mm) B&W 8S45HU type oil engines made by Helsingor Skibsvaerft og Maskinbyggeri AS, Helsingor, geared to a single screw shaft with a controllable pitch propeller. 8,800 bhp. 14.5 kts.

Bulk carrier with six 12-ton Velle type derricks capable of operating grabs carried aboard.
12.1968: Ordered by Gearbulk AS, (Kristian Gerhard Jebsen), Norway, from Lithgows (1969) Ltd., Port Glasgow (Yard No. 1178). 28.1.1971: Launched for Kristian Jebsens Rederi AS, Norway. 1.6.1971: Completed. 1979: Sold to Kampos Companhia Naviera SA, (Frangos Elias & Son Shipping Company, managers) Greece, and renamed KAMPOS. (O.N. 7580). 22.12.1984: Departed from Houston bound for Apapa and Lagos. 14.2.1985: Suffered main machinery failure in the Atlantic. 1.3.1985: Arrived at Curucao in tow of the Dutch salvage tug SMIT LONDON (2,273g. / 75). Cargo subsequently trans-shipped to LA GUAJIRA (18,028g. / 71). 8.8.1986: Delivered at Recife, Brazil for demolition.

FONNES in the New Waterway. (Author's collection)

7113698
48. FONNES (1) (1971 – 1974) Tornes class
1,594g. 1,171n. 3,097d. 262' 4" (BB) x 45' 3" x 17' 4" oa.
16-cyl. 4 S.C.S.A. (250 x 300mm) Normo KVM16 vee type oil engine made by Normo Gruppen AS, Bergen, geared to a controllable pitch propeller. 1,650 bhp. 13.5 kts.
Ice strengthened general cargo vessel with four 5-ton Velle type derricks capable of operating grabs.
16.4.1971: Launched by Batservice Vaerft AS Mandal (Yard No. 572), for Tenax Steamship Company Ltd., London. 30.9.1971: Completed. (O.N. 342904). 1972: Owners restyled as Biovale Ltd. 1973: Owners restyled as Jebsens (UK) Ltd. 1974: Sold to Gallic Estates Ltd., (The Denholm Line Steamers Ltd., managers), London, and renamed GALLIC STREAM. 15.1.1975: Whilst on a voyage from Svelgen to Stjernoy, suffered engine damage and drifted ashore on Bremnesodden, Hamaroy, in a position 68.07.30 N., 15.23.12 E. 16.1.1975: Slipped off and sank.

MORNES in the New Waterway. (W. J. Harvey)

7129233
49. MORNES (1) (1972 – 1974) Tornes class
As built.   1,594g. 1,171n. 3,000d. 262' 6" (BB) x 45' 3" x 17' 5½" oa.
Post 1994:   1,841g. 1,073n. 3,140d.
16-cyl. 4 S.C.S.A. (250 x 300mm) Normo KVM-16 vee type oil engine made by Normo Gruppen AS, Bergen, geared to a controllable pitch propeller. 1,650 bhp. 13.5 kts.
Ice strengthened general cargo vessel with four 5-ton Velle type derricks capable of operating grabs.
26.4.1971: Launched by Batservice Vaerft AS Mandal (Yard No. 574), for Tenax Steamship Company Ltd., London. 14.4.1972: Completed. (O.N. 343127). 1972: Owners restyled as Biovale Ltd. 1973: Owners restyled as Jebsens (UK) Ltd. 1974: Sold to The Denholm Line Steamers Ltd., London, and renamed MONACH. 1983: Sold to Tinasmar SA, Panama, and renamed MONAC. (O.N. 12931-83). 1987: Sold to Vascomar S. A. S., di Scotto di Santono Michele e Ci., Italy, and thence to John Day Maritime Company SA, Sierra Leone, and renamed IBIZA. 1989: Sold to Ripemar S.n.C. di Guardascione Guiseppe e C., Italy, retaining Sierra Leone flag. 1992: Transferred to Italian flag. 1993: Sold to Intermed Shipping Srl, Italy. 1994: Sold to Ionian Shipping Corp., Panama, and renamed AGIOS VISSARION. (O.N. 22201-95C). 7.2002: Sold to Victor de Roche & Louis de Roche, retaining Panama flag. 2003: Sold to Transmed Maritime, Bratislava, Slovakia, (Argo Maritime SA, Varna, Bulgaria, managers), and renamed ASTRA.

FURUNES proceeding on sea trials. (Author's collection / Fr. Lürrsen Werft)

7127596
50. FURUNES (1) (1972 – 1981) Furunes class
As built: 4,851g. 3,629n. 7,580d. 404' 6" (BB) x 56' 1" x 22' 5" oa.
Post 1994: 4,821g. 3,107n. 7,702d.
Post 1997: 4,821g. 3,107n. 7,580d.
Two, 12-cyl. 4 S.C.S.A. (250 x 300mm) KVM-12 vee type oil engines made by Normo Gruppen AS, Bergen, geared to a single controllable pitch propeller. 3,798 bhp. 14.5 kts.
Post 1979: Two, 12-cyl. 4 S.C.S.A. (250 x 300mm) Normo KVM-12 vee type oil engines made by Bergens Mekaniske Verksteder AS, Bergen. 3,800 bhp. 13.25 kts.
Ice strengthened bulk carrier with four 7½-ton Velle type derricks capable of operating grabs carried aboard.
18.12.1971: Launched by Fr. Lürssen Werft GmbH & Company, Bremen-Vegesak (Yard No. 13400), for Tenax Steamship Company Ltd., London. 26.4.1972: Completed. (O.N. 343159). 1972: Owners restyled as Biovale Ltd. 1973: Owners restyled as Kristian Jebsens (UK) Ltd. 1979: Re-engined with similar machinery. 1980: Transferred to Singleton Cia. Naviera SA, (J. Jost, manager), Panama, and renamed FIDUCIA. 1983: Transferred to Jebsens General Malvar SA, (Jebsens Hamburg GmbH & Company KG, Hamburg, managers), Philippines, and renamed GENERAL MALVAR. 1985: Sold to Slobodna Plovidba, Yugoslavia, and renamed DRNIS. 1991: Sold to S. P. Shipping Company Ltd., (Slobodna Plovidba, managers), under Malta flag. 1998: Sold to Alfa Marina, Belize and renamed WAFERAH. 21.6.2004: Demolition commenced at an unspecified location.

7206990
51. SWIFTNES (1) (1972 – 1982) Swiftnes /Saltnes class
As built: 12,982g. 8,041n. 21,916d. 510' 3" (BB) x 75' 2" x 32' 3¼" oa.
Post 1994: 12,668g. 7,464n. 21,916d.
18-cyl. 4 S.C.S.A. (400 x 460mm) Pielstick 18PC2V-400 vee type oil engine made by the shipbuilder at Yokohama. 9,000 bhp. 13.75 kts.
Bulk carrier with five 12-ton Velle type derricks capable of operating grabs carried aboard.
29.2.1972: Launched by Nippon Kokan KK, Shimizu (Yard No. 315), for H. Clarkson & Company Ltd., London. 25.5.1972: Completed. (O.N. 343187). 1974: Sold to Silver Line Ltd., (Denholm Ship Management, managers), London, and by them to Jebsens (UK) Ltd., London. 1974: Transferred to Jebsen, Dillingham Shipping Ltd., (Denholm Ship Management, managers), London. 1979: Transferred to Pacnorse Shipping (UK) Ltd., London. 1981: Transferred to Jebsens Shipping Ltd., London. 1982: Transferred to Botelho Bulk Transport Corp, Philippines, and renamed GENERAL CAPINPIN. (O.N. 12896-83). 1983: Transferred to Aboitiz, Jebsen Bulk Transport Corp., Philippines. 1983: Sold to Advance Steamship Inc., (Kristian Jebsens Rederi AS, managers), Panama. 1985: Transferred to Philippine flag. 1987: Jebsens Ship Management Ltd., appointed as managers. 1988: Sold to Anpo Shipping Company Ltd., Cyprus, and renamed PROTEUS. 1989: Sold to Alpena Navigation Company Ltd., (Anpo Shipping Company Ltd., managers), Cyprus. 20.7.2000: Demolition commenced at an unspecified location.

7206809
52. BRIMNES (2) (1972 – 1974) Brimnes class
22,901g. 14,768n. 32,818d. 585' 0" (BB) x 89' 1" x 34' 0¾" oa
6-cyl. 2 S.C.S.A. (740 x 1,600mm) B&W 6K74EF type oil engine made by J. G. Kincaid & Company Ltd., Greenock. 11,600 bhp. 15.5 kts.
Bulk carrier with five 15-ton cranes capable of operating grabs carried aboard.

2.3.1972: Launched by Lithgows (1969) Ltd., Port Glasgow (Yard No. 1184), for Tenax Steamship Company Ltd., London. 30.6.1972: Completed. (O.N. 343245). 1972: Owners restyled as Biovale Ltd. 1973: Owners restyled as Kristian Jebsens (UK) Ltd. 1974: Transferred to Jebsen, Dillingham Shipping Ltd., (Jebsens (UK) Ltd., managers), London. 1980: Transferred to Pacnorse Shipping (UK) Ltd., (same managers). 1980: Sold to Italmare SpA, Italy, and renamed MARINA DI EQUA. 29.12.1981: Whilst on a voyage from Antwerp to Houston, foundered during a storm at a position 45.41 N., 09.54 W., off the coast of France. All 30 crew perished.

SALTNES (M.R.Dippy)

7216969
53. SALTNES (1) (1972 – 1981) Swiftnes /Saltnes class
As built: 12,982g. 8,046n. 21,916d. 510' 3" (BB) x 75' 2" x 32' 3¼" oa.
Post 1995: 12,794g. 7,483n. 21,916d.
18-cyl. 4 S.C.S.A. (400 x 460mm) Pielstick 18PC2V-400 vee type oil engine made by the shipbuilder at Yokohama. 9,000 bhp. 13.75 kts.
Bulk carrier with five 12-ton Velle type derricks capable of operating grabs carried aboard.
23.5.1972: Launched by Nippon Kokan KK, Shimizu (Yard No. 306), for H. Clarkson & Company Ltd., London. 21.8.1972: Completed for Tenax Steamship Company Ltd., London. (O.N. 358351). 1972: Owner restyled as Biovale Ltd. 1973: Owners restyled as Jebsens (UK) Ltd. 1974: Transferred to Jebsen, Dillingham Shipping Ltd., London. 1980: Transferred to Pacnorse Shipping (UK) Ltd., (Jebsens (UK) Ltd., managers). 1981: Transferred to Skala Navigation Ltd., (same managers), Singapore, and renamed BEAGLE. 1982: Transferred to Jebsens Beagle Shipping (Pte) Ltd., (Kristian Jebsen Singapore Ltd., managers), Singapore. 1984: Sold to Alderney Ltd., (Acomarit Marine Services (UK) Ltd., managers), Gibraltar, and renamed EUROPA POINT. 1988: Removed from management. 1990: Sold to Ciantana Shipping Company Ltd., Malta, and renamed SALVADOR. 1995: Sold to Aegean Steamship Enterprises SA, Panama, and renamed VARNAKOVA. (O.N. 24016-PEXT). 1996: Sold to Intermed Navigation SA, Panama, and renamed GINI I. (O.N. 24016-PEXT1). 1996: Sold to Willow Navigation Ltd., (Unicom Maritime, managers), Bahamian buyers, and renamed JEG FORTUNE. 1997: Sold to Lamer Shipping Inc., (Lamer Chartering Inc., managers), Panama, and renamed GENEVA I. (O.N. 26184-PEXT). 1.1999: Renamed NEVA II (same managers). 2.1999: Renamed EUROPA POINT and sold for $101.5 per light ton displacement, for demolition. 18.2.1999: Raj Metal Works (Private) Ltd., commenced work at Alang.

7211347
54. FJORDNES (1) (1972 – 1981) Furunes class
As built: 4,838g. 3,575n. 7,580d. 404' 4" (BB) x 55' 2" x 22' 4¾" oa.
Post 1994: 4,821g. 3,107n. 7,580d.

Two, 12-cyl. 4 S.C.S.A. (250 x 300mm) Normo KVM-12 vee type oil engines made by Bergens Mekaniske Verksteder AS, Bergen, geared to a single screw shaft with a controllable pitch propeller. 3,800 bhp. 14.5 kts.

Ice strengthened bulk carrier with four 7½-ton Velle type derricks capable of handling grabs carried aboard.

15.4.1972: Launched by Fr. Lürssen Werft GmbH & Company, Bremen-Vegesak (Yard No. 13420), for Kristian Jebsens Rederi AS, Norway. 1.11.1972: Completed. 1981: Transferred to Granby Island Shipping Company SA, Philippines, and renamed GENERAL LUNA. (O.N. 11536-82). 1982: Transferred to Botelho Bulk Transport Corp, Philippines. 1983: Transferred to Aboitiz, Jebsen Bulk Transport Corp, Philippines. 1984: Transferred to Granby Island Shipping Company SA, (Aboitiz, Jebsen Bulk Transport Corp., managers), Philippines. 1985: Sold to Slobodna Plovidba, Yugoslavia, and renamed PRIMOSTEN. 1991: Transferred to S. P. Shipping Company Ltd., Slobodna Plovidba, managers), under S. Vincent and the Grenadines flag. (O.N. 3397). 1998: Sold to P. & S. Shipping N. V. (same, managers), and renamed VALENTINA. 1999: Removed from management. 27.12.2001: Arrived at Mumbai, for demolition.

FJORDNES In the New Waterway. (W. J. Harvey)

SPRAYNES (World Ship Society Photograph Library)

7227279
55. SPRAYNES (1) (1972 – 1974) Swiftnes /Saltnes class
As built: 12,982g.   8,045n.   21,916d.   510' 3" (BB) x 75' 2" x 32' 3¼" oa.

Post 1994: 13,250g. 7,491n. 21,916d.
18-cyl. 4 S.C.S.A. (400 x 460mm) Pielstick 18PC2V-400 oil engine made by the shipbuilder at Yokohama. 9,000 bhp. 14 kts.
Bulk carrier with five 12-ton Velle type derricks capable of operating grabs carried aboard.
22.8.1972: Launched by Nippon Kokan KK, Shimizu (Yard No. 316), for Tenax Steamship Company Ltd., London. 21.11.1972: Completed for Biovale Ltd., London. (O.N. 358649). 1973: Owners restyled as Jebsens (UK) Ltd. 1974: Transferred to Jebsen, Dillingham Shipping Ltd., London. 1980: Transferred to Pacnorse Shipping (UK) Ltd. 1981: Transferred to Jebsens Shipping Ltd., London. 1983: Sold to Salag (Gibraltar) Ltd., (Acomarit Maritime Services SA, managers), Gibraltar, and renamed MONTARIK. 1984: Sold to Alderney Ltd., (Acomarit Maritime Services (UK) Ltd., managers), Gibraltar. 1985: Sold to Acomarit Maritime Services (UK) Ltd. 1988: Sold to Salag (Gibraltar) Ltd. 1990: Acomarit Services Maritimes SA, appointed as managers. 1991: Sold to Elka Shipping Company SA, (Jason Navigation Company Ltd., managers), Greece, and renamed IFIGENEIA. (O.N. 9847). 1993: Renamed GEORGIOS. 10.1.1997: LR Class suspended, laid-up – repairs required. 6.12.1997: Sailed from lay-up at Manila, with repairs still being required. 26.8.1998: Renamed GEORGIOS I, under Honduras flag. (O.N. 119830537-S). 10.9.1998: Arrived at Kaohsiung for demolition. 13.10.1998: Cheng Jen Enterprise Company Ltd., commenced work. 25.11.1998: Honduras registry closed.

BERNES (M. R. Dippy)

7221483
56. BERNES (2) (1972 – 1980) Brimnes class
22,901g. 14,767n. 32,738d. 585' 0" (BB) x 89' 1" x 33' 11" oa.
6-cyl. 2 S.C.S.A. (740 x 1,600mm) B&W 6K74EF type oil engine made by J. G. Kincaid & Company Ltd., Greenock. 10,600 bhp. 15 kts.
Bulk carrier with five 15-ton cranes capable of operating grabs carried aboard.
1972: Ordered by Tenax Steamship Company Ltd., from Lithgows (1969) Ltd., Port Glasgow (Yard No. 1185). 27.6.1972: Launched for Harrisons (Clyde) Ltd., (Tenax Steamship Company Ltd., managers), London. 29.12.1972: Completed for the Nile Steamship Company Ltd., (Biovale Ltd., managers), London. (O.N. 358726). 1973: Managers restyled as Jebsens (UK) Ltd. 1980: Sold to Italmare SpA, Italy, and renamed MARINA DI ALIMURI. (O.N. 108). 1989: Sold to Rubystar Shipping Corp., (Aegeus Shipping SA, managers), Greece, and renamed BOEM. 1993: Sold to Guang Dong Shipping Company Ltd., Shenzhen, Guang Dong Provence, China, and renamed GUANG SHUN.

SEALNES (Author's collection)

7306075
57. SEALNES (1) (1973 – 1983) Swiftnes /Saltnes class
As built: 12,982g. 8,041n. 21,916d.   510' 3" (BB) x 75' 2" x 32' 3¼" oa.
Post 1997: 12,726g. 7,484n. 21,916d.
18-cyl. 4 S.C.S.A. (400 x 460mm) Pielstick 18PC2V-400 oil engine made by the shipbuilder at Yokohama. 9,000 bhp. 14 kts.
Bulk carrier with five 12-ton Velle type derricks capable of operating grabs carried aboard.
24.11.1972: Launched by Nippon, Kokan KK, Shimizu (Yard No. 307), for Biovale Ltd., London.   24.2.1973: Completed for H. Clarkson & Company Ltd., (Biovale Ltd., managers), London. (O.N. 358819).   1974: Transferred to Bishopgate Shipping Company Ltd., (Jebsens (UK) Ltd., managers), London. 1974: Transferred to Jebsen, Dillingham Shipping Ltd., (Denholm Ship Management Ltd., managers), London. 1980: Transferred to Pacnorse Shipping (UK) Ltd., (Jebsens (UK) Ltd., managers). 1981: Transferred to Jebsens Shipping Ltd., London. 1983: Sold to Jordan National Shipping Lines Company Ltd., (Jebsens Ship Management Ltd, managers), Jordan, and renamed HITTEEN. (O.N. 15). 1986: Removed from management. 1989: Jebsens Ship Management Ltd., appointed as managers. 18.10.1990: Sold to Danton Shipping Ltd., Malta, and renamed ECUADOR. (O.N. 2555). 18.7.1994: Sold to Ecuador Shipping Company Ltd., (Goldenport Shipmanagement Ltd., managers), Malta, and renamed ISIDORA. 29.11.1995: Sold to Eurobulker V Shipping Ltd., Honduras, and renamed EUROBULKER V. (O.N. L-0356325). 7.1997: Ilias Shipping Corp., appointed as managers, and Malta flag closed. 22.10.1998: Last reported movement was her arrival at Piraeus. 2001: Sold to unspecified buyers and renamed MED GENERAL under Sao Tome & Principe flag.   5.2005: Still listed in Lloyd's Register without additional change to ownership detail.

FALKNES was based on yhe "Furunes class" hull although fitted with a new design superstructure   (W. J. Harvey)

7229760
58. FALKNES (1) (1973 – 1979) Falknes class

As built: 4,908g. 3,572n. 7,773d.   404' 4" (BB) x 55' 2" x 22' 4¾" oa.
Post 1995: 5,036g. 1,938n. 7,773d.
Two, 12-cyl. 4 S.C.S.A. (250 x 300mm) Normo KVM-12 vee type oil engines made by Bergens Mekaniske Verksteder AS, Bergen, geared to a single screw shaft with a controllable pitch propeller. 3,800 bhp. 13.5 kts
Ice strengthened bulk carrier with four 7.5 ton Velle type derricks capable of handling grabs carried aboard.
19.10.1972: Launched by Fr. Lürssen Werft GmbH & Company, Bremen-Vegesak (Yard No. 13425), for Kristian Jebsens Rederi AS, Norway. 28.3.1973: Completed. 1979: Sold to Oy Partek Ab., (Finska Angfartygs Ab (EFFOA) (Finland Steamship Company Ltd.), managers), Finland, and renamed TAMMO. (O.N. 18007). 1985: Sold to Kelsa Shipping Corp, Panama, and renamed KLEA. 1988: Sold to Polikos Maritime Company, Athens, (Naftitan Maritime and Transportation Enterprises SA, Athens, managers), Greece, converted into a cement carrier, and renamed POLIKOS.

7235989
59. BRAVENES (1) (1973) Brimnes class
As built: 22,906g. 14,790n. 32,818d.   585' 0" (BB) x 89' 1" x 33' 11" oa.
Post 1994: 18,972g. 11,198n. 32,818d.
Post 1996: 18,972g. 11,198n. 32,300d.
6-cyl. 2 S.C.S.A. (740 x 1,600mm) B&W 6K74EF type oil engine made by J. G. Kincaid & Company Ltd., Greenock. 11,600 bhp. 15.5 kts.
Bulk carrier with five 15-ton cranes capable of operating grabs carried aboard..
1972: Ordered by Tenax Steamship Company Ltd., London, from Lithgows (1969) Ltd., Port Glasgow (Yard No. 1186). 20.12.1972: Launched for H. Clarkson & Company Ltd., (Biovale Ltd., managers), London. 4.4.1973: Completed for Bishopgate Shipping Company Ltd., (Jebsens (UK) Ltd., managers), London. (O.N. 357508). 11.4.1973: Delivered as SILVERDON, and Dene Shipping Company Ltd., appointed as managers. 1978: Sold to China Ocean Shipping Company, Shanghai, China, and renamed FEI CUI HAI. 1983: Owner restyled as China Ocean Shipping Company (COSCO). 1984: Transferred to Qingdao Ocean Shipping Company (COSCO QINGDAO). 7.2.1998: Whilst on a voyage from New Mangalore to to Nanjing, with a cargo of iron ore pellets, foundered in the South China Sea in a position 9.28N., 110.33E.

NB The names and dates quoted for completion and delivery were sourced from old shipbuilding records held within Lloyd's Register Archives but appear at variance with other sources that state completed as SILVERDON.

7233577
60. SHARPNES (1) (1973 – 1983) Swiftnes /Saltnes class
As built: 12,982g. 8,045n. 21,916d. 510' 3" (BB) x 75' 2" x 32' 3¼" oa.
Post 1995: 12,631g. 7,490n. 21,916d.
18-cyl. 4 S.C.S.A. (400 x 460mm) Pielstick 18PC2V-400 oil engine made by the shipbuilder at Yokohama. 9,000 bhp. 14 kts.
Bulk carrier with five 12-ton Velle type derricks capable of operating grabs carried aboard.
26.2.1973: Launched by Nippon Kokan KK, Shimizu (Yard No. 308), for H. Clarkson & Company Ltd., London. 25.5.1973: Completed for Jebsens (UK) Ltd., London. (O.N. 358926). 1974: Transferred to Jebsen, Dillingham Shipping Ltd., (same managers), London. 1979: Transferred to Pacnorse Shipping (UK) Ltd., (same managers). 1981: Transferred to Jebsen Shipping Ltd. 1983: Sold to Jordan National Shipping Lines Company Ltd., (Jebsens Ship Management Ltd., managers), Jordan, and renamed AL-KARAMEH. (O.N.16). 1986: Removed from management. 1989: Jebsens Ship Management Ltd., appointed as managers. 1991: Sold to Akaki Marine Company Ltd.,

(Access Shipping Ltd., managers), Cyprus, and renamed KINGFISHER.   3.10.1997: LR class deleted – vessel demolished.

SHARPNES   (Airfoto, Malacca)

SURENES   (Author's collection)

7320473
61. SURENES (1) (1973 – 1983) Swiftnes /Saltnes class
12,982g. 8,045n. 21,916d.   510' 3" (BB) x 75' 2" x 32' 3¼" oa.
18-cyl. 4 S.C.S.A. (400 x 460mm) Pielstick 18PC2V-400 oil engine made by the shipbuilder at Yokohama. 9,000 bhp. 14 kts.
Bulk carrier with five 12-ton Velle type derricks capable of operating grabs carried aboard.
26.5.1973: Launched by Nippon Kokan KK, Shimizu (Yard No. 312), for H. Clarkson & Company Ltd., London. 10.8.1973: Completed for Jebsens (UK) Ltd., London. (O.N. 360684). 1974: Transferred to Jebsen, Dillingham Shipping Ltd., (Jebsens (UK) Ltd., managers), London. 1979: Transferred to Pacnorse Shipping (UK) Ltd., (same managers).   1980: Transferred to Jebsen Shipping Ltd. 1983: Sold to Sohtorik

Denizcilik Sanayi ve Ticaret AS (Sohtorik Shipping and Trading Inc), Turkey, and renamed MED TRANSPORTER. 1998: Sold for demolition.

6723800
62. FRINES (1) (1973 – 1977) Frines class
As built: 2,831g. 1,780n. 4,506d. 314' 4" x 45' 8" x 20' 0¾" oa.
Post 1992: 2,695g. 1,672n. 4,506d.
8-cyl. 4 S.C.S.A. (400 x 580mm) Deutz type oil engine made by Kloeckner-Humboldt-Deutz, Koeln, geared to a controllable pitch propeller. 2,300 bhp. 13 kts.
Ice strengthened general cargo vessel with four 5-ton derricks.
1967: Keel laid as FRINES by Fr. Lürssen Werft GmbH & Company, Bremen-Vegesak (Yard No. 13385), for Kristian Jebsens Rederi AS. 12.7.1967: Launched as FRITRE for Norwegian Rederi AS, Norway. 28.12.1967: Completed for Botvid Ohlsson Partenrederi, Norway. 1972: Owner restyled as I/S Fritre, Norway. 1973: Sold to Kristian Jebsens Rederi AS, Norway, and renamed FRINES. 1977: Transferred to Isskip h/f, Iceland, and renamed ISNES. 1980: Transferred to Nesskip h/f., Iceland. 1982: Sold to Dubhe SpA di Navigazione, Italy, and renamed ALBERTO DORMIO. 1988: Sold to Consorcio Naviero Kariba SA, (Venus Shipping Company (Pte.) Ltd., managers, Greece, and transferred to Costa Rican flag. 1989: Renamed OCEAN WOOD. 1992: Sold to Ocean Wood Srl, Lebanon. 1992: Sold to Leone Compania Naviera SA, St Vincent and The Grenadines, and renamed MARINA I. (O.N. 3762). 1997: Sold to Thalassa International SA, (Nafta Trade Shipping and Commercial SA, managers), St Vincent and The Grenadines, and renamed UNITY X. (O.N. 6753). 24.6.1999: Sold Agios Fanourios Maritime SA, Piraeus, Greece, and renamed ISNES under Cyprus flag. 8.9.1999: Transferred to Greek flag, and renamed FOTINOULA. (O.N. 10666).

7380459
63. BIRKNES (2) (1974 – 1977) Birknes class
18,675g. 12,420n. 35,224d. 177.02 (BB) x 27.84 x 11.151 metres oa.
7-cyl. 2 S.C.S.A. (760 x 1,550mm) Sulzer 7RHD76 type oil engine made by Sumitomo Heavy Industries Ltd., Tamashima, geared to a shaft with a controllable pitch propeller. 14,000 bhp. 15.5 kts.
Bulk carrier with five 16-ton cranes capable of operating grabs carried aboard.
9.9.1974: Launched by Nippon Kokan KK, Shimizu (Yard No. 331), for Kristian Jebsens Rederi AS, Norway. 26.11.1974: Completed. (O.N. 5983). 1977: Transferred to Roxburgh Shipping Ltd., (Kristian Jebsens Rederi AS, managers), Liberia, and renamed BEDOUIN BIRKNES. 1985: Owners restyled as Bedouin Birknes Shipping Ltd., (same managers), Liberia. 1986: Sold to Philippine Jay Shipping Ltd., (Jameel Group) Philippines, and renamed PHILIPPINE JAY. (O.N. 228842). 1988: Sold to Silent Breeze Maritime Ltd., (Skaarup Shipping Corp., managers), Liberia, and renamed DRAGONLAND. 1991: Sold to Reston Shipping SA, Liberia, and renamed CALLIAN S. 1996: Sold to Trinity Marine SA, Liberia, and renamed CHIAN MARINER. 4.1998: Foundered.

7380461
64. BERGNES (1) (1974 – 1975) Birknes class
As built: 20,570g. 12,187n. 35,302d. 177.02 (BB) x 27.84 x 11.151 metres oa.
Post 1994: 20,854g. 11,730n. 35,224d.
7-cyl. 2 S.C.S.A. (760 x 1,550mm) Sulzer 7RHD76 type oil engine made by Sumitoma Heavy Industries Ltd., Tamashima, geared to a shaft with a controllable pitch propeller. 14,000 bhp. 15.5 kts.

Bulk carrier with five 15-ton cranes capable of operating grabs carried aboard.
1973: Ordered by Dillingham, Jebsen Shipping Corp, Liberia, from Nippon Kokan KK, Shimizu (Yard No. 332). 27.11.1974: Launched for Jebsens (UK) Ltd., London. 14.2.1975: Completed. (O.N. 356569). 17.2.1975: Sold to Capricorna Pacific Company Ltd., (Broken Hill Propriety Ltd., managers), Hong Kong, and renamed IRON CAPRICORN. 1988: Sold to County Shipping Company Ltd., (same managers). 1989: Managers restyled as BHP Transport Ltd. 1990: Sold to Athenian Faith SA, (Tsakos Shipping and Trading SA, managers), Greece, and renamed IRENES BLESSING. 1992: Entrust Maritime Company Ltd., appointed as managers. 1993: Sold to Alexander Maritime Inc., (same managers), Greece, and renamed ALEXANDER. 1995: Sold to Arcadia Shipping Private Ltd., India, and renamed ARCADIA PROGRESS. 1999: Lilly Maritime Pvt. Ltd., appointed as managers. 6.2004: Sold to Trust Shipping Enterprises SA, Piraeus, and renamed MARIS, under the India flag.

N.B.
Although Lloyd's Register of Shipping states "launched as BERGNES" and completed as IRON CAPRICORN, Lloyd's Register's own confidential shipbuilding record cards state completed as Bergnes per dates quoted above.

BRAVENES in Canadian waters. (J. K. Byass)

7380502
65. BRAVENES (2) (1975 – 1982) Birknes class
As built: 18,642g. 12,305n. 35,216d. 177.02 (BB) x 27.87 x 11.158 metres oa.
Post 1989: 20,450g. 11,682n. 35,223d.
7-cyl. 2 S.C.S.A. (760 x 1,550mm) Sulzer 7RND76 type oil engine made by Sumitoma Heavy Industries Ltd., Tamashima, geared to a shaft with a controllable pitch propeller. 14,000 bhp. 15.5 kts.
Bulk carrier with five 16-ton cranes capable of operating grabs carried aboard.
1973: Ordered by Dillingham, Jebsen Shipping Corp, Liberia, from Nippon Kokan KK, Shimizu (Yard No. 340). 14.2.1975: Launched. 28.4.1975: Completed. (O.N. 5250). 1981: Transferred to Pacnorse Shipping International Ltd., Liberia. 1982: Transferred to Evans Shipping Ltd., Liberia. 1984: Transferred to Blue Sea Maritime Corp, (Wheelock Marine Services Ltd., managers), Philippines, and renamed MANILA BRAVE. (O.N. 227784). 1985: Transferred to Pacnorse Shipping Three Ltd., (Jebsens Ship Management Ltd., managers) and renamed GENERAL DUQUE thence reverted to Blue Sea Maritime Corp, (same managers). 1989: Chelston Ship Management Ltd., appointed as managers. 1989: Sold to Bulk Partners KS., (Ugland Bulk Carriers AS managers), Norway, and renamed VIVITA. 1991: Ugland Rederi AS (Ugland Group) appointed as managers. 1992: Sold to Resit Kalkavan Denizcilik ve Ticaret Ltd. Sirketi, Turkey, and renamed DENIZATI. 1996: Sold to Denkal Denizcilik Sanayi Sirketi, (Birlesik Yatirim Gurubu Denizcilik Ticaret Ltd., managers), Turkey, and

renamed BEKIR KALKAVAN. 14.12.2000: Demolition commenced at an unspecified location.

REFSNES
(Author's collection / Fotoflite)

7382665
66. REFSNES (1975 – 1983) Rossnes class
As built: 3,842g. 2,414n. 5,699d. 103.49 (BB) x 16.11 x 6.951 metres oa.
Post 1993: 3,883g. 2,133n. 6,167d.
Two, 12-cyl. 4 S.C.S.A. (250 x 300mm) Normo KVM-12 vee type oil engines made by Bergens Mekaniske Verksteder AS, Bergen, geared to a single shaft with a controllable pitch propeller. 3,800 bhp. 13 kts.
Gearless bulk carrier.
15.3.1975: Launched by Kleven Mekaniske Verksteder AS, Ulsteinvik (Yard No. 26), for Kristian Jebsens Rederi AS, Norway. 14.6.1975: Completed. (O.N. 18545). 1982: Transferred to Sameiet Refsnes, (Kristian Jebsens Rederi AS, managers), Norway. 1983: Transferred to Compagnie Generale d'Armements Maritime (C.G.A.M.), France, and renamed SAINT BREVIN. 1989: Transferred to Panama flag. 1990: Transferred to Societe Finisterienne de Cabotage (S.F.C.) and Companhia Naviera Independencia SA, (Jebsens Hamburg GmbH & Company KG, managers). 1993: Jebsens Shipmanagement (Bergen) AS, appointed as managers). (O.N.19541-PEXT4). 1994: Sold to Navale Francaise SA and Compagnie Naviera Independencia SA, (removed from management). (O.N.18790-90C). 1996: Jebsens Shipmanagement (Bergen) AS, appointed as managers. 1997: Managers restyled as Wilson Shipmanagement (Bergen) AS 1998: Transferred to Short Sea Ltd., (same managers), Bergen, under Malta flag. 2000: Renamed REFSNES. 2003: Renamed WILSON REEF. 2.2004: Transferred to Wilson Shipowning AS, Bergen, (same managers), retaining Malta flag.

7382495
67. ROSSNES (1975 – 1983) Rossnes class
As built: 3,842g. 2,414n. 5,699d. 103.49 (BB) x 16.11 x 6.852 metres oa.
Post 1993: 3,842g. 2,414n. 6,167d.

Post 1994: 3,883g. 2,133n. 6,167d.
Post 1998: 3,883g. 2,133n. 6,258d.
Two, 12-cyl. 4 S.C.S.A. (250 x 300mm) Normo KVM-12 vee type oil engines made by Bergens Mekaniske Verksteder AS, Bergen, geared to a single shaft with a controllable pitch propeller. 3,800 bhp. 14 kts.
Gearless bulk carrier.
8.3.1975: Launched by G. Eides, Sonner AS, Hoylandsbygd (Yard No. 100), for Kristian Jebsens Rederi AS, Norway. 21.6.1975: Completed. (O.N. 18549). 1982: Transferred to Partenrederi Rossnes, (Kristian Jebsens Rederi AS, managers), Norway. 1983: Transferred to Compagnie Meridianale de Nav., France, and renamed SAINT BRICE. (O.N.566007A). 1989: Transferred to Panama flag. 1990: Transferred to Societe Finisterienne de Cabotage (S.F.C.) and Compagnie Naviera Independencia SA, (Jebsens Hamburg GmbH & Company KG, managers). (O.N.19565-PEXT4). 1993: Jebsens Shipmanagement (Bergen) AS, appointed as managers). 1994: Sold to Navale Francaise SA and Compagnie Naviera Independencia SA, (removed from management). (O.N.18779-90C). 1996: Jebsens Shipmanagement (Bergen) AS, appointed as managers. 1997: Managers restyled as Wilsons Shipmanagement (Bergen) AS. 1998: Transferred to Short Sea Ltd., (same managers), Malta. 2000: Renamed ROSSNES. 2.2004: Transferred to Wilson Shipowning AS, Bergen, (same managers), and renamed WILSON ROSS, retaining Malta flag.

7341685
68. RISNES (1) (1975 – 1979) Risnes class
As built: 3,645g. 2,297n. 5,699d. 102.27 (BB) x 15.57 x 6.833 metres oa.
Post 1992: 3,341g. 2,297n. 5,790d.
Post 1994: 3,658g. 2,097n. 5,790d.
9-cyl. 4 S.C.S.A. (400 x 460mm) Pielstick 9PC2-2L-400 type oil engine made by Crossley Premier Engines Ltd., Manchester, geared to a shaft with a controllable pitch propeller. 4,500 bhp. 14 kts. (This was the first production unit of this engine model)
Gearless bulk carrier.
10.5.1975: Launched by Appledore Shipbuilders Ltd., Appledore (Yard No. A.S. 105), for Jebsens (UK) Ltd., London. 15.7.1975: Completed. (O.N. 365838). 1979: Transferred to Isskip h/f, Iceland, and renamed SELNES. 3.1990: Transferred to Unistar Shipping Company Ltd., Cyprus.(O.N. 709046). 1999: Osterreichischer Lloyd Ship Management GmbH, appointed as managers. 2004: Renamed WILSON MUUGA.

RAMNES (W. J. Harvey)

7382706
69. RAMNES (1) (1975 – 1983) Rossnes class
As built: 3,842g. 2,414n. 5,699d. 103.56 (BB) x 16.03 x 6.846 metres oa.
Post 1994: 3,883g. 2,133n. 6,258d.

Two, 12-cyl. 4 S.C.S.A. (250 x 300mm) Normo KVM-12 vee type oil engines made by Bergens Mekaniske Verksteder AS, Bergen, geared to a single shaft with a controllable pitch propeller. 3,800 bhp. 13 kts.
Gearless bulk carrier.
12.4.1975: Launched by Brodrene Lothe AS, Haugesund (Yard No. 34), for Kristian Jebsens Rederi AS, Norway. 17.7.1975: Completed. (O.N. 18569). 1982: Transferred to Sameiet Ramnes, (Kristian Jebsens Rederi AS, managers), Norway. 1983: Transferred to Compagnie Meridianale de Nav., France, and renamed SAINT JAMES. 1984: Transferred to Jebsens, France SA, (G.I.E. Maritime Nor-France, managers), France. 1987: Transferred to Jebsens Franco Atlantique SA, (same managers), Philippines, and renamed GENERAL PERALTA. (O.N. 17937-Li). 1990: Transferred to KS Phoenixen, (Jebsens Ship Management (Bergen) AS, managers), Panama, and renamed RAMNES. (O.N. 17937-PEXT 1). 1993: Sold to Portline European SA, (Portline – Transportes Maritimos Internationales SA, managers), Portugal, and renamed EUROPEAN I, retaining Panama flag. (O.N. 17221-87D). 2001: Sold to European Maritime Ltd., Varna, Bulgaria, (Varna Shipping & Trading, managers), and renamed EUROPEAN, under St Vincent and The Grenadines flag.

BELLNES (Airfoto Malacca)

7380485
70. BELLNES (2) (1975 – 1982) Birknes class
As built: 18,642g.   12,305n. 35,685d. 177.02 (BB) x 27.87 x 11.158 metres oa.
Post 1994: 21,828g. 11,073n. 35,223d.
7-cyl. 2 S.C.S.A. (760 x 1,550mm) Sulzer 7RHD76 type oil engine made by Sumitomo Heavy Industry Ltd., Tamashima, geared to a shaft with a controllable pitch propeller. 14,000 bhp. 15.5 kts.
Bulk carrier with five 16-ton cranes capable of operating grabs carried aboard.
1973: Ordered by Dillingham, Jebsen Shipping Corp, Liberia, from Nippon Kokan KK, Shimizu (Yard No. 335). 12.2.1975: Launched. 24.7.1975: Completed. (O.N. 5333).

1981: Transferred to Pacnorse Shipping International Ltd., Liberia. 1982: Transferred to Barnes Shipping Ltd., (Wheelock Marine Services Ltd., managers), Liberia. 1983: Transferred to Merryfield Steamship Inc., (Kristian Jebsens Rederi AS, managers), Liberia. 1984: Transferred to Philippines flag, and renamed MANILA HOPE. (O.N. 225902). 1985: Jebsens Ship Management Ltd., appointed as managers. 1986: Transferred to Pacnorse Shipping Eight Ltd., (same managers), and renamed GENERAL LAPUS thence to Aboitiz, Jebsen Bulk Transport Corp, (same managers). 3.1988: Sold to Octagon Maritime Corp., Greece, and renamed MATUMBA II. 1989: Sold to Chr. J. Reim, then transferred to KS Dixie, (AS Dione, managers), Norway, and renamed DIXIE. 1990: Borgestad-Reim Shipping AS, appointed as managers. 1991: Renamed NOMADIC DIXIE. 1992: Sold to Dixie KS, (Univan Ship Management Ltd., managers). 1994: Nomadic Management AS, appointed as managers, and transferred to Bahamas flag. (O.N. 726115). 1995: Sold to Mete Kardesler Kum, Cakil Pazarlama Kara-Deniz Nakliyati Ve Ticaret Ltd., Istanbul, Turkey, and renamed OSMAN METE.

RINGNES (Author's collection / Fotoflite)

7341697
71. RINGNES (1975 – 1985) Risnes class
3,645g. 2,297n. 5,699d. 102.01 (BB) x 15.85 x 6.833 metres oa.
9-cyl. 4 S.C.S.A. (400 x 460mm) Pielstick 9PC2-2L-400 type oil engine made by Crossley Premier Engines Ltd., Manchester, geared to a shaft with a controllable pitch propeller. 4,500 bhp. 14 kts.
Gearless bulk carrier.
25.7.1975: Launched by Appledore Shipbuilders Ltd., Appledore (Yard No. A.S.106), for Elco Leasing Ltd., (Jebsens (UK) Ltd., managers), London. 30.9.1975: Completed. (O.N. 365929). 1984: Jebsens Ship Management Ltd., appointed as managers. 1985: Sold to Green Light Shipping Corp., Panama, and renamed SANDNES. (O.N. 14704-85). 1987: Transferred to Philippine flag, Jebsens Ship Management AS (JSMA), managers. 1989: Jebsens Ship Management (Bergen) AS appointed as managers. 1991: Transferred to Panama flag. 1992: Transferred to Meridian Bulk Carriers Ltd., renamed RINGNES and transferred to Cyprus flag, (O.N. 709584). 1993: Sold to Corrientes Bulk Carriers Ltd., (Seaplan Shipping Ltd., managers), Cyprus, and renamed MARMON. 1995: Sold to Meridian Bulk Carriers Ltd., (Thorstone Ship Management Ltd., managers), Cyprus. 1997: Sold to Bergen Tug & Salvage AS, Norway and renamed CHARLIE B. 1997: Sold to Vegas Investments Group Inc.,

Portugal, (MAR), and renamed FRANCESCA B. 2000: Renamed SIDER WIND, (Italtech Srl, managers). 6.2.2003: Demolition commenced at an unspecified location.

ROCKNES (Author's collection / Fotoflite)

7341702
72. ROCKNES (1975 - 1993) Risnes class
As built: 3,645g. 2,297n. 5,699d. 102.01 (BB) x 15.85 x 6.833 metres oa.
Post 1993: 3,658g. 2,097n. 5,790d.
9-cyl. 4 S.C.S.A. (400 x 460mm) Pielstick 9PC2-2L-400 type oil engine made by Crossley Premier Engines Ltd., Manchester, geared to a shaft with a controllable pitch propeller. 4,500 bhp. 14 kts.
Gearless bulk carrier.
1.11.1975: Launched by Appledore Shipbuilders Ltd., Appledore (Yard No. A.S. 107), for Elco Leasing Ltd., (Jebsens (UK) Ltd., managers), London. 6.12.1975: Completed. (O.N. 365992). 1983: Transferred to Jebsens (UK) Ltd., (Jebsens Ship Management Ltd., managers), London. 1988: Transferred to Altnacraig Shipping PLC. 1989: Chelston Ship Management Ltd., appointed as managers. 1990: Transferred to Corrientes Bulk Carriers Ltd., (Thorstone Ship Management Ltd., managers), Cyprus. (O.N. 709044). 1992: Jebsens Ship Management (Bergen) AS, appointed as managers. 1993: Seaplan Shipping Ltd., appointed as managers, and renamed ALEXIS. 1998: Sold to Alcamer Shipping Company Ltd., (Wilson Ship Management (Bergen) AS managers). 1999: Sold to Short Sea Ltd., (same managers), Malta, and renamed ROCKNES. 2002: Renamed WILSON MO. 2.2004: Transferred to Wilson Shipowning AS, Bergen, (same managers), retaining Malta flag.

7382500
73. RONNES (1976 – 1986) Rossnes class
As built: 3,842g. 2,414n. 5,699d. 103.56 (BB) x 16.11 x 6.966 metres oa.
Post 1993: 3,890g. 2,048n. 5,699d.
Two, 12-cyl. 4 S.C.S.A. (250 x 300mm) Normo KVM-12 vee type oil engines made by Bergens Mekaniske Verksteder AS, Bergen, geared to a single shaft with a controllable pitch propeller. 3,800 bhp. 13 kts.
Gearless bulk carrier.

6.12.1975: Launched by G. Eides, Sonner AS, Hoylandsbygd (Yard No. 101), for Kristian Jebsens Rederi AS, Norway. 11.2.1976: Completed. (O.N. 18955). 1976: Transferred to Ronnes Shipping Corporation, Liberia. 1977: Transferred to Kristian Jebsens Rederi AS, Norway. 1981: Transferred to Sameiet Ronnes, (Kristian Jebsens Rederi AS, managers), Norway. 1983: Transferred to Kristian Jebsens Rederi AS, Norway. 1986: Transferred to Granby Island Shipping Company SA, (Kristian Jebsens Rederi AS, managers), Philippines, and renamed GENERAL LUNA. (O.N. 17057-Li). 1987: Jebsens Ship Management AS (JSMA), appointed as managers, under Panama flag. 1990: Sold to Altnacraig Shipping Plc., (Chelston Ship Management Ltd., managers), London, and renamed RISNES. (O.N. 717469). 1993: Sold to Geralia Shipping Company Ltd., (Jebsen Shipmanagement (London) Ltd., managers), Cyprus. (O.N. 710021). 1996: Sold to Kriti Silver Shipping Company Ltd., (Donnelly Ship Management Ltd., managers), Cyprus. 2000: Tordenskjold Marine Haugesund AS, appointed as managers. 2001: Sold to Franklin Shipping AS., (same managers), and transferred to Bahamas flag. 6.2003: Transferred to Actinor Bulk AS, Bergen, (Wilson Shipmanagement AS, Bergen, managers), renamed WILSON RIGA, and transferred to Barbados flag.

RONNES (W. J. Harvey)

ROLLNES (W.J. Harvey)

7366013
74. ROLLNES (1976 – 2002) Risnes class
As built: 3,645g. 2,297n. 5,699d. 102.04 (BB) x 15.85 x 6.851 metres oa.
Post 1993: 3,658g. 2,097n. 5,789d.

9-cyl. 4 S.C.S.A. (400 x 460mm) Pielstick 9PC2-2L-400 type oil engine made by Crossley Premier Engines Ltd., Manchester, geared to a shaft with a controllable pitch propeller. 4,500 bhp. 14 kts.
Gearless bulk carrier.
17.1.1976: Launched by Appledore Shipbuilding Company Ltd., Appledore (Yard No. A.S. 108), for Hambros Bank Ltd., (Jebsens (UK) Ltd., managers), London. 1.3.1976: Completed. (O.N. 366050). 1983: Jebsens Ship Management Ltd., appointed as managers. 1988: Transferred to Altnacraig Shipping Plc. 1989: Chelston Ship Management Ltd., appointed as managers. 1991: Transferred to Baltimore Shipping Company SA, (Jebsens Ship Management (Bergen) AS, appointed as managers), Panama. (O.N. 20878-Li). 5.1996: Sold to Pan Journey Shipping Company Ltd., (Donnelly Ship Management Ltd., managers), Cyprus. (O.N. 710834). 2000: Tordenskjold Marine Gdynia Sp.z.o.o., appointed as managers. 2001: Sold to Franklin Shipping AS, (same managers), Norway, retaining flag. 19.2.2002: Whilst in a position 60.08N., 05.17E., on a ballast voyage from Odda to Slovaag, suffered an engine-room fire that spread to her accommodation. The fire was extinguished and she arrived in tow at Bergen, next day. She was later reported lying at Aagotnes near Bergen, and to be sold for demolition. 6.2003: Sold to Esper / Kanafi, North Korea, and renamed AMIR AHMAD.

RIKNES

(Author's collection / Fotoflite)

7382677
75. RIKNES (1976 – 1983) Rossnes class
As built: 3,845g.   2,416n. 6,250d. 103.56 (BB) x 16.01 x 6.833 metres oa.
Post 1993: 3,839g.   2,137n. 6,258d.
Post 1995: 3,839g.   2,133n. 6,258d.
Two, 12-cyl. 4 S.C.S.A. (250 x 300mm) Normo KVM-12 vee type oil engines made by Bergens Mekaniske Verksteder AS, Bergen, geared to a single shaft with a controllable pitch propeller. 3,800 bhp. 13 kts.
Gearless bulk carrier.
20.11.1975: Launched by Kleven Mekaniske Verksteder AS, Ulsteinvik (Yard No. 27), for Kristian Jebsens Rederi AS, Norway. 23.4.1976: Completed. (O.N. 18744). 1982: Transferred to Partenrederi Riknes, (Kristian Jebsens Rederi AS, managers), Norway. 1983: Transferred to Jebsens France SA, (G.I.E. Maritime Norfrance, managers), France, and renamed SAINT JEAN. (O.N. 609478-V). 1987: Transferred to Jebsens, Franco-Atlantique SA, (same managers), Philippines, and renamed GENERAL PAPA.

(O.N. 17920-Li). 1990: Transferred to Jebsens France SA and Jebsens Franco-Atlantique SA, (Jebsens Ship Management (Bergen) AS managers), Philippines. 1992: Transferred to Govil Management Inc., (same managers), Philippines, and reverted to RIKNES. 1993: To Panama flag. (O.N. 17174-87B). 1995: Transferred to D. L. Marine 1 (Malta) Ltd., (Phoenocean Ltd., managers), Malta, and renamed NORNES. (O.N. 4019). 12.1997: Sold to Bundle Shipping Ltd., Malta. 12.1998: Sold to Olady Ventures Inc., Portugal, and renamed LUCILLIA. 12.2003: Sold to Wilson Shipowning AS, Bergen, (Wilson Shipmanagement AS, Bergen, managers), and renamed WILSON RYE, under the Barbados flag. 2004: Sold to Bongo AS., Bergen, (same managers).

ROGNES (W. J. Harvey)

7382718
76. ROGNES (1976 – 1987) Rossnes class
3,845g. 2,417n. 6,100d. 103.56 (BB) x 16.01 x 6.833 metres oa.
Two, 12-cyl. 4 S.C.S.A. (250 x 300mm) Normo KVM-12 vee type oil engines made by Bergens Mekaniske Verksteder AS, Bergen, geared to a single shaft with a controllable pitch propeller. 3,800 bhp. 13 kts.
Gearless bulk carrier.
31.1.1976: Launched by Brodrene Lothe AS, Haugesund (Yard No. 35), for Kristian Jebsens Rederi AS, Norway. 4.5.1976: Completed. (O.N. 18753). 1982: Transferred to Sameiet Rognes, (Kristian Jebsens Rederi AS, managers), Norway. 1983: Transferred to Kristian Jebsens Rederi AS, Norway. 1987: Transferred to Cromer Shipping Corp, (Jebsens Ship Management AS (JSMA), managers), Philippines, and renamed GENERAL AQUINO. (O.N. 17939-Li). 1990: Transferred to Panama flag. (O.N. 17939-PEXT3). 1992: Transferred Jebsens Thun Short Sea SA, (Jebsens Thun Management AS, managers), and renamed ROGNES. 1993: (Jebsens Ship Management (Bergen) AS, managers). 1995: Sold to Sameiet Rognes (same managers). (O.N. 17227-87CH). 1998: Transferred to Netherlands flag. 1998: Wilson Ship Management (Bergen) AS appointed as managers. 2000: Sold to Garibaldi Srl Cooperativa di Navigazione, Italy. 2003: Renamed CAPTAIN DANIEL. 11.2003: Sold to Bolami Sea Line Srl, Ravenna, Italy.

7533032
77. BAYNES (2) (1976 – 1982) Baynes class
As built: 19,153g. 12,571n. 34,541d. 180.02 (BB) x 28.45 x 10.891 metres oa.
Post 1992: 20,663g. 11,706n. 34,541d.

7-cyl. 2 S.C.S.A. (760 x 1,550) Sulzer 7RND76 type oil engine made by the shipbuilder at Tamashima, geared to a shaft with a controllable pitch propeller. 14,000 bhp. 15.5 kts.
Bulk carrier with four 15-ton cranes capable of operating grabs carried aboard.
11.12.1975: Ordered by Dillingham, Jebsen Shipping Corporation, Liberia, from Sumitomo Heavy Industries Ltd., Uraga (Yard No. 989). 28.5.1976: Launched. 17.9.1976: Completed. (O.N. 5694). 1981: Transferred to Pacnorse Shipping International Ltd., Liberia. 1982: Transferred to Blackwell Shipping Ltd., (Kristian Jebsens Rederi AS, managers), Liberia, and renamed GENERAL SEGUNDO, under Philippine flag. (O.N. 226195). 1985: Transferred to Pacnorse Shipping Six Ltd., (Jebsens Ship Management AS (JSMA), managers), Philippines. 1987: Sold to Ocean Jay Marine Ltd., (Jameel Group) and renamed OCEAN JAY, under Cyprus flag. 1988: Sold to Great Cosmos Navigation SA, Panama, and renamed TRANS FORTUNE. 1993: Dae Yang Shipping Company Ltd., appointed as managers. 1994: Sold to Halk Finansal Kiralama AS (Asian Transmarin Cemicilik Ticaret ve Endustri AS (Asian Transmarin Shipping Trading and Industry Company Inc), Turkey, and renamed MERKUR. 5.2002: Renamed MERK, for final voyage. 29.5.2002: Beached at Alang for demolition.

RAFNES (W. J. Harvey)

7414183
78. RAFNES (1976 – 1987) Rossnes class
As built: 3,843g. 2,416n. 6,250d. 103.56 (BB) x 16.01 x 6.83 metres oa.
Post 1998: 3,885g. 2,048n. 6,351d.
Two, 12-cyl. 4 S.C.S.A. (250 x 300mm) Normo KVM-12 vee type oil engines made by Normo Gruppen AS, Bergen, geared to a single shaft with a controllable pitch propeller. 3,800 bhp. 14 kts.
Gearless bulk carrier.
30.6.1976: Launched by Kleven Mekaniske Verksteder AS, Ulsteinvik (Yard No. 28), for Kristian Jebsens Rederi AS, Norway. 9.10.1976: Completed. (O.N. 18846). 1982: Transferred to Sameiet Rafnes, (same managers), Norway. 1987: Transferred to Marvelstone SA, (Jebsens Ship Management AS (JSMA), managers), Philippines, and renamed GENERAL GARCIA. 1990: Sold to Altnacraig Shipping Plc, (Chelston Ship Management Ltd., managers), London, and renamed RAFNES. (O.N. 717390). 1993: Sold to Geralia Shipping Company Ltd., (Jebsens Shipmanagement (London) Ltd, managers), Cyprus. (O.N. 710020). 1996: Sold to Cosmaris Navigation Company Ltd., (Donnelly Shipmanagement Ltd., managers), Cyprus. 2000: Tordenskjold Marine Haugesund AS, appointed as managers, and transferred to Bahamas flag. 7.2003: Transferred to Actinor Bulk AS, Bergen, (Wilson Shipmanagement AS, Bergen, managers), renamed WILSON ROUEN, under Barbados flag.

BOLNES (Authors collection / Airfoto Malacca)

7426227
79. BOLNES (2) (1976 – 1981) Birknes class
As built: 20,094g. 12,718n. 35,208d. 177.02 (BB x 27.87 x 11.158 metres oa.
Post 1995: 20,350g. 11,622n. 35,208d.
7-cyl. 2 S.C.S.A. (760 x 1,550mm) Sulzer 7RHD76 type oil engine made by Sumitomo Heavy Industries Ltd., Tamashima, geared to a shaft with a controllable pitch propeller. 14,000 bhp. 15.5 kts.
Bulk carrier with five 15-ton cranes capable of operating grabs carried aboard
1974: Ordered by Jebsen, Dillingham Shipping Ltd., London, from Nippon Kokan KK, Shimizu, Shizouka Pref. (Yard No. 351). 12.7.1976: Launched. 18.11.1976: Completed. (O.N. 366314). 1979: Transferred to Pacnorse Shipping (UK) Ltd. 1981: Transferred to Birbirry Shipping Corp, Liberia. 1982: Transferred to Doyle Shipping Ltd., Liberia, and renamed EASTERN ALLIANCE. 1982: Transferred to Eastern Alliance Ltd., (Union Steamship Company of New Zealand Ltd., managers), Bermuda, and renamed NEW ZEALAND ALLIANCE. 1983: Transferred to Zealand Ltd., (same managers). 1984: Transferred to Pacnorse Shipping Two Ltd., (Kristian Jebsens Rederi AS, managers), Philippines, and renamed GENERAL TINIO. (O.N. 12682-Li). 1985: Jebsens Ship Management Ltd., appointed as managers. 1986: Sold to Roll Branch Ltd., Gibraltar, and renamed KINDLY. (O.N. 366314). 1987: Sold to Great City Navigation SA, Panama, and renamed TRANS COMFORT. (O.N. 18230-PEXT). 1996: Sold to Leodas Shipping SA, Panama, and renamed LEODAS. 2000: Cavo Doro Navigation, appointed as managers, and renamed TIGER V. 2003: New Hope Marine, appointed as managers. 2003: Midas Shipping Navigation, Taipei, appointed as managers, and renamed MIDAS. 5.2003: Sold to Midas Shipping Navigation, Taipei, Taiwan, (Waywiser Marine Shipping, Taipei, managers), retaining Panama flag.

7419200
80. RADNES (1976 – 1984) Rossnes class

As built: 3,924g. 2,417n. 5,750d. 103.56 (BB) x 16.11 x 6.97 metres oa.
Post 1993: 3,885g. 2,048n. 6,258d.
Two, 12-cyl. 4 S.C.S.A. (250 x 300mm) Normo KVM-12 vee type oil engines made by Normo Gruppen AS Bergen, geared to a single shaft with a controllable pitch propeller. 3,800 bhp. 14 kts.
Gearless bulk carrier.
12.10.1976: Launched by G. Eides, Sonner AS, Hoylandsbygd (Yard No. 102), for Kristian Jebsens Rederi AS, Norway. 11.12.1976: Completed. (O.N. 18883). 1982: Transferred to Partenrederi Radnes, (Kristian Jebsens Rederi AS, managers), Norway. 1984: Sold Massoel SA, (Acomarit Services Maritimes SA, managers), Switzerland, and renamed LUGANO. (O.N. 123). 1986: Sold to Masstransport MT SA, Switzerland. 1990: Transferred to Radnes Shipping Inc., (Jebsens Ship Management (Bergen) AS managers), and renamed RADNES, under Panama flag. (O.N. 19545-PEXT). 1994: Sold to Altnamara Shipping Plc., (Jebsens Shipmanagement (London) Ltd., managers), London. (O.N. 725771). 1998: Transferred to Radnes Shipping Ltd., (Wilsons Shipmanagement (Bergen) AS, managers), under Malta flag. 2003: Sold to Wilson Shipowning AS, Bergen, (Wilson Shipmanagement AS, Bergen, managers), renamed WILSON ROUGH, retaining Malta flag.

RADNES leaving Immingham. (J. K. Byass)

8750077
81. ALADDIN (1976 – 1990)
8,308g. 4,879n. 320 x 293 x 128 feet rectangular platform.
Two, turbo charged engines of EMD 16-645-E9 type made by General Motors Corp, Detroit, driving two, 2,100 Kilowatt, 600 volts A.C. generators, each connected to two electric 2,000 shp., motors geared to twin screw shafts. 6 kts.
"Ocean Voyager" class/design self-propelled semi submersible drilling rig.
1973: Completed as WAAGE DRILL 1 by the Avondale Shipyards Inc., New Orleans, for KS Waage Drilling AS & Company, Norway. 1976: Sold to Aladdin drilling Activities AS, Norway, and renamed ALADDIN. (O.N. 18155). 1979: Sold to Jebsen Drilling Ltd., Norway. 1980: Transferred to Jebsen Drilling Plc., London. (O.N. 379944). 1990: Sold to J. Lauritzen AS, (Lauritzen Offshore AS, managers), Denmark, and renamed DAN BARONESS, under Bahamas flag. (O.N. 379944). 1993: Transferred to Lauritzen Shipping (Bahamas) Ltd., (same managers). 1996: Sold to Diamond Offshore

Corporation, Houston, Texas, and renamed OCEAN BARONESS. 1997: Transferred to Panama flag (O.N. 23460-97). 2003: Transferred to Diamond Offshore Drilling Ltd., Aberdeen, (Diamond Offshore Corporation, Houston, managers), under Marshal Islands flag.

ALADDIN.

(Jebsens)

SINBAD

(Jebsens)

8755388
82. SINBAD (1976 – 1979)
8,721g. 5,292n. 320 x 293 x 128 feet rectangular platform.
Two, turbo charged engines of EMD 16-645-E9 type made by General Motors Corp, Detroit, driving two, 2,100 Kilowatt, 600 volts A.C. generators, each connected to two electric 2,000 shp., motors geared to twin screw shafts. 6 kts.

"Ocean Voyager" class/design self-propelled semi submersible drilling rig.
1973: Completed as WAAGE DRILL II by the Avondale Shipyards Inc., New Orleans, for KS Waage Drilling AS & Company, Norway. 1976: Sold to Aladdin Drilling Activities AS, Norway, and renamed SINBAD. 1979: Transferred to Simgood Ltd., London, and renamed SINBAD SAXON. (O.N. 379945). 1979: Sold to Jebsen Drilling Ltd., Norway. 1980: Transferred to Jebsen Drilling Plc., London. 1990: Sold to J. Lauritzen AS, (Lauritzen Offshore AS, managers), Denmark, and renamed DAN COUNTESS, under Bahamas flag. (O.N. 379944). 1994: Sold to Diamond Offshore Corporation, Houston, Texas, and renamed OCEAN COUNTESS 1996: Transferred to Diamond Offshore (USA) Inc, Houston, Texas, and to Panama flag (O.N. 22764-96). 2001: Diamond Offshore Drilling Services Inc, appointed as managers. 2004: Transferred to Diamond Offshore Services Corporation, Houston, (Diamond Offshore Corporation Inc., Houston, managers), and renamed OCEAN STAR, under the Marshall Islands flag.

83. JENNES   (1976 – 1977) see ship No. 39 above.

BERGNES (M. R. Dippy)

7600225
84. BERGNES (2) (1977 – 1985) Baynes class
As built: 20,473g. 12,571n. 34,503d. 180.02 (BB) x 28.15 x 10.302 metres oa.
Post 1989:   19,134g. 12,601n. 34,503d.
Post 1994:   20,594g. 11,764n. 34,503d.
7-cyl. 2 S.C.S.A. (760 x 1,550mm) Sulzer 7RND76 type oil engine made by the shipbuilder at Tamashima, geared to a shaft with a controllable pitch propeller. 14,000 bhp. 15.5 kts.
Bulk carrier with four 15-ton cranes capable of operating grabs carried aboard
1976: Ordered by International Marine Corp. from Sumitomo Heavy Industries Ltd., Uraga (Yard No. 1000). 17.9.1976: Launched for Kristian Jebsens Rederi AS, Norway. 11.1.1977: Completed. (O.N. 18903). 1982: Transferred to Panama flag / Hamburg flag. 1985: Transferred Pacnorse Shipping Five Ltd., and renamed GENERAL LACUNA, thence to Magic Overseas Inc., Panama, (Reederei J. Jost, Flensburg, W. Germany, managers), under Philippines flag. (O.N. 228361). 1987: Jebsens Hamburg GmbH & Company KG, appointed as managers. 1989: Transferred to KS Bergnes, (Jebsens Ship Management (Bergen) AS, managers), Norway, and reverted to BERGNES. 1990: Univan Ship Management Ltd., appointed managers. 1995: Trans-Pacific Shipping

Company, Yangon, Union of Myanmar, (Lasco Shipping Company, Portland, Oregon, USA, managers), and renamed JADE ORIENT. 1995: Clipper Bulk Portland Inc., appointed as managers. 2002: Sold to Ally Marine Company Ltd., Taipei, Taiwan, (New Amego Shipping, Taipei, managers), and renamed ALLY II, under Panama flag. 2004: Waywiser Marine Shipping, Taipei, appointed as managers.

BROOKNES (World Ship Society Photograph Library)

7426239
85. BROOKNES (2) (1977 – 1986) Birknes class
20,164g. 12,514n. 35,138d. 177.02 (BB) x 27.84 x 11.131 metres oa.
7-cyl. 2 S.C.S.A. (760 x 1,550mm) Sulzer 7RND76 type oil engine made by Sumitomo Heavy Industries Ltd., Tamashima, geared to a shaft with a controllable pitch propeller. 12,600 bhp. 15.5 kts.
Bulk carrier with five 15-ton cranes capable of operating grabs carried aboard
1974: Ordered by Kristian Jebsens Rederi AS, Norway, from Nippon Kokan KK, Shimizu, Shizouka Pref. (Yard No. 352). 13.7.1976: Launched for Reederei J. Jost, Flensburg, W. Germany. 1.4.1977: Completed. 1978: Owners restyled as J. Jost O. H. G., (Reederei J. Jost, managers). 1980: Transferred to Reederei J. Jost, under Panama flag. 1985: Transferred to Jebsens Brooknes GmbH & Company KG, (Jebsens Hamburg GmbH & Company KG, managers), Panama. (O.N. 8874-HA-F). 1986: Transferred to the Philippines flag, and renamed GENERAL ESTRELLA. (O.N. 18704-Li). 1987: Aboitiz, Jebsen Bulk Transport Corp., appointed as managers. 1988: Sold to Chester Universal II Inc., (Kristian Gerhard Jebsens GmbH & Company KG, managers), Panama. 1990: Transferred to Sicaal Jebsens Ships India Ltd., India, and renamed PEARL LUCK. (O.N. 2425). 1993: Sold to Pearl Ships Ltd., India. 31.3.2001: Demolition commenced at an unspecified location.

BRUNES (J. K. Byass)

7617620
86. BRUNES (3) (1977) Baynes class
As built: 19,158g. 12,659n. 34,488d. 180.02 (BB) x 28.45 x 10.897 metres oa.
Post 1997: 20,589g. 11,810n. 34,488d.
7-cyl. 2 S.C.S.A. (760 x 1,550mm) Sulzer 7RND76 type oil engine made by the shipbuilder at Tamashima, geared to a shaft with a controllable pitch propeller. 14,000 bhp. 15.5 kts.
Bulk carrier with four 15-ton cranes capable of operating grabs carried aboard.
30.1.1977: Launched by Sumitomo Heavy Industries Ltd., Uraga (Yard No. 1047), for Sameiet Brunes, (AS Atle Jebsen Rederi, managers), Norway. 27.4.1977: Completed for Renfrew Shipping Ltd., (Kristian Gerhard Jebsen SA, managers), Liberia. (O.N. 6120). 1977: Renamed BEDOUIN BRUNES, (Kristian Jebsens Rederi AS, managers). 1983: Removed from management. 1985: Transferred to Bedouin Brunes Shipping Ltd., Liberia. 1985: Sold to the USSR-Black Sea Shipping Company, Russia, and renamed DNEPROGES. 1996: Sold to Tailwind Shipping Inc., (Blasco UK Ltd., managers), under Liberia flag, and renamed KOKTEBEL. 2000: Sold to Emporio Navigation Ltd., (Agro Shipping & Trading (UK) Ltd., managers), and renamed MELINI, retaining Liberia flag. 12.2003: Sold to Salvinia Navigation, Odessa, Ukraine, (Intresco Ltd, Odessa, managers), and renamed SALVINIA, retaining Liberia flag.

BINSNES (M. R. Dippy)

7426203
87. BINSNES (3) (1977 – 1982) Baynes class
As built: 19,196g. 12,572n. 34,544d. 180.02 (BB) x 28.45 x 10.891 metres oa.

Post 1997: 20,589g. 11,810n. 34,545d.
7-cyl. 2 S.C.S.A. (760 x 1,550mm) Sulzer 7RND76 type oil engine made by the shipbuilder at Tamashima, geared to a shaft with a controllable pitch propeller. 14,000 bhp. 15.5 kts.
Bulk carrier with four 15-ton cranes capable of operating grabs carried aboard.
1974: Ordered by Dillingham, Jebsen Shipping Corp, Liberia, from Sumitomo Heavy Industries Ltd., Uraga (Yard No. 986). 3.12.1976: Launched. 27.4.1977: Completed. (O.N. 6815). 1981: Transferred to Pacnorse Shipping International Ltd. 1982: Transferred to Sanders Shipping Ltd., (Kristian Jebsens Rederi AS, managers), Philippines, and renamed GENERAL ROXAS. 1986: Transferred to Pacnorse Shipping Nine Ltd., (same managers). 1986: Sold to the USSR-Black Sea Shipping Company, Russia, and renamed VASILIY AZHAYEV. 1997: Hero Maritime Ltd., (Ocean Agencies Ltd., managers), St Vincent and The Grenadines, and renamed KARAGOL. 1999: Sold to Flagship Company Ltd., (Barclay Shipping Ltd., managers), and renamed MILTIADIS M, under Malta flag. 2004: Sold to Da Tong Shipping Company, Quingdao, China, and renamed SHUN YING, under Panama flag.

BORGNES in Australian waters, grabs ready for work. (M. R. Dippy)

7600768
88. BORGNES (2) (1977 – 1983) Birknes class
20,384g. 12,307n. 35,271d. 177.02 (BB) x 27.84 x 11.158 metres oa.
7-cyl. 2 S.C.S.A. (760 x 1,550mm) Sulzer 7RHD76 type oil engine made by Sumitomo Heavy Industries Ltd., Tamashima, geared to a shaft with a controllable pitch propeller. 14,000 bhp. 15.5 kts.
Bulk carrier with five 15-ton cranes capable of operating grabs carried aboard.
1976: Ordered by Jebsens (UK) Ltd., from Nippon Kokan KK, Shimizu, Shizouka Pref. (Yard No. 359). 16.1.1977: Launched. 12.5.1977: Completed. (O.N. 377274). 1983: Sold to the USSR-Black Sea Shipping Company, Russia, and renamed VLADIMIR GAVRILOV. 1996: Sold to Gavrilov Shipping Corp., (Blasco UK Ltd., managers), Liberia. 1997: Sold to Magellan Shipping Inc., (Poseidon Schiffarhts GmbH, Lubeck, W. Germany, managers), Liberia, and renamed KANEV. 1999: Sold to Amalthea Maritime Ltd., London, (Seven Seas Maritime Ltd., London, managers), and renamed AMALIA, under Malta flag.

89. FJELLNES (1)   (1977 – 1981) see ship No. 39 above.

FJELLNES
at Hull.

(Chriss Reynolds collection)

ISNES

(J. K. Byass)

90. ISNES (1)   **(1977 – 1983)** see ship No. 53 above.

FOSSNES

(Author's collection / Airfoto Malacca)

91. FOSSNES (1)   **(1977 – 1981)** see ship No. 41 above.

BESSNES at Vancouver on 6 September 1983. (Chriss Reynolds collection)

7426215
92. BESSNES   (1977 – 1984) Baynes class
As built: 19,196g. 12,572n. 33,750d. 180.02 (BB) x 28.43 x 10.302 metres oa.
Post 1989: 20,619g. 11,907n. 34,537d.
7-cyl. 2 S.C.S.A. (760 x 1,550mm) Sulzer 7RHD76 type oil engine made by the shipbuilder at Tamashima, geared to a shaft with a controllable pitch propeller. 14,000 bhp. 15.5 kts.
Bulk carrier with four 15-ton cranes capable of operating grabs carried aboard.
1974: Ordered by Dillingham, Jebsen Shipping Corporation, Liberia, from Sumitomo Heavy Industries Ltd., Uraga (Yard No. 987). 26.3.1977: Launched. 7.7.1977: Completed. (O.N. 6005). 1981: Transferred to Pacnorse Shipping International Ltd., Liberia. 1982: Transferred to Elmslie Shipping Ltd., (Kristian Jebsens Rederi AS, managers), Liberia. 1983: Transferred to Pacnorse Shipping International Ltd., (same managers). 1984: Transferred to Pacnorse Shipping Seven (Pte) Ltd., (same managers), Singapore, and renamed BEAVER. (O.N. 382716). 1986: Transferred to M. N. Campos & Company, (same managers), Singapore, and renamed GENERAL VILLA. 1987: Transferred to Philippine flag. (O.N. 229636). 1987: Sold to Asian Prosperity Lines Inc., (Acomarit Maritime Services (UK) Ltd., managers), Philippines, and renamed AMATISTA. 1988: Sold to KS Sydship V (Ugland Marine AS, managers), and renamed LIVANITA. 1989: Ugland Bulk Carriers AS, appointed as managers. 1990: Ugland Rederi AS (Ugland Group), appointed as managers. 1995: Sold to Trans-Pacific Shipping Company, Yangon, Union of Myanmar, (Lasco Shipping Company, Portland, Oregon, USA, managers) Liberia, and renamed JADE PACIFIC. 2002: Sold to Jeannie Marine Corporation SA, Taipei, Taiwan, and renamed JEANNIE III, under Panama flag. 2004: Waywiser Marine Shipping, Taipei, appointed as managers.

7411375
93. REKSNES (1977 – 1987) Rossnes class
3,844g. 2,417n. 5,750d. 103.56 (BB) x 16.01 x 6.851 metres oa.

Two, 12-cyl. 4 S.C.S.A. (250 x 300mm) Normo KVM-12 vee type oil engines made by Bergens Mekaniske Verksteder AS, Bergen, geared to a single shaft with a controllable pitch propeller. 3,800 bhp. 14 kts.

Gearless bulk carrier. Subsequently fitted with a travelling diesel powered mechanical shovel.

9.10.1976: Launched by Brodrene Lothe AS, Haugesund (Yard No. 36), for Kristian Jebsens Rederi AS, Norway. 8.1977: Completed. (O.N. 18901). 1982: Transferred to Partenrederi Reksnes, (Kristian Jebsens Rederi AS, managers), Norway. 1987: Transferred to Marinefield SA, (same managers), Philippines, and renamed GENERAL VALERIANO. 1988: Jebsens Ship Management AS (JSMA), appointed as managers. 1989: Jebsens Ship Management (Bergen) AS, appointed as managers. 1990: Transferred to Panama flag. 1992: Renamed REKSNES. 1996: Sold to Jebsen Short Sea SA, (Jebsens Ship Management (Bergen) AS, managers). (O.N. 17118-87C). 1997: Transferred to Jebsens Industrial Shipping Services AS, Bergen, and removed from management. (O.N. 17118-87D). 2004: Transferred to Wilson Industrial Shipping Services AS, Bergen, (Wilson Shipmanagement (Bergen) AS, managers), retaining Panama flag.

REKSNES (W. J. Harvey)

DON ANTONIO BOTELHO 6 January 1984 in Australian waters. (World Ship Society Photograph Library)

7632670
94. DON ANTONIO BOTELHO (1977 – 1992)
4,318g. 3,120n. 7,678d. 109.5 x 17.02 x 7.101 metres oa.

6-cyl. 4 S.C.S.A. (470 x 760mm) Makita KSLH647 type oil engine made by Makita Diesel Company Ltd., Takamatsu. 4,100 bhp. 14.5 kts.
General cargo vessel with one 20-ton and three 15-ton derricks.
14.12.1976: Keel laid by Mie Shipyard Company Ltd., Yokkaichi (Yard No. 181), for Suraga Kaiji KK, Japan. Due to the financial insolvency of the shipbuilder the shipowner became bankrupt. 3.3.1977: Launched as DON ANTONIO for Botelho Bulk Transport Corp, Philippines. 29.6.1977: Completed. (O.N. 223511). 1977: Transferred to Aboitiz, Jebsen Bulk Transport Corp., Philippines, and renamed DON ANTONIO BOTELHO. 1980: Transferred to W. G. & A. Jebsens Shipmanagement, Manila. 1992: Sold to Vinland Trading Company, Panama, and renamed MUFADDAL. 2.1993: Sold to Mufaddal Shipping Ltd., (United Ship Management Ltd., managers), Panama. 4.1999: Sold to Everest Maritime Ltd., Panama, and renamed ALEXANDER I. 8.1999: Sold to Jalal Embrahimi, Panama, and renamed AL MUJEER. 2000: Sold to Nasser Ibrahimi Company, Dubai, and renamed GALATIC DOLPHIN, under Panama flag. 2001: Sold to E. & W. Freights & Logistics Inc., and transferred to Belize flag. 2003: Sold to Cat Nhat Transport, Haiphong, Vietnam, and renamed ALPHA, under the Mongolia flag. 10.2004: Reported as sold to unspecified Vietnam flag buyers, (Eastern Dragon Shipping, Haiphong, managers), retaining Mongolia flag.

7636066
95. CLYDENES (1) (1977 – 1982) Clydenes class
As built: 2,351g.   1,414n. 3,564d. 87.03 x 13.75 x 5.65 metres oa.
Post 1990:   1,582g.   837n. 3,564d.
Post 1996:   2,430g.   1,452n. 3,564d.
12-cyl. 4 S.C.S.A. (325 x 370mm) Allen 12VS37-F vee type oil engines made by A. P. E. Allen Ltd., Bedford, reverse reduction geared to shaft. 2,700 bhp. 12.5 kts.
Bulk carrier with four 12-ton derricks.
14.10.1976: Ordered by Jebsens (UK) Ltd. from Ferguson Brothers (Port Glasgow) Ltd., Port Glasgow (Yard No. 475). Work subcontracted to Scotts Shipbuilding Company Ltd., Greenock (Yard No. 748). 28.1.1977: Keel laid. 30.9.1977: Launched for H. Clarkson & Company Ltd., London. 29.12.1977: Completed for Scandinavian Leasing Ltd., (Jebsens (UK) Ltd., managers), London. (O.N. 377477). 1982: Transferred to Massoel SA, (Acomarit Maritime Services SA, managers), Switzerland, and renamed SARINE. (O.N. 116). 1990: Sold to Kytheraiki Marine Company Ltd., Glyfada, Athens, and renamed GEORGIOS XII, under Cyprus flag. 1991: Sold to Sealpha Shipping Ltd., Nicosia, Cyprus, (Kytheraiki Marine Company Ltd., Athens, managers). (O.N. 708977). 1994: Managers restyled as Kytheraiki Shipmanagement Inc. 1999: Sold to Golden Post Marine Inc., Athens, (same managers), under Panama flag. (O.N. 27242-00) 2003: Renamed GEORGIOS X. II. 4.2005: Sold to Kalk Finansal (Kermatrans International, Istanbul, managers), Turkey, and renamed VILDIRIM K.

BEDOUIN BRUNES

(M.R. Dippy)

96. BEDOUIN BRUNES (1977 – 1985) see ship No. 86 above.

BEDOUIN BIRKNES

(J. K. Byass)

97. BEDOUIN BIRKNES (1977 – 1986) see ship No. 63 above.

FRAMNES returning from acceptance trials. (Author's collection / Fr. Lürrsen Werft)

7610103
98. FRAMNES (1978 – 1998) Fonnes class
As built: 3,083g. 2,073n. 4,350d. 93.48 x 15.42 x 6.42 metres oa.
Post 1984: 3,949g. 2,307n. 5,800d. 105.70 x 15.42 x 6.881 metres oa.
8-cyl 4 S.C.S.A. (400 x 460mm) Pielstick 8PC2-2L-400 type oil engine made by Blohm & Voss AG, Hamburg. 4,000 bhp. 13.5 kts.
Bulk carrier with two 12½-ton cranes capable of operating grabs carried aboard.
17.8.1977: Launched by Fr. Lürssen Werft GmbH & Company, Bremen-Vegesak (Yard No. 13455), for Brema Reederei GmbH & Company KG, (Reederei J. Jost, Flensburg, managers), W. Germany. 17.1.1978: Completed. 1984: Transferred to Reederei J. Jost, and lengthened. 1985: Transferred to Brema Reederei GmbH & Company KG, (Reederei J. Jost, managers), under Panama flag. 1988: Jebsens Hamburg GmbH & Company KG, appointed as managers. 1990: Jebsens Ship Management (Bergen) AS appointed as managers. 1991: Transferred to Lancelot Shipping Corp., (Jebsens Thun Management AS, managers), Norway (NIS). 1992: Aboitiz, Jebsen Bulk Transport Corp., appointed as managers. 1994: Transferred to Philippines flag. 1997: Sold to Aboitiz, Jebsen Shipmanagement. 1998: Sold to Amagi Shipping Company Ltd., (Wilson Ship Management (Bergen) Ltd. AS, managers), Cyprus, and renamed FROMNES. 2000: Sold to Short Sea Ltd., (same managers), Malta. (O.N. 6881).

14.4.2003: Renamed WILSON MARIN. 2.2004: Sold to Wilson Shipowning AS, Bergen, (same managers), retaining Malta flag.

CLARKNES leaving the Manchester Ship Canal. (W. J. Harvey)

7620457
99. CLARKNES (1978 – 1983) Clydenes class
2,351g. 1,414g. 3,564d. 87.03 x 13.75 x 5.65 metres oa.
As built: 12-cyl. 4 S.C.S.A. (325 x 370mm) Allen 12VS37-F vee type oil engine made by A. P. E. Allen Ltd., Bedford, reverse reduction geared to shaft. 2,700 bhp. 12.5 kts.
Post 1998: 8-cyl. 4 S.C.S.A. (256 x 310mm) A.B.C.-8MDZC type oil engine made by Anglo-Belgian Corp N. V. Ghent. 1,986 bhp. 12.5 kts.
Bulk carrier with four 12-ton derricks.
1976: Ordered by Jebsens (UK) Ltd. from Ferguson Brothers (Port Glasgow) Ltd., Port Glasgow (Yard No. 474). 5.9.1977: Launched for H. Clarkson & Company Ltd., London. 20.1.1978: Completed, Jebsens (UK) Ltd., managers. (O.N. 377346). 1983: Sold to Massoel SA, (Acomarit Services Maritimes SA, managers), Switzerland, and renamed FRIBOURG. (O.N. 121). 1993: Sold to Vectis Shipping Ltd., (Carisbrooke Shipping Company Ltd., managers), Cowes, and renamed VECTIS FALCON. 6.1998: Re-engined. 1998: Sold to Baybreak Ltd., and Dynaship Maritime Ltd., (Carisbrooke Shipping Plc, managers), under Barbados flag. 1999: Managers restyled as Carisbrooke Shipping Ltd. 2000: Carisbrooke Shipping (Management) Ltd., appointed as managers. 2001: Transferred to Baybreak Ltd. 4.2003: Sold to Tsafson Shipping SA., Athens, Greece, (Meadway Shipping SA., Glyfada, Greece, managers), and renamed CHRISTOS, under the Georgia flag. 12.2004: Sold to Sesame Shipping LLC, Odessa, (Private Enterprise Svetoch, Odessa, managers), and renamed ANNA, under the Comoros flag.

7426241
100. BECKNES (1978 – 1983) Birknes class
As built: 20,164g. 12,514n. 35,164d. 177.02 (BB) x 27.84 x 11.131 metres oa.
Post 1997: 20,352g. 11,562n. 35,165d.

7-cyl. 2 S.C.S.A. (760 x 1,550mm) Sulzer 7RND76 type oil engine made by Sumitomo Heavy Industries Ltd., Tamashima, geared to a shaft with a controllable pitch propeller. 14,000 bhp. 15.5 kts.
Bulk carrier with five 15-ton cranes capable of operating grabs carried aboard.
1974: Ordered by Dillingham, Jebsen Shipping Corp, Liberia, from Nippon Kokan KK, Shimizu, Shizouka Pref. (Yard No. 354). 28.3.1977: Launched for Atle Jebsen AS, Norway. 21.1.1978: Completed for Jebsens Hamburg GmbH & Company KG, (J. Jost, Flensburg, manager). 1979: Transferred to Panama flag. 1983: Sold to USSR-Black Sea Shipping Company, Russia, and renamed PYOTR SMORODIN. 1996: Sold to Arctic Shipping Company Ltd., (Poseidon Schiffarhts GmbH, managers), Liberia, and renamed KAGARLYK. 1999: Sold to Alkestis Maritime Ltd., London, (Seven Seas Maritime Ltd., London, managers), and renamed ALYCIA, under the Malta flag.

BECKNES (M. R. Dippy)

BRISKNES June 1980   (World Ship Society Photograph Library)

7507485
101. BRISKNES (2) (1978 – 1982) Birknes class
As built: 18,640g.   12,317n. 35,246d. 177.02 (BB) x 27.87 x 11.164 metres oa.
Post 1997: 20,352g.   11,562n. 35,246d.
7-cyl. 2 S.C.S.A. (760 x 1,550mm) Sulzer 7RHD76 type oil engine made by Sumitomo Heavy Industries Ltd., Tamashima, geared to a shaft with a controllable pitch propeller. 14,000 bhp. 15.5 kts.
Bulk carrier with five 15-ton cranes capable of operating grabs carried aboard.
1975: Ordered by Dillingham, Jebsen Shipping Corp, Liberia, from Nippon Kokan KK, Shimizu, Shizouka Pref. (Yard No. 355). 17.6.1977: Launched. 31.1.1978: Completed. (O.N. 6175). 1981: Transferred to Pacnorse Shipping International Ltd. 1982: Transferred to Maybray Shipping Ltd., (Kristian Jebsens Rederi AS, managers),

Liberia. 1983: Transferred to Pacnorse Shipping Four Ltd., (same managers), and renamed GENERAL MASCARDO. (O.N. 227603). 1985: Sold to USSR-Black Sea Shipping Company, Russia, and renamed MIKHAIL STELMAKH. 1996: Sold to Atlantic Shipping Company Ltd., (Poseidon Schiffarhts GmbH, managers), Liberia, and renamed KOROSTEN. 1999: Renamed KAROSEL. 1999: Renamed LADY LORY. 1999: Sold to Evryalos Maritime SA., Piraeus, and renamed MICHAEL S, under the Malta flag. 2000: Arion Shipping SA, Piraeus, appointed as managers. 2003: Bright Navigation SA., Piraeus, appointed as managers.

BARKNES arriving on the River Thames in November 1978. (World Ship Society Photograph Library)

7501699
102. BARKNES (1978 – 1982) Baynes class
As built: 19,196g. 12,572n. 34,556d. 180.02 (BB) x 28.45 x 10.891 metres oa.
Post 1995: 20,644g. 11,763n. 34,544d.
7-cyl. 2 S.C.S.A. (760 x 1,550mm) Sulzer type 7RND76 oil engine made by the shipbuilders at Tamashima, geared to a shaft with a controllable pitch propeller. 14,000 bhp. 15.5 kts.
Bulk carrier with four 15-ton cranes capable of operating grabs carried aboard.
1975: Ordered by Dillingham, Jebsen Shipping Corp, Liberia, from Sumitomo Heavy Industries Ltd., Uraga (Yard No. 988). 2.6.1977: Launched. 29.3.1978: Completed. (O.N. 6201). 1981: Transferred to Pacnorse Shipping International Ltd. 1982: Transferred to Cairns Shipping Ltd., (Kristian Jebsens Rederi AS, managers), Liberia, thence to Brockway Shipping Ltd., (Wheelock Marine Services, managers), Liberia. 1983: Transferred to Chios Crown Corp, (same managers). 1985: Transferred to Blue Sea Maritime Corp, (Fenwick Shipping Services Ltd., managers), Philippines, and renamed MANILA SUCCESS. 1987: Transferred to Pacnorse Shipping One Ltd., (same managers), and renamed GENERAL ROXAS. 1988: Jebsens (UK) Ltd., appointed as managers. 1988: Renamed RENKO, (Chelston Ship Management Ltd., managers), Panama. 1990: Transferred to Sicaal Jebsens Ships India Ltd., India, and renamed PEARL PROSPERITY. (O.N. 2424). 1993: Sold to Pearl Ships Inc., India. 5.4.2003: Demolition commenced at an unspecified location.

7632876
103. FRINES (2) (1978 – 1988) Frines class
8,098g. 5,088n. 12,358d. 134.52 x 20.71 x 8.688 metres oa.
12-cyl. 4 S.C.S.A. (400 x 460mm) Pielstick 12PC2-2V-400 vee type oil engine made by Sumitomo Heavy Industries Ltd., Tamashima. 6,000 bhp. 14.75 kts.
Bulk carrier with three 15-ton cranes capable of operating grabs carried aboard.

1976: Ordered, by Atle Jebsen, from Nippon Kokan KK, Shimizu, Shizouka Pref. (Yard No. 371). 20.1.1978: Launched for Kristian Jebsens Rederi AS. 30.3.1978: Completed for Thurso Shipping Ltd., (Kristian Jebsens Rederi AS, managers), Liberia. (O.N. 6230). 1983: Transferred to J. J. Shipping Ltd., (same managers). 1.1988: Renamed FREENES, (Jebsens Ship Management AS (JSMA), managers), Philippines. 1989: Transferred to Altnacraig Shipping Plc, (Chelston Ship Management Ltd., managers), London, (O.N. 717274). 1990: Transferred to Worldwide Maritime Corporation Inc., (Jebsens Ship Management (Bergen) AS, managers), Panama. 1991: Chelston Ship Management Ltd., appointed as managers. 1991: Jebsens Ship Management (Bergen) AS, appointed as managers. 1992: Transferred to J. A. Shipping Ltd., (same managers), Norway, and reverted to FRINES, (O.N. N-01244). 1993: Transferred to Panama flag. 1995: Sold to Trieres Shipping Company Ltd., (same managers), Cyprus. 1996: Sold to Jangade Shipping Company Ltd., Limassol, (Donnelly Ship Management Ltd., managers). 1999: Storesund Management AS, appointed as managers. 2000: Tordenskjold Marine Haugesund AS appointed as managers. 2001: Sold to Fulton Bulk AS, Bergen, (same managers), and to Bahamas flag, (O.N. 8000285). 2003: Temaco Shipmanagement AS, appointed as managers. 2004: Sold to Megoni Shipping Ltd., (Melissa Shipping Ltd., Auckland, and renamed MEGONI, under Panama flag. 2004: Sold to Neptune Investments Ltd., Auckland, (Neptune Shipping Agency, Auckland, managers), and renamed CAPITAINE COOK II, retaining Panama flag.

7610098
104. FONNES (2) (1978 – 1988) Fonnes class
As built: 3,083g. 2,074n. 4,350d. 93.48 x 15.42 x 6.420 metres oa.
Post 1984: 3,971g. 2,333n. 5,753d. 105.7 x 15.42 x 6.881 metres oa.
Post 1996: 3,980g. 2,370n. 5,753d.
8-cyl. 4 S.C.S.A. (400 x 460mm) Pielstick 8PC2-2L-400 type oil engine made by Blohm & Voss AG, Hamburg. 4,000 bhp. 13.5 kts.
Bulk carrier with two 12½ -ton cranes capable of operating grabs carried aboard.
17.1.1978: Launched by Fr. Lürssen Werft GmbH & Company, Bremen-Vegesak (Yard No. 13454), for Brema Reederei GmbH & Company KG, (Reederei J. Jost, Flensburg, managers), W. Germany. 28.4.1978: Completed. 1982: Transferred to Reederei J. Jost. 1984: Lengthened, and transferred to Brema Reederei GmbH & Company KG, (Reederei J. Jost, managers). 1986: Transferred to Panama flag. 1988: Transferred to Philippine flag, and renamed GENERAL ROMULO, (Jebsens Hamburg GmbH & Company KG, managers). 1989: Renamed FONNES, under Panama flag. 1991: Jebsens Ship Management (Bergen) AS, appointed as managers. 1991: Transferred to Mersol Maritime Inc., (same managers). 1995: Sold to Jebsens Thun Short Sea SA, (same manager). 1996: Sold to Frederiksberg Bulk KS (Donnelly Shipmanagement Ltd., managers), Bergen, under St Vincent and The Grenadines flag. 2000: Tordenskjold Marine Gdynia Sp z.o.o., appointed as managers. 2003: Sold to Premier Ventures Inc., (Reliance Transport Ltd., managers), and renamed ELPIS, retaining St Vincent and The Grenadines flag. 2004: Sold to Rocafield Maritime Corporation, Limassol, (NV Vega Shipping Company Ltd., Limassol, managers), and renamed LADY FOX, retaining St Vincent and The Grenadines flag.

7632888
105. FINNSNES (1978 – 1988) Frines class
As built: 8,098g. 5,088n. 9,300d. 134.52 x 20.55 x 8.668 metres oa.
Post 1996: 8,967g. 4,542n. 12,394d.
12-cyl. 4 S.C.S.A. (400 x 460mm) Pielstick 12PC2-2V-400 vee type oil engine made by the shipbuilder at Yokohama. 6,000 bhp. 13.75 kts.
Bulk carrier with three 15-ton cranes capable of operating grabs carried aboard.

1976: Ordered, by Atle Jebsen, from Nippon Kokan KK, Shimizu, Shizouka Pref. (Yard No. 372). 28.4.1978: Launched for Kristian Jebsens Rederi AS, Liberia. 8.8.1978: Completed for Rothway Shipping Ltd., (Kristian Jebsens Rederi AS, managers), Liberia. (O.N. 6320). 1983: Transferred to J. J. Shipping Ltd., (same managers), Liberia. 1988: Transferred to Philippine flag, and renamed FAIRNES, (Jebsens Ship Management AS (JSMA), managers). 1989: Chelston Ship Management Ltd., appointed as managers. 1990: Jebsens Ship Management (Bergen) AS, appointed as managers. 1992: Transferred to the Liberian flag. 1992: Transferred to Norway flag, and reverted to FINNSNES, (O.N. N-01198). 1994: Transferred to Panama flag. 1995: Sold to Trieres Shipping Company Ltd., (same managers), Cyprus. 1996: Sold to Clarineto Shipping Company Ltd., Limassol, (Donnelly Ship Management Ltd., managers), St Vincent and The Grenadines flag. 2000: Storesund Management AS, appointed as managers. 2000: Tordenskjold Marine Haugesund AS appointed as managers. 2001: Sold to Fulton Bulk AS, Bergen, (same managers), under Bahamas flag. (O.N. 8000284). 2003: Temaco Shipmanagement AS, appointed as managers. 2004: Sold to unspecified North Korea flag buyers, and renamed MARIMAR.

FINNSNES (Airfoto Malacca)

7700556
106. ALTNES (3) (1978 – 1986) Altnes class
As built: 3,002g. 1,877n. 4,500d. 92.03 x 15.02 x 6.401 metres oa.
Post 1980: 3,929g. 2,591n. 5,995d. 107.40 x 15.02 x 6.751 metres oa.
6-cyl. 4 S.C.S.A. (410 x 470) Werkspoor 6TM410 type oil engine made by Stork-Werkspoor Diesel BV, Amsterdam. 4,000 bhp. 13.5 kts.
Bulk carrier with two 12½ -ton cranes capable of operating grabs carried aboard.

23.6.1978: Launched by Kleven Mekaniske Verksteder AS, Ulsteinvik (Yard No. 32), for, Kristian Jebsens Rederi AS, Norway. 7.10.1978: Completed. (O.N. 19214). 1980: Lengthened. 1984: Transferred to Partenrederi Altnes, (Kristian Jebsens Rederi AS, managers), Norway. 1986: Transferred to Isskip h/f., Iceland, and renamed SALTNES. 1987: Transferred to the Panama flag. 1988: Transferred to the Iceland flag. 1990: Transferred to Jebsens North Sea KS, (Jebsens Ship Management (Bergen) AS, managers), and reverted to ALTNES. 1991: Aboitiz, Jebsen Bulk Transport Corp., appointed as managers. 1992: Transferred to Jebsens Thun Short Sea SA, (same managers). 1996: Sold to Frederiksberg Bulk KS, Bergen, (Donnelly Tanker Management Ltd., managers), St Vincent and The Grenadines. 13.1.1998: Capsized and sank following collision.

ALTNES on the River Ouse, leaving Goole 24 May 1979, before lengthening Compare with the later photograph on page 25 above. (J. K. Byass)

7805370
107. FARNES (1979 – 1988) Farnes class
As built: 8,115g. 5,104n. 12,961d.   134.52 x 20.73 x 8.668 metres oa.
Post 1992. 8,960g. 4,548n. 12,274d.
12-cyl. 4 S.C.S.A. (400 x 460mm) Pielstick 12PC2-2V-400 vee type oil engine made by the shipbuilder at Yokohama. 6,000 bhp. 14.75 kts.
Bulk carrier with one 15-ton and two 25-ton cranes capable of operating grabs carried aboard. The two forward mounted 25-ton cranes can work in tandem to lift 50-tons.
8.8.1978: Launched by Nippon Kokan KK, Shimizu, Shizouka Pref. (Yard No. 379), for Kristian Jebsens Rederi AS, Liberia. 12.1.1979: Completed for Baltic Mercury Transport Ltd., (Jebsens (UK) Ltd., managers), Liberia. (O.N. 6431). 1988: Transferred to Long Beach Shipping Corp, (Chelston Ship Management Ltd., managers), Philippines, and renamed FULLNES. 1990: Jebsens Ship Management (Bergen) AS, appointed as managers. 1991: Transferred to Liberian flag. 1992: Transferred to J. A. Shipping Ltd., (same managers), Norway, (O.N. N-01197). 1994: Transferred to Panama flag. 1995: Sold to Trieres Shipping Company Ltd., (same managers), Cyprus flag. 1996: Sold to Morosaco Shipping Company Ltd., Limassol, (Donnelly Ship Management Ltd., Limassol, managers), Cyprus flag. 2000: Tordenskjold Marine Haugesund AS, Bergen, appointed as managers.   2001: Sold to Fulton Bulk AS, Bergen, (same managers), under Bahamas flag. (O.N. 8000283). 2001: Converted into a cement carrier, and renamed CEM K. 2003: Temaco Shipmanagement AS appointed as managers. 2003: Sold to Grosvenor Ventures SA, Piraeus, (Sekur Holdings SA, Piraeus, managers), and renamed LUCKY ARROW, under Panama flag.

VIGSNES At Immingham, after lengthening. (W.J. Harvey)

7700544
108. VIGSNES (4) (1979 – 1986) Altnes class
As built: 3,002g. 1,877n. 4,500d.   92.03 x 15.02 x 6.401 metres oa.
Post 1980: 3,924g. 2,591n. 5,995d. 107.40 x 15.02 x 6.401 metres oa.
6-cyl. 4 S.C.S.A. (410 x 470mm) Werkspoor 6TM410 type oil engine made by Stork-Werkspoor Diesel BV, Amsterdam. 4,000 bhp. 13.5 kts.
Bulk carrier with two 12½ -ton cranes capable of operating grabs carried aboard.
15.12.1978: Launched by Kleven Mekaniske Verksteder AS, Ulsteinvik (Yard No. 33), for, Kristian Jebsens Rederi AS, Norway. 9.3.1979: Completed. (O.N. 19305). 1980: Lengthened. 1981: Transferred to Partenrederi Vigsnes, (Kristian Jebsens Rederi AS, managers), Norway. 1983: Kristian Gerhard Jebsen Skipsrederi AS, appointed as managers. 1985: Kristian Jebsens Rederi AS, appointed as managers. 1986: Transferred to the Argo Caribbean Group SA, (Jebsens Hamburg GmbH & Company KG GmbH, managers), Philippines, and renamed GENERAL JACINTO. (O.N. 15815-86). 5.2.1987: Collided with the motor tanker PALAMIS (1,738g. /86) in a position 50.25 N., 00.30 E., in the English Channel, and was holed. Subsequently beached off Bexhill, Sussex. 7.2.1987: Having jettisoned part of her cargo with her own grabs she was refloated and proceeded under tow to Dover for temporary repairs and then to Bremerhaven for permanent repairs. 1990: Aboitiz, Jebsen Bulk Transport Corp., appointed as managers, under Panama flag. 1992: Transferred to Jebsens Thun Short Sea SA, (Jebsens Thun Management AS, managers), and renamed VIGSNES. 1995: Sold to Frederiksberg Bulk KS, (Donnelly Ship Management Ltd., managers), Bergen, under St Vincent and The Grenadines flag. 2000: Tordenskjold Marine Gdynia Sp. z.o.o., appointed as managers2003: Sold to Eurobulk AS, Bergen, (Temaco Shipmanagement AS, managers). 12.2004: Sold to Nordic Transport AS, Bergen, (Seagate Transport Inc., Liberia, managers), and renamed ALEXANDROS S, under the Georgia flag.

FIRMNES (W. J. Harvey)

7805382
109. FIRMNES (1979 – 1988) Farnes class
As built: 8,116g. 5,104n. 12,374d. 134.52 x 20.73 x 8.668 metres oa.
Post 1992. 8,960g. 4,548n. 12,274d.
12-cyl. 4 S.C.S.A. (400 x 460mm) Pielstick 12PC2-2V-400 vee type oil engine made by the shipbuilder at Yokohama. 6,000 bhp. 13.75 kts.
Bulk carrier with one 15-ton and two 25-ton cranes capable of operating grabs carried aboard. The two forward mounted 25-ton cranes can work in tandem to lift 50-tons.
5.12.1978: Launched by Nippon Kokan KK, Shimizu, Shizouka Pref. (Yard No. 380), for Kristian Jebsens Rederi AS, Liberia. 20.3.1979: Completed for Baltic Venus Transport Ltd., (Jebsens (UK) Ltd., managers), Liberia. (O.N. 6461). 1988: Transferred to Long Beach Shipping Corp., (Chelston Ship Management Ltd., managers), Philippines, and renamed FURUNES. 1990: Jebsens Ship Management (Bergen) AS, appointed as managers. 1991: Transferred to Liberian Flag. 1992: Transferred to A. J. Shipping Ltd., (same managers), Norway, (O.N. N-01196). 1994: Transferred to Panama flag. 1995: Sold to Wide Source Maritime Inc., (Aboitiz, Jebsens Shipmanagement, managers), Philippines. 1997: Sold to Aboitiz, Jebsens Far East Shipping SA, (W. G. & A. Jebsens Shipping Corporation Inc., managers), Philippines. 1998: Sold to AJFE Cement Carrier 1 Inc., (Aboitiz, Jebsen Bulk Transport Corp., managers), converted into a self-unloading bulk cement carrier, and renamed ALCEM CALACA. (O.N. MNLD010162). 2002: Sold to Emblem Shipping Pty Ltd, Brisbane, (Cementco Shipping Inc, Brisbane, managers), under the Australia flag.

7418880
110. PACNORSE 1 (1979 – 1996)
9,872g. 4,809n. 9,200d. 153.65 x 23.5 x 8.021 metres oa.
Five, 12-cyl. 4 S.C.S.A. (280 x 290mm) 3,600 bhp. Pielstick 12PA6V280 vee type oil engines made by Chantiers de L'Atlantique, St. Denis, powering five generators, each powering four electric motors of 1,750 shp., connected to twin main drive shafts with controllable pitch propellers. 13 kts. Three thwartship thrust propellers forward, and two thwartship thrust propellers aft.
Dynamically positioned self-propelled drilling ship.
26.6.1974: Ordered by Santa Fe International Corp. (later transferred to Ocean Drilling Corp I) from Scotts Shipbuilding Company Ltd., Greenock (Yard No. 746). 3.4.1975: Keel laid. 7.4.1979: Launched for Pacnorse Drilling Bermuda Corp., Bermuda. 10.6.1979: Trials. 21.6.1979: Completed for Pacnorse Drilling Corporation 1 Ltd., (Kristian Jebsens Rederi AS, managers), Liberia. (O.N. 6333). 1987: Jebsen Offshore Drilling Company Ltd., appointed as managers. 1988: Transferred to

GARNES 8 July 1996   (World Ship Society Photograph Library)

7810210
115. GARNES (4) (1980 – 1986) Korsnes class
As built: 2,991g. 1,874n. 4,599d.   91.65 x 15.04 x 6.485 metres oa.
Post 1983: 3,967g. 2,212n. 6,105d. 107.01 x 15.04 x 6.485 metres oa.
6-cyl. 4 S.C.S.A. (410 x 470mm) Werkspoor 6TM410 type oil engine made by Stork-Werkspoor Diesel BV, Amsterdam, geared to a controllable pitch propeller. 4,000 bhp. 13 kts.
Gearless bulk carrier.
2.6.1979: Keel laid by Storviks Mekaniske Verksteder AS, Kristiansand (Yard No. 91), for Kristian Jebsens Rederi AS, Norway. 2.1.1980: Launched. 7.6.1980: Completed for Partenrederi Garnes, (Kristian Jebsens Rederi AS, managers), Norway. (O.N. 19464). 1983: Lengthened by Fosen Mekaniske Verksteder AS, Fevak. 1986: Transferred to Cameco Shipping Company, (Jebsens Hamburg GmbH & Company KG, managers), Philippines, and renamed GENERAL CAMPOS. (O.N. 228670). 1990: Transferred to Panama flag, and Jebsens Ship Management (Bergen) AS, appointed as managers. 1992: Transferred to Jebsens Thun Short Sea SA, (Jebsens Thun Management Ltd., managers), and renamed GARNES. 1996: Sold to Frederiksberg Bulk KS, Bergen, (Donnelly Ship Management Ltd., Limassol, managers), St Vincent and The Grenadines flag. 2000: Tordenskjold Marine Gdynia Sp. z.o.o., appointed as managers. 2002: Sold to Short Sea Ltd., Malta, and renamed WILSON MALM, retaining St Vincent and The Grenadines flag.. 2003: Transferred to Wilson Shipowning AS, Bergen, (Wilson Shipmanagement AS, Bergen, managers), under Malta flag.

7825576
116. EDCO (1980 -   )
As built: 22,605g. 14,213n. 38,300d. 185.40 x 26.24 x 11.772 metres oa.
Post 1995: 22,530g. 13,016n. 38,300d.
6-cyl. 2 S.C.S.A. (670 x 1,700mm) B&W 6L67GB type oil engine made by AS Fredriksstad Mekaniske Verksteder Fredriksstad. 11,200 bhp. 16 kts.
Bulk carrier with three 15-ton cranes capable of operating grabs carried aboard.
3.1978: Ordered by Kristian Jebsens Rederi AS from Stord Verft AS, Stord (Yard No. 808), for Misr Edco Shipping Company Ltd., Alexandria, Egypt. 4.2.1980: Keel laid. 23.8.1980: Launched. 5.10.1980: Completed.

EDCO (M. R. Dippy)

117. FIDUCIA (2)   **(1980 – 1983)** see ship No. 50 above

118. GENERAL LIM (1)   **(1980 – 1986)** see ship No. 39 above.

7719820
119. EL TOR   (1981 – 1991)
4,609g. 2,162n. 1,046d. 105.97 (BB) x 17.30 x 4.120 metres oa.
Four, 12-cyl. 4 S.C.S.A. (250 x 300mm) Normo KVM-12 vee type oil engines made by the shipbuilder, geared in pairs to twin shafts with controllable pitch propellers. 9,900 bhp. 15 kts.   Thwartship thrust propeller forward.
412 berthed, 660 deck passenger / roro cargo ferry with a stern door ramp.
9.1977: Ordered by Kristian Jebsens Rederi AS from Bergens Mekaniske Verksteder AS, Bergen (Yard No. 794), for Misr Edco Shipping Company Ltd., Egypt. 23.9.1980: Launched. 31.3.1981: Completed. 1991: Renamed EL ARISH – EL TOR. 1999: Sold to Sayed Nasr Navigation Lines, Cairo, (International Ship Management (ISM), Cairo, appointed as managers), Egypt, and renamed EL-ARISH. 1999: Arab Ship Management, Cairo, appointed as managers. 2000: Removed from management.

7810222
120. RAKNES (3) (1981 – 1986) Korsnes class
3,955g. 2,614n. 6,186d. 107.4 x 15.04 x 6.651 metres oa.
6-cyl. 4 S.C.S.A. (410 x 470mm) Werkspoor 6TM410 vee type oil engine made by Stork-Werkspoor Diesel BV, Amsterdam, geared to a controllable pitch propeller. 3,600 bhp. 13.5 kts.
Gearless bulk carrier.
24.4.1981: Launched by Storviks Mekaniske Verksteder AS, Kristiansund (Yard No. 92), for Partenrederi Raknes, (Kristian Jebsens Rederi AS, managers), Norway. 11.7.1981: Completed. (O.N. 19593). 1986: Transferred to Amstelstroom Management Company Ltd., (Jebsens Ship Management Ltd., managers), Holland, and renamed EEMNES. 1988: Jebsens Ship Management AS (JSMA) appointed as managers. 1989: Jebsens Ship Management (Bergen) AS, appointed as managers. 1991: Transferred to Panama flag, (O.N.19671-91A). 1992: Renamed RAKNES. 6.1995: Sold to Almar Shipping Company Ltd., Bergen, (same managers), under Cyprus flag, and renamed RAMNES. 2004: Renamed WILSON MERSIN, (Wilson Shipmanagement AS, Bergen, managers).

RAKNES (Author's collection / Fotoflite)

7924889
121. KRISLOCK (1981 – 1983) Krislock class
29,761g. 21,414n. 61,190d. 223.15 (BB) x 32.26 x 13.020 metres oa.
7-cyl. 2 S.C.S.A. (670 x 1,700mm) B&W 7L67GFCA type oil engine made by Mitsui Engineering & Shipbuilding Company Ltd., Tamano. 13,100 bhp. 14.5 kts.
Bulk carrier with six 15-ton cranes capable of operating grabs carried aboard.
1979: Ordered by the World Wide Shipping Group, Hong Kong, from Koyo Dockyard Company Ltd., Mihara, Japan (Yard No.1013). 25.8.1981: Launched for Liberian Totem Transports Inc., (Wallem Ship Management Ltd., managers), Liberia. 4.11.1981: Completed. (O.N. 7073). 1982: Wheelock Marine Services Inc., appointed as managers. 1983: Transferred to Manila Bulk Carriers Inc., (same managers), Philippines, and renamed MANILA PEACE. (O.N.227548). 1985: Fenwick Shipping Services Ltd., appointed as managers. 1986: Transferred to Pacnorse Shipping Nine Ltd., Manila. 1986: Sold to the Maersk Company (Singapore) Pte. Ltd., Singapore, and renamed MAERSK SEMAKAU. (O.N.383483). 1986: Sold to Midnight Star Shipping Inc., Bahamas, and renamed ASTERIX, (O.N.383453). 1987: Transferred to Greek flag. (O.N.9212). 1989: Sold to Sea Velvet Marine Ltd., (Iolcos Hellenic Maritime Enterprises Company Ltd., managers), Cyprus, and renamed THEMIS PETRAKIS. 10.2000: Sold to P. T. Perusahaan Pelayaran Samudera Khusus Arpeni Pratama Ocean Line, Indonesia, and renamed DEWI UMAYI. (O.N. 081/MI/10/2000).

8720840
122. ALI BABA (1981 – 1989)
7,644g. 4,490n. 355 x 221 x 120 feet rectangular platform.
Four, V18A type oil engines made by Hedamora Diesel Company, Japan, driving generators each powering four electric motors geared to twin screw shafts. 9 kts.
Akers H-3 design self-propelled, semi-submersible drilling rig.
1976: Completed as NORTROLL by Trosvik-Framnaes, Sandefjord, for KS Golar-Nor Oceanics AS & Company, Norway. 1981: Sold to Jebsen Drilling Ltd., London, and

renamed ALI BABA. (O.N. 399051). 1981: Transferred to Jebsen Drilling Plc., London. 1989: Sold to Davy Offshore Ltd., Middlesbrough. 1990: Renamed EMERALD PRODUCER. 1995: Sold to The Cunard Steam Ship Company Plc, (Trafalgar House Offshore Fabricators Ltd., Glasgow, managers), London. 1996: Sold to Seatankers Management Company Ltd., (Atlantic Power & Gas Ltd., managers), Aberdeen, and renamed NORTHERN PRODUCER. 1997: Atlantic Floating Production Ltd., appointed as managers. 1998: Sold to Northern Offshore ASA, (same managers), Norway, and transferred to Cyprus flag. 1999: PGS Atlantic Power Ltd., appointed as managers. 2000: PGS Production Ltd., appointed as managers. 2002: Sold to Qualimar Shipping Company Ltd., Cyprus. 2004: Sold to Northern Offshore Management AS, Oslo.

ALI BABA undergoing overhaul in foggy conditions.

(W. J. Harvey)

GENERAL LUNA at Felixstowe in 1982 wearing Botelho Bulk funnel markings.
(World Ship Society Photograph Library)

123. GENERAL LUNA (1)   **(1981 – 1985)** see ship No. 54 above.

BEAGLE At Avonmouth in May 1982 (World Ship Society Photograph Library)

124. BEAGLE   **(1981 – 1984)** see ship No. 53 above.

AKRANES (J. K. Byass)

125. AKRANES   **(1981 – 1995)** see ship No. 41 above.

EASTERN ALLIANCE (World Ship Society Photograph Library)

126. EASTERN ALLIANCE   **(1981 – 1982)** see ship No. 79 above.

8000472

127. LIMELOCK (1982) Limelock class

29,759g. 21,414n. 61,315d. 223.15 (BB) x 32.26 x 12.451 metres oa.

7-cyl. 2 S.C.S.A. (670 x 1,700mm) B&W 7L67GFCA type oil engine made by Mitsui Engineering & Shipbuilding Company Ltd., Tamano. 13,100 bhp. 14.5 kts.

Bulk carrier with four 25-ton cranes capable of operating grabs carried aboard.

1980: Ordered by the World Wide Shipping Group, Hong Kong, from Koyo Dockyard Company Ltd., Mihara, Japan (Yard No.1015). 5.12.1981: Launched for Stratton Shipping Ltd., (Kristian Jebsens Rederi AS, managers), Hong Kong. 18.2.1982: Completed. 1982: Renamed GENERAL AGUINALDO, (Pacific Norse Shipping Ltd., Bermuda, managers), and transferred to Philippine flag. (O.N.228633). 1985: Sold to Pacnorse Shipping Ten Ltd., (Kristian Jebsens Rederi AS, managers). 1986: Sold to the Maersk Company (Singapore) Pte. Ltd., Singapore, and renamed MAERSK SERAYA. (O.N.383473). 1988: Owners restyled as A. P. Moller (Singapore) Pte. Ltd. 1992: Sold to Pandesia Maritime Inc., (Magna Marine Inc., managers), Greece, and renamed PANDESIA. 2001: Sold to KDB Capital Corp., Soeul, South Korea, (Seven Mountain Shipping, Seoul, managers), and renamed GREAT SKY, under South Korea flag.

8001024

128. TELNES (5) (1982 -   ) Telnes class

As built: 6,793g. 4,248n. 10,110d. 117.71 x 20.55 x 8.481 metres oa.

Post 1983: 4,793g.

6-cyl. 4 S.C.S.A. (410 x 470mm) Werkspoor 6TM410 type oil engine made by Stork-Werkspoor Diesel B.V. Amsterdam, geared to a controllable pitch propeller. Thwartship thrust propeller forward. 4,600 bhp. 14 kts.

Belt-unloading bulk carrier.

17.10.1981: Launched by Kleven Mekaniske Verksteder AS, Ulsteinvik (Yard No. 38), for Partenrederi Telnes, (Kristian Jebsens Rederi AS, managers), Norway. 27.2.1982: Completed. (O.N. 19682). 1983: Transferred to Jebsens Shipping Ltd., (Jebsens Ship Management Ltd., managers), London, (O.N. 703309). 1986: Transferred to Jebsens (UK) Ltd., (same managers). 1987: Transferred to Telnes Shipping Ltd., (same managers), Hong Kong. 1988: Chelston Ship Management Ltd., appointed as managers. 1989: Transferred to Jebsens Thun Beltships Investments Inc., (same managers). 9.1997: Sold to Telnes Panama SA, (Wilson Shipmanagement (Bergen) AS, managers), under Panama flag. 10.2003: Transferred to Telnes Panama AS, Bergen, (AJ Ship Management, Leer, Germany, managers), under Antigua and Barbuda flag.

8014162

129. NORSELOCK / MANILA PACIFIC (1982 – 1986) Limelock class

29,759g. 21,414n. 61,000d. 223.15 (BB) x 32.26 x 13.02 metres oa.

7-cyl. 2 S.C.S.A. (670 x 1,700mm) B&W 7L67GFCA type oil engine made by Mitsui Engineering & Shipbuilding Company Ltd., Tamano. 13,100 bhp. 14.5 kts.

Bulk carrier with four 25-ton cranes capable of operating grabs carried aboard.

1980: Ordered by the World Wide Shipping Group, Hong Kong, from Koyo Dockyard Company Ltd., Mihara, Japan (Yard No. 1025). 18.6.1982: Launched as NORSELOCK for Shilton Shipping Company, Hong Kong. 21.9.1982: Completed as MANILA PACIFIC for Baliwag Navigation Inc., (Wheelock Marine Services Inc., managers), Philippines. (O.N. 226969). 1985: Fenwick Shipping Services Ltd., appointed as managers. 1986: Transferred to Pacnorse Shipping Eight Ltd., (same managers). 1986: Sold to The Maersk Company (Singapore) Pte. Ltd., Singapore, and renamed MAERSK SENANG. (O.N.383493). 1987: Owner restyled as A. P. Moller (Singapore)

Pte. Ltd. 1992: Sold to Panoria Maritime Inc., (Magna Marine Inc., managers), Greece, and renamed PANORIA. 2000: Sold to Seven Mountain Shipping Company Ltd., South Korea, and renamed MONARCH. (O.N. ICR-002772). 6.2004: Sold to Formosa Allstar Marine, Taipei, Taiwan, (Formosa Plastics Marine, Taipei, managers), and renamed FORMOSABULK No. 3, under Liberia flag.

8116960
130. FJELLNES (2) (1982 – 1986) Fjellnes class
As built: 7,367g. 4,995n. 12,334d. 129.04 (BB) x 20.05 x 8.419 metres oa.
Post 1994: 8,351g. 4,305n. 12,296d.
Post 1995: 8,351g. 4,305n. 12,334d.
9-cyl. 4 S.C.S.A. (400 x 460mm) Pielstick 9PC2-5L-400 type oil engine made by Nippon Kokan KK, Yokohama. 5,850 bhp. 13.75 kts.
Bulk carrier with two 15-ton cranes capable of operating grabs carried aboard.
26.4.1982: Launched by Miho Zosensho KK, Shimizu, Shizouka Pref (Yard No. 1209), for Kristian Jebsens Rederi AS, Panama. 5.8.1982: Completed for Sangrail Companhia Naviera SA, (Kristian Jebsens Rederi AS, managers), Panama. (O.N. 11170). 1985: Transferred to Jebsens Fjellnes Shipping SA, (same managers). 1986: Transferred to Philippines flag, and renamed FASTNES, (Jebsens Ship Management AS (JSMA), managers). 1989: Jebsens Ship Management (Bergen) AS, appointed as managers. 1990: Chelston Ship Management Ltd., appointed as managers. 1992: Transferred to Panama flag, (Jebsens Ship Management (Bergen) AS, managers). 1993: Sold to Massoel SA, Switzerland, and renamed SARINE 2. 1994: Acomarit Services Maritimes SA, appointed as managers and transferred to Switzerland flag. 1996: Sold to Harbor Fair Shipping SA, (Perpetual Shipmanagement International Inc., managers), Panama, and renamed DIANE GREEN. 1997: Harbor Fair Development Ltd., appointed as managers. 3.2000: Purchased at an auction in Trinidad, via their bankers by Arklow Shipping Ltd. 7.2000: Dry-docked for overhaul at Dublin, transferred to Coastal Shipping Plc (Arklow Shipping Ltd., managers), Arklow and renamed ARKLOW DAY. (O.N. 402889). 6.11.2003: Sold to Castor Maritime, Piraeus, (Sea Observer Shipping, Piraeus, managers), Greece, and renamed CASTOR under Malta flag.

FOSSNES Off Cuxhaven. (W.J. Harvey)

8116972
131. FOSSNES (2) (1982 – 1987) Fjellnes class
As built: 7,363g. 4,793n. 12,200d. 129.32 (BB) x 20.35 x 8.419 metres oa.
Post 1990: 8,300g. 4,296n. 12,078d.
9-cyl. 4 S.C.S.A. (400 x 460mm) Pielstick 9PC2-5L-400 type oil engine made by Nippon Kokan KK, Yokohama. 5,850 bhp. 14.5 kts.
Bulk carrier with two 15-ton cranes capable of operating grabs carried aboard.

1981: Ordered by the Jameel Organization from Miho Zosensho KK, Shimizu, Shizouka Pref (Yard No.1210), for New Jay Shipping Inc., Liberia. 5.8.1982: Launched. 11.11.1982: Completed for Fossnes Shipping Ltd., Liberia. (O.N.7311). 1987: Transferred to Sun Jay Shipping Ltd., Cyprus, and renamed SUN JAY. 1987: Transferred to Sunshine Shipping Ltd., Cyprus, and renamed SUN KING. 1990: Transferred to Desford Investments Ltd., (Fenwick Shipping Services Ltd., managers), Hong Kong, and renamed FANLING. 1998: Sold to Zirkel Verwaltungs GmbH, Brake, Germany, and renamed HEA, under Antigua and Barbuda Flag. 2000: Sold to Hea Navigation Ltd., (Zirkel Verwaltungs GmbH, managers). 10.2002: Sold to Ahmad Shipping Company, Tartous, Syria, (Samin Shipping Ltd, Limassol, Cyprus, managers), and renamed AHMAD S, under the Syria flag.

132. NEW ZEALAND ALLIANCE   **(1982 – 1984)** see ship No. 79 above.

133. GENERAL ROXAS (1)   **(1982 – 1986)** see ship No. 87 above.

134. GENERAL AGUINALDO   **(1982 – 1986)** see ship No. 127 above.

GENERAL CAPINPIN   3 September 1986 in Australian waters. (World Ship Society Photograph Library)

135. GENERAL CAPINPIN   **(1982 – 1988)** see ship No. 51 above.

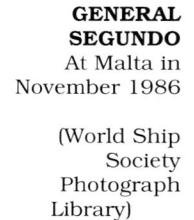

GENERAL SEGUNDO
At Malta in November 1986

(World Ship Society Photograph Library)

136. GENERAL SEGUNDO   **(1982 – 1987)** see ship No. 77 above.

SARINE in February 1987   (Chriss Reynolds collection)

137. SARINE   **(1982 – 1987)** see ship No. 95 above.

FRIBOURG In April 1984   (Chriss Reynolds collection)

138. FRIBOURG   **(1982 – 1987)** see ship No. 99 above.

TINNES on the River Medway   (Chriss Reynolds collection)

8008450
139. TINNES (3)   **(1983 – 1987)** Telnes class
As built: 6,792g. 4,281n. 10,110d. 117.71 x 20.58 x 8.481 metres oa.
Post 1992:   5,829g. 4,120n. 10,110d.
Post 1994:   6,944g. 2,710n. 10,110d.

6-cyl. 4 S.C.S.A. (410 x 470mm) Werkspoor 6TM410 type oil engine made by Stork-Werkspoor Diesel B.V. Amsterdam, geared to a controllable pitch propeller. Thwartship thrust propeller forward. 4,600 bhp. 14 kts.
Belt-unloading bulk carrier.
2.10.1982: Launched by Kleven Mekaniske Verksteder AS, Ulsteinvik (Yard No. 39), for Partenrederi Tinnes, (Kristian Jebsens Rederi AS, managers), Norway. 15.1.1983: Completed. (O.N. 19682). 1987: Transferred to Oceanside Shipping Corp., (same managers), Philippines, and renamed GENERAL BONIFACIO. 1988: Transferred to Tinnes Shipping Ltd., (Jebsens (UK) Ltd., managers), London, and renamed TINNES, (O.N. 717038). 1989: Transferred to Jebsens Thun Beltships Investments Inc., (Chelston Ship Management Ltd., managers). 1992: Transferred to Norway (NIS) flag, (O.N. N-01194). 1996: Transferred to Panama flag. 1997: Transferred to Beltunloaders Shipping AS, Bergen. 1997: Sold to Tinnes Panama S. A. (Jebsens Shipmanagement (Bergen) AS, managers), Panama. 2003: Transferred to Erste Belt Shipping AG, Leer, Germany, (AJ Ship Management, Leer, Germany, managers), under Antigua and Barbuda flag.

FALKNES – anchored in the English channel, 11 May 1983, whilst bound to Govan with a deck cargo of equipment destined for two new Company L-class ships under construction on the Clyde. Note the tripped starboard anchor and painter's platform secured to it.
(Authors collection / Fotoflite)

8116984
140. FALKNES (2) (1983 – 1986) Fjellnes class
As built:-   7,944g. 5,104n. 12,078d. 129.04 (BB) x 20.05 x 8.419 metres oa.
Post 1994:   8,353g. 4,305n. 12,296d.
Post 1995:   8,353g. 4,305n. 12,271d.
9-cyl. 4 S.C.S.A. (400 x 460mm) Pielstick 9PC2-5L-400 type oil engine made by Nippon Kokan KK, Yokohama. 5,850 bhp. 13.5 kts.
Bulk carrier with two 15-ton cranes capable of operating grabs carried aboard.
12.11.1982: Launched by Miho Zosensho KK, Shimizu, Shizouka Pref. (Yard No. 1211), for Partenrederi Falknes, (Kristian Jebsens Rederi AS, managers), Norway.

24.2.1983: Completed. (O.N. 19844). 1986: Transferred to Emporium Shipping Corp., (same managers), Philippines, and renamed GENERAL FITNES * then FITNES, (O.N. 228976). 1987: Jebsens Ship Management AS (JSMA), appointed as managers. 1988: Renamed FALKNES. 1989: Jebsens Ship Management (Bergen) AS, appointed as managers. 1990: Transferred to Panama flag (Chelston Ship Management Ltd., managers) (O.N. 17095-87B). 1991: Jebsens Ship Management (Bergen) AS, appointed as managers. 1993: Sold to Massoel SA, Switzerland, and renamed URI. 1993: Acomarit Services Maritimes SA, appointed as managers and transferred to Switzerland flag. 1996: Sold to Masstransport MT SA, (same managers). 1997: Sold to Golden Fair Shipping SA, (Harbor Fair Development Ltd., managers), Panama, and renamed DAISY GREEN. 1999/2000: Purchased at a Rotterdam auction by Coastal Shipping Ltd., (Arklow Shipping Ltd., managers), Republic of Ireland, and renamed ARKLOW DAWN, retaining Panama flag. 2000: Transferred to Arklow flag. (O.N. 402888). 10.2000: Dry-docked at Dublin for first overhaul since purchase. 16.12.2003: Sold to Polydefkis Maritime SA., Piraeus, (Sea Observer Shipping, Piraeus, managers), and renamed POLYDEFKIS under Malta flag.

* GENERAL FITNES was quoted in Lloyds register for a period before being amended to FITNES. This was believed to be "human error" when GENERAL was added to follow suit of the other renamings. Also a play on the term "general fitness" with two "s".

GENERAL VALDEZ

(World Ship Society Photograph Library)

7027071
141. GENERAL VALDEZ (1983 – 1987)
As built: 4,734g. 3,261n. 7,078d. 115.07 (BB) x 17.25 x 6.96 metres oa.
Post 1995: 5,413g. 3,247n. 7,018d.
8-cyl. 4 S.C.S.A. (550 x 900mm) oil engine made by Ito Tekkosho, Shimizu. 5,400 bhp. 14 kts.
General cargo vessel with a container capacity of 150 TEU.
17.3.1970: Keel laid as SANTA ISABELA by Hayashikane Zosen, Shimonoseki (Yard No. 752), for Citadel Lines Inc., Philippines. 6.7.1970: Launched. 28.8.1970: Completed. 1983: Sold to Aboitiz, Jebsen Bulk Transport Corp., Philippines, and renamed GENERAL VALDEZ. (O.N. 213915). 1987: Renamed ABOITIZ SUPER CONCARRIER I, (Aboitiz Shipping Corp. managers). 1994: Aboitiz Transport System, Manila, appointed as managers. 1996: Sold to Aboitiz, Jebsens Shipmanagement, Manila.

FJORDNES (World Ship Society Photograph Library)

8116996
142. FJORDNES (2) (1983 – 1987) Fjellnes class
As built:-   7,393g. 4,962n. 12,319d. 129.04 (BB) x 20.02 x 8.419 metres oa.
Post 1990: 8,300g. 4,296n. 12,352d.
Post 1996: 8,300g. 4,296n. 12,296d.
9-cyl. 4 S.C.S.A. (400 x 460mm) Pielstick 9PC2-5L-400 type oil engine made by Nippon Kokan KK, Yokohama. 5,850 bhp. 14.5 kts.
Bulk carrier with two 15-ton cranes capable of operating grabs carried aboard.
1981: Ordered by the Jameel Organization from Miho Zosensho KK, Shimizu, Shizouka Pref. (Yard No. 1212), for Star Jay Shipping Inc., (Kristian Jebsens Rederi AS, managers), Liberia. 28.2.1983: Launched. 27.5.1983: Completed for Fjordnes Shipping Ltd., Liberia. (O.N. 7393). 1987: Renamed STAR JAY. 1987: Transferred to Elpis Shipping Ltd., Cyprus, and renamed ELPIS. (O.N. 708388). 1990: Transferred to Stateville Company Ltd., London, (Fenwick Shipping Services Ltd., Hong Kong, managers), and renamed KAMTIN. (O.N. 715735). 1995: Transferred to Hong Kong flag. 1996: Sold to Libmar Shipping SA, Panama City, (Phoenocean Ltd., Tolworth, Surrey, managers), Bahamas, and renamed FALKNES. (O.N. 728063). 2000: Renamed DEMI GREEN. 2002: Sold to Lia Navigation GmbH & Company KG, Germany, and renamed LIA, under Antigua and Barbuda flag. 2003: Sold to Krios Maritime SA, Piraeus, (Sea Observer Shipping SA, Piraeus, managers), and renamed KRIOS, under the Malta flag.

BINSNES In November 1986. (World Ship Society Photograph Library)

7928067
143. BINSNES (4) (1983 – 1989) Bolnes class
As built:-   16,421g. 11,411n. 26,354d. 175.14 (BB) x 25.53 x 9.964 metres oa.
Post 1989:   15,743g. 11,888n. 26,354d.
Post 1994:   16,097g. 9,951n. 26,354d.
6-cyl. 2 S.C.S.A. (740 x 1,600mm) B&W 6K74EF type oil engine made by J. G. Kincaid & Company Ltd., Greenock. 11,600 bhp. 15.5 kts.
Bulk carrier with five 25-ton cranes capable of operating grabs carried aboard and with a container capacity of 682 TEU.
1979: Ordered by Shadeberry Ltd. from Govan Shipbuilders Ltd., Govan (Yard No. 252). 5.2.1981: Launched as LORD JELLICOE, for Liberty Maritime Agency Ltd. 10.4.1981: Completed as LORD CURZON for Bishopgate Marine Hire Purchase Ltd., (H. Scullard & Sons Ltd., managers), London. (O.N. 390944). 1983: Renamed BINSNES, (Jebsens Ship Management Ltd., managers). 1988: Transferred to Panama flag. 1989: Sold to Celis World Shipping Inc., (V. Ships Norway AS, managers), Panama, and renamed WANI FALCON. 1990: Thorvald Klaveness & Company AS, appointed as managers. 1991: Renamed BANAK. 1992: Sold to Guybulk Shipping Ltd., (same managers). 1993: Renamed BAMIA. 1997: Sold to Alcinoe Shipping SA, Athens, (Eurobulk SA, Athens, managers), and renamed PANTELIS P, under the Cyprus flag.

BOLNES In Australian waters 21 June 1988. (World Ship Society Photograph Library)

7928055
144. BOLNES (3) (1983 – 1989) Bolnes class
As built:-   16,421g. 11,411n. 26,354d. 175.14 (BB) x 25.53 x 9.964 metres oa.
Post 1989:   15,743g. 11,888n. 26,354d.
Post 1994:   16,079g. 9,951n. 26,354d.
6-cyl. 2 S.C.S.A. (740 x 1,600mm) B&W 6K74EF type oil engine made by J. G. Kincaid & Company Ltd., Greenock. 11,600 bhp. 15.5 kts.
Bulk carrier with five 25-ton cranes capable of operating grabs carried aboard and with a container capacity of 682 TEU.
1979: Ordered by Groomcharm Ltd. from Govan Shipbuilders Ltd., Govan (Yard No. 251). 2.4.1980: Keel laid. 12.11.1980: Launched as LORD BYRON for Liberty Maritime Agency Ltd. 23.2.1981: Completed for Bishopgate Marine Hire Purchase Ltd., (H. Scullard & Sons Ltd., managers), London. (O.N. 390832). 1983: Renamed BOLNES, (Jebsens Ship Management Ltd., managers). 1988: Transferred to Panama flag. 1989: Sold to Celis World Shipping Inc., (V. Ships Norway AS, managers), Panama flag, and

renamed WANI BIRD. 1990: Thorvald Klaveness & Company AS, appointed as managers. 1991: Renamed BALSA. 1992: Sold to Balsa Partner AS, (same managers), and transferred to Norway (NIS) flag, (O.N. N-01206). 1997: Sold to Aspida Navigation SA, Piraeus, (Eurobulk SA, Piraeus, managers), and renamed IOANNIS A. P., under the Cyprus flag. 1998: Sold to Oceanpride Shipping SA, Piraeus, (same managers), and renamed JOHN P, retaining Cyprus flag.

SAINT BRICE

(Author's collection / Fotoflite)

145. SAINT BRICE   **(1983 – 1997)** see ship No. 67 above.

SAINT BREVIN
In November 1987

(Chriss Reynolds collection)

146. SAINT BREVIN   **(1983 – 1997)** see ship No. 66 above.

SAINT JAMES

(Author's collection / Fotoflite)

147. SAINT JAMES (1983 – 1987) see ship No. 69 above.

SAINT JEAN

(Author's collection / Fotoflite)

148. SAINT JEAN	**(1983 – 1987)**	see ship No. 75 above.
149. MANILA PEACE	**(1983 – 1986)**	see ship No. 121 above.
150. GENERAL MALVAR	**(1983 – 1985)**	see ship No. 50 above.
151. GENERAL MASCARDO (1)	**(1983 – 1985)**	see ship No. 101 above.
152. MANILA HOPE	**(1983 – 1985)**	see ship No. 70 above.

MANILA HOPE At Malta 20 September 1985 (World Ship Society Photograph Library)

LAKENES on 8 February 1984 on builders trials. (World Ship Society Photograph Library)

8126630
153. LAKENES (1984 – 1985) Lakenes class
25,965g. 14,942n. 45,090d. 183.01 (BB) x 31.04 x 11.939 metres
4-cyl. 2 S.C.S.A. (760 x 1,600mm) Sulzer 4RLB76 type oil engine made by Clark, Hawthorn Ltd., Wallsend. 9,800 bhp. 14 kts.
Bulk carrier with four 25-ton cranes capable of operating grabs carried aboard.
1981: Ordered by Pacnorse Shipping (UK) Ltd., London from Govan Shipbuilders Ltd., Govan (Yard No. 260). 9.11.1983: Launched for Investors In Industry Plc, (Jebsens (UK) Ltd., managers). 12.3.1984: Completed. (O.N. 705511). 1985: Transferred to Manufacturer's Hanover Trust Company, (same managers). 1987: Transferred to Ascot Leasing Ltd., (Jebsens Ship Management Ltd., managers). 1988: Transferred to Panama flag. (O.N. 18965-PEXT). 1990: Jebsens Ship Management (Bergen) AS, appointed as managers. 1993: Sold to Millgate Shipping Corporation, Greece, and renamed FAETHON. 2002: Sold to Bolero Trading SA, Piraeus, (Adelfia Shipping SA, Piraeus, managers), and renamed ANTONIS, under Greece flag.

LOFTNES
6 July 1984.

(World Ship Society Photograph Library)

8126642
154. LOFTNES (1984 – 1987) Lakenes class
25,965g. 14,942n. 45,090d. 183.01 (BB) x 31.04 x 11.939 metres
4-cyl. 2 S.C.S.A. (760 x 1,600mm) Sulzer 4RLB76 type oil engine made by Clark, Hawthorn Ltd., Wallsend. 9,800 bhp. 14 kts.
Bulk carrier with four 25-ton cranes capable of operating grabs carried aboard.
1981: Ordered by Pacnorse Shipping (UK) Ltd., London, from Govan Shipbuilders Ltd., Govan (Yard No. 261). 20.3.1984: Launched for Jebsens (UK) Ltd. 14.7.1984: Completed for Priorhouse Ltd., and Capital Leasing Ltd., (Jebsens (UK) Ltd., managers), London. (O.N. 705511). 1987: Transferred to Edilsea Maritime Company SA, (same managers), Panama, and renamed GENERAL LUKBAN. (O.N. 18146-Li). 1988: Chelston Ship Management Ltd., appointed as managers. 1989: Transferred to Celis World Shipping Inc., Panama, and renamed WANI RIVER. 1989: Sold to KS Havtjeld, (AS Havtor, manager), Norway, and renamed HAVTJELD. 1995: Sold to China Progress Inc., Panama City, (Fortune Power & Shipping Enterprise Company Ltd., managers), Panama, and renamed CHINA PROGRESS. (O.N. 22876-96A). 2001: Sold to Huaxing Maritime SA, Panama, and renamed HUAXING HAI. 2004: Sold to Master Shipping Inc., Athens, (World Carrier SA, Athens, managers), and renamed SALOOS, under Panama flag.

SWIFTNES on 4 October 1991 inward to Rotterdam on the New Waterway. (World Ship Society Photograph Library)

8300614
155. SWIFTNES (2) (1984 – 1995) Swiftnes class

As built: 19,353g. 9,134n. 30,036d. 170.03 (BB) x 27.56 x 10.002 metres oa.
Post 1998; 18,284g. 6,750n. 30,036d.
6-cyl. 2 S.C.S.A. (580 x 1,700mm) Sulzer 6RTA58 type oil engine made by the shipbuilder at Kobe. 7,500 bhp. 14 kts.
Bulk carrier with three 25-ton cranes capable of operating grabs carried aboard and with a container capacity of 514 TEU.
1983: Ordered by the Mitsubishi Corporation from Mitsubishi Heavy Industries Ltd., Nagasaki (Yard No. 1922) for lease to Atle Jebsen Rederi. 29.5.1984: Launched for Ryoshin Lease KK, Japan. 11.9.1984: Completed. (O.N. 128103). 1985: Transferred to MTBC Leasing Company Ltd., (Sankyo Kaiun KK, (Sankyo Line), managers), Japan. 1988: Sold to Altamar International Shipping Company Ltd., Philippines. (O.N. 229651). 1989: Transferred to S-Ships S. A. (Jebsens Ship Management (Bergen) AS, managers), Norway, (O.N. N-00822). 1992: Sold to Larkspur Investments SA, Bergen, (same managers). 1995: Renamed WESTERN OSPREY. 1996: Aboitiz, Jebsens Shipmanagement appointed as managers. 1998: Sold to AFJE Cement Carrier II Inc., (Aboitiz, Jebsen bulk Transport Corp., managers), converted into a self-unloading bulk cement carrier, and renamed ALCEM LUGAIT. 1998: Transferred to Aboitiz, Jebsen Far East II Inc., Manila, (same managers). 2000: Sold to Tilbury Shipping Inc., Manila, (LMS Manila Inc, managers), under Panama flag. (O.N. 24584-PEXT3). 2003: Belden Ship Management, Manila, appointed as managers. 2005: Sold to unspecified operators, (Belden Shipping Ltd., Singapore, managers), under Singapore flag.

TORNES   (Jebsens)

8321888
156. TORNES (3) (1984 – 1999) Tornes class
6,389g. 2,946n. 8,721d. 113.01 (BB) x 20.22 x 8.263 metres oa.

6-cyl. 4 S.C.S.A. (400 x 460mm) Pielstick 6PC2-3L-400 type oil engine made by Nippon Kokan KK, Yokohama. 3,510 bhp. 15 kts. Thwartship thrust controllable pitch propeller forward.
Belt-unloading bulk carrier.
3.4.1984: Keel laid by Mitsubishi Heavy Industries Ltd., Shimonoseki (Yard No. 867). 13.6.1984: Launched for AS Jebsens Self Unloaders, (Kristian Jebsens Rederi AS, managers), Norway. 1.11.1984: Completed. (O.N. 20026). 1985: Transferred to KS AS Jebsen Tornes, (same managers), Norway. 1987: Jebsens Ship Management AS (JSMA), appointed as managers and transferred to Norway (NIS) flag, (O.N. N-00095). 1989: Jebsens Ship Management (Bergen) AS, appointed as managers. 1990: Transferred to Jebsens Thun Beltships Investments Inc., (same managers). 1995: Sold to Beltships SA, (same managers) Panama. 1997: Sold to Tornes Panama S. A. (Jebsen Shipmanagement (London) Ltd., managers). 1998: Wilson Shipmanagement (Bergen) AS appointed as managers. 5.2000: Sold to Beltships Luxembourg SA, (same managers), Luxembourg, and renamed TABA. 2002: Sold to Beltships Shipping AS, Bergen, and reverted to TORNES. 2004: Transferred to Zweite Belt Shipping AG, Leer, Germany, (AJ Ship Management, Leer, Germany, managers), under the Portugal flag

SPRAYNES on 13 March 1993. (World Ship Society Photograph Library)

8300626
157. SPRAYNES (2) (1984 – 1989) Swiftnes class
As built: 19,353g. 9,134n. 30,036d. 170.03 (BB) x 27.56 x 10.002 metres oa.
Post 1992: 19,385g. 9,134n. 30,027d.
6-cyl. 2 S.C.S.A. (580 x 1,700mm) Sulzer 6RTA58 type oil engine made by the shipbuilder. 7,500 bhp. 14 kts.
Bulk carrier with three 25-ton cranes capable of operating grabs carried aboard and with a container capacity of 514 TEU.
1983: Ordered by the Mitsubishi Corporation from Mitsubishi Heavy Industries Ltd., Nagasaki (Yard No. 1923), for lease to Atle Jebsen Rederi. 10.8.1984: Launched for Ryoshin Lease KK, Japan. 12.11.1984: Completed for MTBC Leasing Company Ltd., (Sankyo Kaiun KK, (Sankyo Line), managers), Japan. (O.N. 128123). 1988: Sold to Leonis Navigation Company Inc., Philippines. (O.N. 229431). 1989: Renamed WANI TIGER. 1990: Sold to KS Barkald, (Thorvald Klaveness & Company AS, managers), Norway, and renamed BARKALD, (O.N. N-00739). 1992: Sold to Solombala Shipping SA, (Northern Shipping Company, Russia, managers), and reverted to SPRAYNES, under St Vincent and The Grenadines flag,(O.N. 3729). 1993: Jebsens

Shipmanagement (Bergen) AS, appointed as management. 1995: Renamed WESTERN FALCON. 1998: Renamed GRUMANT, (Wilson Ship Management (Bergen) AS, managers). 2002: Malta Ship Management Ltd., Malta, appointed as managers. 2004: Sold to Primal Shipping Ltd., Glasgow, (ASP Seascot Shipmanagement Ltd., Glasgow, managers), and renamed OCEANIC LAND, under St Vincent and The Grenadines flag. 2005: Owners and managers relocated to London.

GENERAL SANTOS Departing Hobart on 22 December 1989. (World Ship Society Photograph Library)

8118554
158. LOCKNES / GENERAL SANTOS (1984 – 1991) Locknes class
27,798g. 15,973n. 47,879d. 189.08 (BB) x 32.24 x 12.001 metres
6-cyl. 2 S.C.S.A. (660 x 1,400mm) Sulzer 6RLB66 type oil engine made by Mitsubishi Heavy Industries Ltd., Kobe. 10,000 bhp. 14.75 kts.
Bulk carrier with three 25-ton cranes capable of operating grabs carried aboard.
1981: Ordered by Pacnorse Shipping International Ltd., Philippines from Namura Shipbuilding Company Ltd., Imari (Yard No. 869). 5.8.1983: Launched as LOCKNES for Broomhill Shipping Company Ltd., (Aboitiz, Jebsen Bulk Transport Corp., managers), Philippines. (O.N. 227619). 17.2.1984: Completed as GENERAL SANTOS for Broomhill Ltd., (Kristian Jebsens Rederi AS, managers), Philippines. 1986: Transferred to Pascal (No.1) Shipping Corp., (same managers). 1987: Jebsens Ship Management AS (JSMA), appointed as managers. 1989: Aboitiz, Jebsen Bulk Transport Corp, appointed as managers. 1991: Transferred to Discovery Management Inc. (same managers), and renamed LUNINGNING. 1991: Sold to Colakoglu Metalurji AS, (Denak Depoculuk ve Nakliyecilik AS, Istanbul, Turkey, and renamed BIBI M. 1992: Sold to Denak Depoculuk ve Nakliyecilik AS, Istanbul, Turkey.

8118566
159. LINDNES (1) (1984 – 1986) Locknes class
27,798g. 15,973n. 47,932d. 189.08 (BB) x 32.24 x 12.001 metres
6-cyl. 2 S.C.S.A. (660 x 1,400mm) Sulzer 6RLB66 type oil engine made by Mitsubishi Heavy Industries Ltd., Kobe. 10,000 bhp. 14.75 kts.
Bulk carrier with three 25-ton cranes capable of operating grabs carried aboard.
1981: Ordered by Pacnorse Shipping International Ltd., Philippines from Namura Shipbuilding Company, Imari (Yard No. 870). 25.11.1983: Launched for First RL (Bermuda) Company Ltd., (Aboitiz, Jebsen Bulk Transport Corp., managers), Panama. 23.2.1984: Completed for R L Kingdom (Panama) SA, (Kristian Jebsens Rederi AS, managers), Panama. (O.N. 12325YJ). 1986: Renamed GENERAL LIM. 1987: Daido Kaiun KK, appointed as managers. 5.1988: Sold to Warby Ltd., Anglo Eastern Management Services Ltd., managers), Hong Kong, and renamed URSUYA, (O.N.

711269). 1989: Transferred to Mission Shipping Ltd., (Anglo Eastern Ship Management Ltd., managers). 1993: Sold to Colakoglu Metalurji AS, (Denak Depoculuk ve Nakliyecilik AS, (Deniz Shipping Agency), managers), Turkey, and renamed FEYZA. 2004: Sold to Denak Depoculuk ve Nakliyecilik AS, Istanbul.

8201337
160. PHILIPPINE KAMIA / ST AUBIN (1984 – 1989) Kamia class
12,539g. 7,897n. 18,100d. 160.03 x 22.20 x 8.818 metres oa.
5-cyl. 2 S.C.S.A. (550 x 1,380mm) B&W 5L55GFCA type oil engine made by Hudong Shipyard, Shanghai. 6,700 bhp. 13.75 kts.
Bulk carrier with four 15-ton cranes capable of operating grabs carried aboard.
1982: Ordered by Wheelock Marden & Company Ltd., Hong Kong, from Guangzhou Shipyard, Guangzhou / Canton (Yard No. 1105). 25.3.1983: Keel laid as PHILIPPINE KAMIA. 5.3.1984: Launched for Poole Shipping Ltd., (Wheelock Marine Ltd., managers), Hong Kong. 30.11.1984: Completed as ST. AUBIN for Yorkshire Bank Leasing Ltd., (Turnbull, Scott Management Ltd., managers), Hong Kong. (O.N.708292). 1985: Owners restyled as Yorkshire Bank Lease Management Ltd., (same managers). 1989: Sold to Triple-Crown Company Inc., (Fenwick Shipping Services Ltd., Hong Kong, managers), Philippines, and renamed CALATAGAN. 1995: Sold to Botelho Shipping Corporation, Philippines, (same managers). 1999: Sold to Galaxy Shipping Ltd., Hong Kong, (same managers), and renamed ST. AUBIN. 2002: Sold to Thymus Shipping Ltd., Dubai, (Tradeline Inc, Dubai, managers), and renamed REGAL STAR, under St Vincent and The Grenadines flag.

GENERAL HIZON on 28 May 1984. (World Ship Society Photograph Library)

8118578
161. LANGNES / GENERAL HIZON (1984 – 1989) Locknes class
27,798g. 15,973n. 47,879d. 189.08 (BB) x 32.24 x 12.070 metres
6-cyl. 2 S.C.S.A. (660 x 1,400mm) Sulzer 6RLB66 type oil engine made by Mitsubishi Heavy Industries Ltd., Kobe. 10,000 bhp. 14.75 kts.
Bulk carrier with three 25-ton cranes capable of operating grabs carried aboard.
1981: Ordered as LANGNES by Pacnorse Shipping International Ltd., Philippines, from Namura Shipbuilding Company Ltd., Imari (Yard No. 865). 28.9.1983: Launched. 15.5.1984: Completed as GENERAL HIZON, for Pisces Maritime SA, (Aboitiz, Jebsen Bulk Transport Corp., managers), Philippines. (O.N. 227760). 1989: Sold to Jovian Maritime SA, (Vermilion Overseas Management Company Ltd., managers), Philippines, and renamed JOVIAN LIBERTY. 1992: Sold to Mauritius Steam Navigation Company

Ltd., (Rogers & Company Ltd., managers), Mauritius, renamed RIAMBEL. 1994: Sold to Sutherland Navigation Inc., Bahamas, and renamed PILION. 1995: Sold to India Cements Ltd., India, and renamed ICL RAJA MAHENDRA. 2002: Sold to Web Shipping Ltd., Valletta, Malta, (Barclay Shipping SA, Piraeus, managers), and renamed GIORGOS, under Malta flag. 2005: Capital Ship Management SA, Piraeus, appointed as managers.

BEAVER on 29 May 1986. (World Ship Society Photograph Library)

162. BEAVER   **(1984 – 1986)** see ship No. 92 above.

163. MANILA BRAVE   **(1984 – 1985)** see ship No. 65 above.

164. GENERAL TINIO   **(1984 – 1986)** see ship No. 79 above.

LUGANO
(World Ship Society Photograph Library)

165. LUGANO   **(1984 – 1990)** see ship No. 80 above.

166. GENERAL LACUNA   **(1985 – 1989)** see ship No. 84 above.

GENERAL LACUNA July 1986.

(World Ship Society Photograph Library)

SHARPNES (World Ship Society Photograph Library)

8307935
167. SHARPNES (2) (1985 – 2005) Swiftnes class
As built: 18,977g. 9,298n. 29,402d. 170.03 (BB) x 27.56 x 10.002 metres oa.
Post 1995: 18,993g. 9,293n. 29,402d.
6-cyl. 2 S.C.S.A. (580 x 1,700mm) Sulzer 6RTA58 type oil engine made by the shipbuilder at Tamashima. 7,500 bhp. 14 kts.
Bulk carrier with three 25-ton cranes capable of operating grabs carried aboard and with a container capacity of 514 TEU.
1983: Ordered by Ryoshin Lease KK, Japan, from Sumitomo Heavy Industries Ltd., Yokosuka (Yard No. 1121), for lease to Atle Jebsen Rederi. 12.6.1984: Keel laid. 8.9.1984: Launched. 9.1.1985: Completed for MTBC Leasing Company Ltd., (Sankyo Kaiun KK, (Sankyo Line), managers), Japan. (O.N. 128142). 1988: Sold to Altamar International Shipping Company Ltd., Philippines. (O.N. 229652). 1989: Transferred to Comboship International SA, (Jebsens Ship Management (Bergen) AS, managers), Norway, (O.N. N-00838). 1992: Transferred to Jebsens Thun Lumber Ship SA, (Same managers). 1993: Sold to Maimaksa Shipping SA, (same managers), St Vincent and The Grenadines. 1994: Sold to Jebsen Pitch Carriers (same managers), under Panama flag. 1998: Transferred to Aluventure Sharpnes Shipping Company SA, Leer,

Germany, (Wilson Ship Management (Bergen) AS, Bergen, managers), retaining Panama flag. 2003: AJ Ship Management, Leer, appointed as managers. 2005: Sold to Gearbulk Shipping Ltd., Bergen, (Kristian Gerhard Jebsen, Bergen, manager), and renamed ASPEN ARROW.

TERTNES as built   (Author's collection)

TERTNES converted for seabed pipeline operations. Note the extended accommodation block aft and the tower above it, and her modified bow
(Author's collection).

8315554
168. TERTNES (1985 -   ) Tertnes class
As built: 6,259g. 2,566n. 8,999d. 112.02 (BB) x 20.53 x 8.214 metres oa.
Post 1992: 7,845g. 3,111n. 11,546d. 129.04 (BB) x 20.53 x 8.650 metres oa.
8-cyl. 4 S.C.S.A. (320 x 350mm) 8R32D type oil engine made by Oy Wartsila Ab, Vaasa/Vasa, geared to a controllable pitch propeller.   3,800 bhp. 15 kts.
Post 1992: Twin thwartship thrust controllable-pitch propellers forward and aft.
Belt-unloading bulk carrier.

29.9.1984: Launched by Kleven Mekaniske Verksteder AS, Ulsteinvik (Yard No. 92), for Kristian Jebsens Rederi AS, Norway. 26.1.1985: Completed for KS AS Jebsens Tertnes, (Kristian Jebsens Rederi AS, managers), Norway. 1987: Jebsens Ship Management AS (JSMA), appointed as managers, and Transferred to Norway (NIS) flag, (O.N. N-00097). 1988: Transferred to Panama flag, (O.N. 18632-PEXT4). 1989: Jebsens Ship Management (Bergen) AS, appointed as managers. 1992: Transferred to Van Oord ACZ BV, Holland, and subsequently lengthened and converted into a stone carrier sea-pipe-discharger. 1993: Transferred to Jebsens Ship Management (Bergen) AS, and to Norway flag. 1995: Sold to Van Oord Marine Services BV, Rotterdam, (Van Oord ACZ BV, Rotterdam, managers). 1997: Jebsens Ship Management (Bergen) AS, Bergen, appointed as managers. 1998: Transferred to Netherlands flag. 2005: Sold to Tertnes BV, Leer, Germany, (AJ Ship Management, Leer, managers), retaining Netherlands flag.

8312734
169. SEALNES (2) (1985 – 1989) Swiftnes class
19,385g. 9,134n. 30,027d. 170.39 (BB) x 27.56 x 10.002 metres oa.
6-cyl. 2 S.C.S.A. (580 x 1,700mm) Sulzer 6RTA58 type oil engine made by the shipbuilder at Kobe. 7,500 bhp. 14 kts.
Bulk carrier with three 25-ton cranes capable of operating grabs carried aboard and with a container capacity of 514 TEU.
1983: Ordered by Kristian Jebsens Rederi AS from Mitsubishi Heavy Industries Ltd., Nagasaki (Yard No. 1929). 14.6.1984: Keel laid. 2.11.1984: Launched for Ryoshin Lease KK, (R. C. Tsavliris, manager), Japan. 26.1.1985: Completed for MTBC Leasing Company Ltd., (Sankyo Kaiun KK, (Sankyo Line), managers), Japan. (O.N. 128149). 1987: Sold to Leonis Navigation Company Inc., Philippines. (O.N. 229430). 1989: Renamed WANI HUNTER, (Thorvald Klaveness & Company AS, managers). 1990: Sold to Dyvi Bulkshipping III AS, Norway, and renamed DYVI OCEANIC, (O.N. N-00753). 1991: Jan-Erik Dyvi appointed as manager. 1991: Purchased by Jebsen Ship Management Holdings AS, (Aboitiz, Jebsen Bulk Transport Corp., managers), and reverted to SEALNES. 1992: Transferred to Anglia Maritime SA, (Jebsens Thun Management AS, managers). 1992: Aboitiz, Jebsen Bulk Transport Corp, Manila, appointed as managers. 1995: Renamed WESTERN CONDOR. 1996: Sold to Aboitiz, Jebsen Shipmanagement, Manila, Philippines. 1999: Renamed CONDOR, (Aboitiz, Jebsens Bulk Transport Corporation, managers). 1999: Sold to Anglia Maritime SA, (same managers), and renamed SEALNES, under the Philippines flag. (O.N. MNLA000209). 2002: Transferred to Hong Kong flag. 2004: Sold to Ership Internacional SA, Madrid, Spain, and renamed FENIX, under Panama flag.

8307636
170. JEBSEN TAURANGA (1985 – 1988) Tauranga class
19,510g. 9,105n. 29,095d. 174.81 (BB) 27.52 x 10.002 metres oa.
6-cyl. 4 S.C.S.A. (750 x 620mm) Pielstick 6PC4-2L-570 type oil engine made by the shipbuilder at Yokohama. 7,240 bhp. 14 kts. Thwartship controllable pitch propeller forward.
Bulk carrier with one 25-ton crane and two travelling 30.5 ton gantry cranes to handle a container capacity of 920 TEU.
1983: Ordered by Kristian Jebsens Rederi AS from Nippon Kokan KK, Tsu (Yard No. 90). 2.8.1984: Launched for Viking Marine (Bermuda) Ltd., Bermuda. 21.2.1985: Completed, (Kristian Jebsens Rederi AS, managers), Hong Kong. (O.N. 706958). 1987: Jebsens Ship Management AS (JSMA), appointed as managers. 1988: Renamed GENERAL TIRONA. 1989: Renamed LANKA AMILA. 1990: Transferred to Jebsen Containership AS, (Jebsens Ship Management (Bergen) AS, managers). 1992:

Renamed GENERAL TIRONA. 1995: Transferred to Viking International Carriers Inc,. Philippines, (same managers). 7.3.1996: Suffered machinery problems off Cape Agulhas and was towed to Cape Town by the salvage tug WOLRAAD WOLTEMADE. 18.3.1996: Departed Cape Town following repairs. 1998: Aboitiz, Jebsen Bulk Transport Corp., appointed as managers. 2000: Sold to Wallock Enterprises Corporation, (same managers), and renamed WILLIAM OLDENDORFF. (O.N. MNLA000088). 2002: Sold to Viking International Carriers Inc., (same managers), Phillipines, and renamed GENERAL TIRONA. 2002: Sold to China Shipping International, Shanghai, and renamed HAI NUN. 2003: Sold to Shanghai Time Shipping Company, Guangzhou, and renamed HAI NENG.

JEBSEN TAURANGA

(Author's collection / Jebsens)

8321890
171. TORGNES (1985 – 1996) Tornes class
6,389g. 2,946n. 8,721d. 113.01 (BB) x 20.22 x 8.267 metres oa.
6-cyl. 4 S.C.S.A. (400 x 460mm) Pielstick 6PC2-3L-400 type oil engine made by Nippon Kokan KK, Yokohama. 3,510 bhp. 15 kts. Thwartship thrust propeller forward.
Belt-unloading bulk carrier.
30.8.1984: Launched by Mitsubishi Heavy Industries Ltd., Shimonoseki (Yard No. 868), for AS Jebsens Self Unloaders, (Kristian Jebsens Rederi AS, managers), Norway. 22.2.1985: Completed for Amoroso Ltd., (Jebsens Ship Management Ltd., managers), Isle of Man. (O.N. 704559). 1986: Transferred to Diomedes Navigation SA, (same managers), Panama. 1987: Transferred to Norway (NIS) flag, (O.N. N-00150). 1988: Owners restyled as Diomedes World SA, (same managers). 1989: Transferred to Jebsens Thun Beltships Investment Inc., (Jebsens Ship Management (Bergen) AS, appointed as managers). 1996: Renamed ENTERPRISE. 1997: Sold to Belt Unloaders Shipping SA, (same managers). 1999: Brambles Ship Management, Australia, appointed as managers. 1999: Toll Shipping Pty. Ltd, appointed as managers. 2003:

Sold to Enterpan Pty. Ltd., Melbourne, (ASP Ship Management, Melbourne, managers), under Antigua and Barbuda flag. 2005: Sold to Zweite Belt Shipping AG, Leer, Germany, (AJ Ship Management, Leer, managers), retaining Antigua and Barbuda flag.

GENERAL MATA on 30 September 1985 in the New Waterway inward to Rotterdam
(World Ship Society Photograph Library)

8313221
172. SALTNES (2) / GENERAL MATA (1985 – 1989) Swiftnes class
As built: 18,977g. 9,359n. 29,446d. 174.81 (BB) x 27.56 x 10.002 metres oa.
Post 1998: 18,977g. 9,539n. 27,939d.
6-cyl. 2 S.C.S.A. (580 x 1,700mm) Sulzer 6RTA58 type oil engine made by the shipbuilder at Tamashima. 7,500 bhp. 14 kts.
Bulk carrier with three 25-ton cranes capable of operating grabs carried aboard and with a container capacity of 514 TEU.
1983: Ordered by Ryoshin Lease KK, Japan, from Sumitomo Heavy Industries Ltd., Yokosuka (Yard No. 1123), for lease to Atle Jebsen Rederi. 8.9.1984: Launched as SALTNES. 25.2.1985: Completed as GENERAL MATA for RL Kingdom (Panama) SA, (Kristian Jebsens Rederi AS, managers), Philippines. (O.N. 14902-85). 1987: Transferred to Aboitiz, Jebsen Bulk Transport Corp., (Jebsens Ship Management AS (JSMA), managers). 1989: Transferred to General Mata Inc., (Havtor AS, managers), Norway, and renamed WANI LAKE. (O.N. N-00871). 1993: Transferred to Bakarista Shipping SA, and renamed SHEERNES, under St Vincent and The Grenadines flag. (O.N. 3805). 1995: Renamed WESTERN EAGLE. 1998: Wilson Ship Management (Bergen) AS, Bergen, appointed as managers. 1998: Renamed EAGLE. 2001: Sold to Spalmex Marine BV, Rotterdam, (Confidence Ship Management BV, Rotterdam, managers), and renamed BRAZILIAN CONFIDENCE, under Cyprus flag. 2004: Sold to Revenge Shipping Corporation, Rotterdam, (same managers), and transferred to Panama flag. 2005: Sold to Spalmex Marine SA, Piraeus, (Hellas Marine Services SA, Piraeus, managers), and transferred to Cyprus flag.

8201351
173. MANILA SPIRIT / ST.CLOUD (1985 – 1994) Kamia class
12,519g. 6,153n. 18,411d. 160.0 x 22.05 x 8.802 metres oa.
5-cyl. 2 S.C.S.A. (550 x 1,380mm) B&W 5L55GFCA type oil engine made by Hudong Shipyard, Shanghai. 6,700 bhp. 13.75 kts.
Bulk carrier with four 15-ton cranes capable of operating grabs carried aboard.
1982: Ordered by Wheelock Marden & Company Ltd., Hong Kong, from Guangzhou Shipyard, Guangzhou/Canton (Yard No. 1107). 24.8.1984: Keel laid as hull sub-contract by Dalien Shipyard, Dalien (Yard No. B.270/7). 24.1.1985: Launched as

MANILA SPIRIT for Wheelock Marden & Company, Hong Kong. 29.3.1985: Completed as ST. CLOUD by Guangzhou Shipyard, Guangzhou/Canton (Yard No. 1107), for Yorkshire Bank Lease Management Ltd., (Turnbull, Scott Management Ltd., managers), Hong Kong. (O.N. 708319). 1991: Fenwick Shipping Services Ltd., appointed as managers. 1994: Sold to Breton Ltd., Hong Kong, (same managers). 2002: Sold to Zhoushan Zhongchang Shipping Company, Zhoushan, China, retaining Hong Kong flag.

SURENES at Port Adelaide 3 December 1990. (World Ship Society Photograph Library)

8307947
174. SURENES (2) (1985 - 1995) Swiftnes class
18,977g. 9,296n. 29,319d. 170.01 (BB) x 27.54 x 10.002 metres oa.
6-cyl. 2 S.C.S.A. (580 x 1,700mm) Sulzer 6RTA58 type oil engine made by the shipbuilder at Tamashima. 7,500 bhp. 14 kts.
Bulk carrier with three 25-ton cranes capable of operating grabs carried aboard and with a container capacity of 514 TEU.
1983: Ordered by Ryoshin Lease KK, Japan, from Sumitomo Heavy Industries Ltd., Yokosuka (Yard No. 1122), for lease to Atle Jebsen Rederi. 12.6.1984: Keel laid. 13.10.1984: Launched. 28.3.1985: Completed for MTBC Leasing Company Ltd., (Sankyo Kaiun KK, (Sankyo Line), managers), Japan. (O.N. 127662). 1987: Sold to Oriman Shipping Corp., Philippines. (O.N. 229310). 1989: Transferred to Heskin Development Inc., (Aboitiz, Jebsen Bulk Transport Corp, managers), Panama. 1992: Transferred to the Philippine flag, (O.N. 230284). 1995: Renamed WESTERN HAWK. 1997: Aboitiz, Jebsen Shipmanagement appointed as managers. 1998: Transferred to Overseas Bulk Transport Inc., (Aboitiz, Jebsen Bulk Transport Corp., managers). 1999: Renamed HAWK. 1999: Sold to Heskin Development Inc., (same managers), and renamed SURENES. 2004: Sold to Ership Internacional SA, Madrid, and renamed CICLOPE, under Panama flag..

8307648
175. JEBSEN NAPIER (1985 – 1988) Tauranga class
19,510g. 9,109n. 28,936d. 174.81 (BB) 27.52 x 10.062 metres oa.

6-cyl. 4 S.C.S.A. (750 x 620mm) Pielstick 6PC4-2L-570 type oil engine made by the shipbuilder at Yokohama. 7,240 bhp. 14.75 kts. Thwartship controllable pitch propeller forward.
Bulk carrier with one 25-ton crane and two travelling 30.5 ton gantry cranes to handle a container capacity of 920 TEU.
1983: Ordered by Kristian Jebsens Rederi AS from Nippon Kokan KK, Tsu (Yard No. 91). 19.1.1985: Launched for Glacier Maritime (Bermuda) Ltd., Bermuda. 5.6.1985: Completed for Sun Iris Marine SA, (Kristian Jebsens Rederi AS, managers), Philippines. (O.N. 228212). 1987: Jebsens Ship Management AS (JSMA), appointed as managers. 1988: Renamed GENERAL DELGADO. 1989: Renamed LANKA ARUNA. 1990: Transferred to Jebsen Containership AS, (Jebsens Ship Management (Bergen) AS, managers). 1992: Transferred to Sun Iris Marine SA, (same managers), and renamed GENERAL DELGADO. 1995: Sold to Wallock Enterprises Corporation (same managers). 1998: Sold to Nor-Phil Ocean Shipping Inc., (Aboitiz, Jebsen Bulk Shipping Corp, appointed as managers). 2000: Sold to Wallock Enterprises Corporation, (same managers), and renamed FREDERIKE OLDENDORFF. (O.N. 000085). 2002: Renamed GENERAL DELGADO. 2004: Sold to Tanixo Shipping SA, Piraeus, (Generals Shipmanagement SA, Piraeus, managers), under Cyprus flag.

TROLLNES Fitted for seabed pipeline operations. Note the extended accommodation block aft.
(Chriss Reynolds collection)

8315566
176. TROLLNES (1985 -   ) Tertnes class
6,398g. 2,517n. 8,734d. 112.02 (BB) x 20.53 x 9.61 metres oa.
6-cyl. 4 S.C.S.A. (320 x 350mm) Wartsila 8R32 type oil engine made by Oy Wartsila Ab, Vaasa/Vasa. 3,800 bhp. 14.75 kts. Thwartship thrust propeller forward.
Belt-unloading bulk carrier.
15.3.1985: Launched by Kleven Mekaniske Verksteder AS, Ulsteinvik (Yard No. 93), for KS AS Jebsens Trollnes, (Kristian Jebsens Rederi AS, managers), Norway. 12.6.1985: Completed. 1987: Jebsens Ship Management AS (JSMA), appointed as managers. (O.N. 20083). 1989: Jebsens Ship Management (Bergen) AS, appointed as managers. 1990: Transferred to Jebsens Thun Beltships Investments Inc., (same managers). 1993: Sold to Van Oord ACZ BV., (same managers). 1995: Sold to Van Oord Marine Services BV (Van Oord ACZ BV managers), and converted into a self-discharging pipe stone carrier. 1996: Jebsens Ship Management (Bergen) AS appointed as managers. 1997: Sold to Trollnes Panama Ltd., (same managers), Panama. 2002: Aboitiz, Jebsen Ship Management, Manila, appointed managers. 2004: Sold to Zweite Belt Shipping AG, Leer, Germany, (AJ Ship Management, Leer, managers), under Antigua and Barbuda flag. 2005: Transferred to Portugal flag.

GENERAL VARGAS
(Internet source)

7510286
177. GENERAL VARGAS (1985 – 1994)
8,341g. 4,341n. 12,100d. 145.88 (BB) x 19.62 x 7.924 metres oa.
9-cyl. 4 S.C.S.A. (450 x 550mm) MaK 9M551AK type oil engine made by MaK Maschinenbau GmbH, Kiel. 6,000 bhp. 15.5 kts.
Ice strengthened bulk carrier with two 16-ton cranes capable of operating grabs carried aboard.
4.9.1976: Keel laid as BRUNTO by Schiffs.u Masch. Paul Lindenau GmbH & Company KG, Kiel (Yard No. 170), for AS Westray, (J. Brunvall, manager), Norway. 17.1.1977: Launched. 11.3.1977: Completed. 6.1985: Sold to Hillgrey Shipping SA, (Kristian Jebsens Rederi AS, managers), Philippines, and renamed GENERAL VARGAS. (O.N. 228247). 1987: Transferred to Marinefield SA, (Jebsens Ship Management AS (JSMA), managers), Philippines. 1989: Jebsens Ship Management (Bergen) AS, appointed as managers. 1994: Sold to Partenrederi Brunto ANS (same managers), Norway, and renamed BRUNTO. 1998: Wilson Shipmanagement (Bergen) AS, appointed as managers. 2002: Sold to Ahilleos Maritime, Varna, Bulgaria, and renamed LINDEN, under the Bolivia flag. 2003: Sold to Pineks Tekstil Deri Pazarlama, Istanbul, and renamed C. AYDIN, under Turkey flag. 2004: Sold to Linden Shipping Ltd., Varna, Bulgaria, (Ahilleos Ship Management Ltd., Varna, managers), and renamed LINDEN, under Slovakia flag.

7503518
178. GENERAL CABAL (1985 - 2000)
7,952g. 4,999n. 12,100d. 145.50 (BB) x 19.59 x 7.924 metres oa.
9-cyl. 4 S.C.S.A. (450 x 550mm) MaK 9M551AK type oil engine made by MaK Maschinenbau GmbH, Kiel. 6,000 bhp. 15.5 kts.
Ice strengthened bulk carrier with two 16-ton cranes capable of operating grabs carried aboard.
29.4.1976: Keel laid as BRUNI by Schiffs.u Masch. Paul Lindenau GmbH & Company KG, Kiel (Yard No. 169), for AS Westray, (J. Brunvall, manager), Norway. 26.9.1976: Launched. 2.12.1976: Completed. 5.1.1977: Delivered. 6.1985: Sold to Hillgrey Shipping SA, (Kristian Jebsens Rederi AS, managers), Philippines, and renamed GENERAL CABAL. (O.N. 228246). 1987: Jebsens Ship Management AS (JSMA), appointed as managers. 1989: Jebsens Ship Management (Bergen) AS, appointed as managers. 1992: Sold to Gallic Shipping International SA, (same managers), Panama. 1995: Sold to Aboitiz, Jebsen Transport Corporation (same managers). 1996: Sold to

Gallic Shipping International SA, (same managers), Panama. 1997: Jebsen Ship Management (London) Ltd., appointed as managers. 1998: Sold to Filscan Shipping Inc., (ASP Seascot Shipmanagement Ltd., Glasgow, managers). 2000: Sold to Irene Shipping Ltd., (Ahilleos Maritime Enterprises Ltd, Varna, managers), and renamed NORDEN, under Malta flag. (O.N. 6820). 2003: Sold to Norden Shipping Ltd., Varna, (Ahilleos Ship Management Ltd., Varna, managers), under Slovakia flag.

GENERAL CABAL (Internet source)

JEBSEN TIMARU This class carried the largest funnels ever in the fleet. (World Ship Society Photograph Library)

8313025
179. JEBSEN TIMARU (1985 – 1988) Tauranga class
19,510g. 8,949n. 29,153d. 174.81 (BB) 27.52 x 10.062 metres oa.
6-cyl. 4 S.C.S.A. (750 x 620mm) Pielstick 6PC4-2L-570 type oil engine made by the shipbuilder at Yokohama. 7,240 bhp. 15 kts. Thwartship controllable pitch propeller forward.
Bulk carrier with one 25-ton crane and two travelling 30.5 ton gantry cranes to handle a container capacity of 920 TEU.
1983: Ordered by Kristian Jebsens Rederi AS from Nippon Kokan K.K., Tsu (Yard No. 92). 1.4.1985: Launched for Fjord Marine (Bermuda) Ltd., Bermuda. 31.7.1985: Completed for Sun Iris Marine SA, (Kristian Jebsens Rederi AS, managers), Philippines. (O.N. 228288). 1987: Jebsens Ship Management AS (JSMA), appointed as managers. 1988: Renamed GENERAL VILLA. 1989: Renamed LANKA ASITHA. 1990: Transferred to Jebsen Containership AS, (Jebsens Ship Management (Bergen) AS, managers). 1992: Renamed GENERAL VILLA. 1995: Sold to Wallock Enterprises Corporation (same managers). 1998: Sold to Nor-Phil Ocean Shipping Inc., Aboitiz,

Jebsen Bulk Transport Corp, appointed as managers). 2000: Transferred to Wallock Enterprises Corp., (same managers). (O.N. MNLA000089). 2004: Sold to Blue Crest Shipping SA, Piraeus, (Generals Shipmanagement AS, Piraeus, managers), under Cyprus flag.

GENERAL MOJICA on 20 July 1993, at Falmouth. (Chriss Reynolds collection)

8201349
180. GENERAL MOJICA (1985 – 1999) Kamia class
12,539g. 6,143n. 18,411d. 160.0 x 22.05 x 8.816 metres oa.
5-cyl. 2 S.C.S.A. (550 x 1,380mm) B&W 5L55GFCA type oil engine made by Hudong Shipyard, Shanghai. 6,700 bhp. 13.75 kts.
Bulk carrier with four 15-ton cranes capable of operating grabs carried aboard.
1982: Ordered by Wheelock Marden & Company Ltd., Hong Kong, from Guangzhou Shipyard, Guangzhou/Canton (Yard No. 1106). 25.10.1983: Keel laid for Wheelock Marine Ltd., Hong Kong. 31.7.1984: Launched for Jebsens Maritime Agencies Inc., (Jebsens (UK) Ltd., managers, Hong Kong. 23.9.1985: Completed for Snowdon Shipping Corp, (Aboitiz, Jebsen Bulk Transport Corp., managers), Philippines. (O.N. 17058). 1990: Transferred to Melbourne Navigation SA, Panama, (O.N. 15417-86B). 1992: Sold to New Bandera Ltd., (Fenwick Shipping Services Ltd., Hong Kong, managers), Philippines, (O.N. 232086). 1999: Sold to United Asia Shipping Ltd., Hong Kong, (same managers), and renamed ST. CROIX. 2002: Sold to Taizhou Shipping Company, Taizhou, China, and renamed ZHE HAI 323, under Republic of China flag.

8108585
181. GENERAL CRUZ (1) (1985 – 1987)
36,209g. 25,953n. 63,800d. 225.03 (BB) x 32.31 x 13.080 metres oa.
5-cyl. 2 S.C.S.A. (800 x 1,950mm) B&W 5L80GFCA type oil engine made by Mitsui Engineering & Shipbuilding Company Ltd., Tamano. 12,600 bhp. 15 kts.
Bulk carrier with one 35-ton and three 25-ton cranes and with a container capacity of 891 TEU.
1981: Ordered as RANGELOCK from Burmeister & Wain Skibsvaerft AS, Kobenhavn (Yard No. 909), by Alberton Shipping Corporation, (Wheelock Marden Group). 13.9.1982: Keel laid. 5.11.1982: Launched for Wheelock Maritime International (UK) Ltd., (Wheelock Marine Services Ltd., managers), Hong Kong. 6.1.1982: Completed. (O.N. 17138). 1985: Transferred to Hardyship Ltd., (Kristian Jebsens Rederi AS, managers), Panama, and renamed GENERAL CRUZ. 1986: Transferred to General Cruz KS, (same managers), Philippines. 1987: Sold to Jayel Shipping Pte. Ltd., (Pacific

Carriers Pte. Ltd., managers), Singapore, and renamed IKAN BILIS. (O.N. 383714). 1995: Sold to Ikan Bilis Shipping Private Ltd., (PACC Ship Managers Private Ltd., managers), Singapore. 1996: Sold to Pacific Carriers Private Ltd., (same managers), Singapore. 1997: Sold to Silver Yang Navigation Inc., Panama, and renamed SILVER YANG. 2000: China Shipping (HK) Marine Company Ltd., Hong Kong, appointed as managers. 2004: Sold to Yin Hua Shipping Ltd., Hong Kong, (same managers), retaining Panama flag.

182. MANILA SUCCESS   (1985 – 1987) see ship No. 102 above.

SANDNES at Ghent in 1985.

(Chriss Reynolds)

183. SANDNES (1)   **(1985 – 1992)** see ship No. 71 above.

184. GENERAL DUQUE   **(1985 – 1989)** see ship No. 65 above.

TRONES on the River Weser in May 1998.   (Chriss Reynolds)

8422163
185. TRONES (1986 -   ) Trones class
7,556g. 3,199n. 11,339d. 121.80 (BB) x 20.53 x 11.61 metres oa.
8-cyl. 4 S.C.S.A. (320 x 350mm) Wartsila 8R32 type oil engine made by Oy Wartsila Ab., Vaasa/Vasa, geared to a controllable pitch propeller. 3,800 bhp. 14.75 kts. Thwartship thrust controllable pitch propeller forward.
Belt-unloading bulk carrier.
14.1.1985: Keel laid by Kleven Mekaniske Verksteder AS, Ulsteinvik (Yard No. 94) for Atle Jebsen Rederi. 2.11.1985: Launched for Partenrederi Trones Rederi. (Kristian

Jebsens Rederi AS, managers), Panama. 15.3.1986: Completed for Sapco Overseas SA, (same managers), Panama. (O.N. 1567). 5.1986: Delivered. 1987: Jebsens Industrial Shipping Services AS, Bergen, appointed as managers, and transferred to Norway (NIS) flag, (O.N. N-00001). 1988: Jebsens Ship Management (Bergen) AS, appointed as managers. 1990: Transferred to Jebsens Thun Beltships Investment Inc., (same managers). 1997: Sold to Trones Panama Ltd., (same managers), Panama. 2002: Transferred to E.T.M. Luxemburg, (Wilson Shipmanagement (Bergen) AS, Bergen, managers), under Luxembourg flag. 2003: Transferred to E.T.M. Luxemburg and Trones Panama Ltd., (same managers), under Panama flag. 2003: Transferred to Portugal flag. 2004: Transferred to Erste Belt Shipping AG, Leer, Germany, (AJ Shipmanagement, Leer, managers), retaining Portugal flag.

186. GENERAL LUNA (2)   (**1986 – 1990**) see ship No. 73 above.

187. FASTNES   (**1986 – 1992**) see ship No. 130 above.

GENERAL CAMPOS

(World Ship Society Photograph Library)

188. GENERAL CAMPOS   (**1986 – 1991**) see ship No. 115 above.

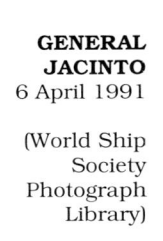

GENERAL JACINTO
6 April 1991

(World Ship Society Photograph Library)

189. GENERAL JACINTO   **(1986 – 1992)** see ship No. 108 above.

190. GENERAL LIM (2)   **(1986 – 1988)** see ship No. 159 above.

GENERAL RICARTE At Immongham October 1989   (W. J. Harvey)

191. GENERAL RICARTE   **(1986 – 1991)** see ship No. 111 above.

FITNES   (Chriss Reynolds collection)

182. GENERAL FITNES /
        FITNES (1986 – 1988) see ship No. 140 above.

EEMNES In May 1988   (Chriss Reynolds collection)

193. EEMNES   **(1986 – 1991)** see ship No. 120 above.

SALTNES In December 1987 (Chriss Reynolds collection)

194. SALTNES (2)	**(1986 – 1990)**	see ship No. 106 above.
195. GENERAL VILLA (1)	**(1986 – 1987)**	see ship No. 91 above.
196. GENERAL ESTRELLA	**(1986 – 1990)**	see ship No. 85 above.
197. GENERAL LAPUS	**(1986 – 1988)**	see ship No. 70 above.
198. GENERAL ROXAS (2)	**(1987 – 1988)**	see ship No. 102 above.
199. GENERAL LUKBAN	**(1987 – 1989)**	see ship No. 153 above.

GENERAL BONIFACIO (Chriss Reynolds collection)

200. GENERAL BONIFACIO   **(1987 – 1988)** see ship No. 139 above.

GENERAL VALERIANO on the River Maas 12 May 1989. Note the travelling crane that has been added.
(World Ship Society Photograph Library)

201. GENERAL VALERIANO   (1987 – 1991) see ship No. 93 above.

GENERAL GARCIA at Immingham.

(W.J.Harvey)

202. GENERAL GARCIA   (1987 – 1990) see ship No. 78 above.
203. ABOITIZ SUPERCONCARRIER 1   (1987 –   ) see ship No. 141 above.

GENERAL AQUINO with travelling deck crane added.

(Chriss Reynolds collection)

204. GENERAL AQUINO   (1987 – 1991) see ship No. 76 above.

GENERAL PAPA (World Ship Society Photograph Library)

205. GENERAL PAPA   (1987 – 1992) see ship No. 75 above.

GENERAL PERALTA At Avonmouth on 25 June 1988   (World Ship Society Photograph Library)

206. GENERAL PERALTA   (1987 – 1990) see ship No. 69 above.

7521132
207. ISNES (2) (1987 – 1994)
As built;   2,868g. 1,974n. 4,420d. 91.09 x 14.56 x 6.909 metre.
Post 1994: 2,978g. 1,268n. 4,450d.
Post 1995: 2,978g. 1,268n. 4,001d.
6-cyl. 4 S.C.S.A. (370 x 400) Deutz RSBV6M540 type oil engine made by Kloeckner-Humboldt-Deutz, Voerde. 3,000 bhp. 13 kts. Thwartship Thrust propeller forward.
Ice strengthened general cargo vessel with a 20-ton travelling crane and with a container capacity of 155 TEU.
29.9.1975: Keel laid as DOLLART by Schulte & Bruns, Emden (Yard No. 282), for Schulte & Bruns 'Dollart' Schiffahrtsges. KG, W. Germany. 15.4.1976: Launched. 26.6.1976: Completed. 1979: Sold to Dollart-Reederei GmbH & Company KG, W. Germany. 1980: Thien & Heyenga Bereederungs-und-Befrachtungsgesellschaft m.b.H., appointed as managers. 1987: Sold to Nesskip h/f., Iceland, and renamed ISNES. 1991: Transferred to Norway registration, (Jebsens Ship Management AS

(JSMA), appointed as managers), (O.N. N-01058). 1994: Sold to Gards Rederi AS, (Gard Shipping AS, managers), Norway, and renamed GARDSKY. 1999: Sold to Gustav Walter Invest AS, (Wani Norse Management AS, managers). 2003: Sold to Anchor Marine Ltd., Cardiff, (Willie Shipping Ltd., Cardiff, managers), and renamed CELTIC SPIRIT, under Bahamas flag.

ISNES 8 January 1994. (World Ship Society Photograph Library)

7718022
208. GENERAL LIM (3) (1988 – 1989)
As built: 14,091g. 9,275n. 23,777d. 159.82 (BB) x 24.62 x 9.954 metres oa.
Post 1989: 16,118g. 14,344n. 23,777d.
Post 1990: 14,387g. 8,537n. 23,777d.
6-cyl. 2 S.C.S.A. (680 x 1,250mm) Sulzer 6RND68 type oil engine made by Mitsubishi Heavy Industries Ltd., Kobe. 9,900 bhp. 14.5 kts.
Bulk carrier with four 25-ton cranes.
1.7.1977: Keel laid as OCEAN LAND by Imabari Zosen, Marugame (Yard No. 1045), for Shoyo Kisen KK, Japan. 27.7.1977: Launched. 30.9.1977: Completed. 1983: Sold to Dejal Shipping SA, Panama, (proposal to rename GLORY BON was abandoned). 1985: Sold to Million Maritime Company SA, Panama, and renamed MILLION TRADER. 1988: Sold to Sochin Maritime Inc., Panama, and renamed GENERAL LIM. (O.N. 11976). 1989: Sold to General Lim Inc., (AS Havtor Management, managers), and renamed WANI SWAN. 1990: Thorvald Klaveness & Company AS, appointed as managers. 1990: Converted into a self unloading bulk carrier. 1995: Sold to Wani Swan Shipping Inc., (same managers). 2000: Wani-Norse Management AS, appointed as managers. (O.N. 13733-84H). 2003: Sold to Ever Dragon Shipping Company, Fuzhou, China, (Fujian Xinan Shipping Company, Fuzhou, managers), and renamed RAMBLE CLOUD, under Panama flag.

7709320
209. GENERAL MASCARDO (2) (1988 – 1989)
As built: 20,288g. 14,604n. 35,343d. 182.33 (BB) x 26.04 x 11.251 metres oa.

Post 1989: 20,700g. 12,583n. 35,343d.
7-cyl. 2 S.C.S.A. (680 x 1,250mm) Sulzer 7RND68 type oil engine made by Mitsubishi Heavy Industries Ltd., Kobe. 11,550 bhp. 14.25 kts.
Bulk carrier with four 15-ton and one 5-ton cranes.
30.6.1977: Keel laid as NIKKEI CENTRAL by Imabari Zosen, Marugame (Yard No. 1052), for T. S. Central Shipping Company Ltd., Liberia. 20.2.1978: Launched. 9.5.1978: Completed. 1985: Sold to Cyr Transport and Marine Services Inc., Philippines. (O.N. 228406). 1986: Transferred to Panama flag (O.N. 15389-86). 1988: Sold to Satinsea Maritime Company Ltd., (Transatlantic Seaways, SA, managers), Cyprus, and renamed PROTAGONIST II. 1988: Sold to Z. B. S. World Corp., (Jebsens Ship Management AS (JSMA), managers), Panama, and renamed GENERAL MASCARDO. (O.N. 18811-PEXT). 1989: Renamed WANI HILL, (Thorvald Klaveness & Company AS, managers). 1990: Transferred to General Mascardo Shipping Inc. (same managers). 1991: Sold to Almaris Shipping Company Ltd., (Atlantis Management Inc., managers), Cyprus, and renamed ARISTI. 1.9.1993: Sold to Almi Marine Management SA, Cyprus. 1994: Renamed ARISTI D. 2.1999: Sold to Sunflower Shipping Company Ltd., (Barclay Shipping Ltd., managers), and renamed EXPRESS REBEL. 4.7.2001: Sold to Shun Tong Shipping SA, Quingdao, China, and renamed CHANG TONG under Panama flag. (O.N. 29768-PEXT).

7533056
210. BULKNES (2) (1988 – 1989)
As built: 15,256g. 10,675n. 28,362d. 178.11 (BB) x 22.92 x 10.902 metres oa.
Post 1989: 15,573g. 10,159n. 28,362d.
Post 1995: 15,578g. 10,484n. 28,406d.
Post 1996: 15,573g. 11,161n. 27,082d.
6-cyl. 2 S.C.S.A. (680 x 1,250mm) Sulzer 6RND68 type oil engine made by Sumitomo Heavy Industries Ltd., Tamashima. 9,900 bhp. 15.5 kts.
Bulk carrier with four 15-ton cranes.
1975: Ordered by Drechtships N.V. Netherlands, from Nippon Kokan KK, Tsurumi Shipyard, Yokohama (Yard No. 950). 20.10.1976: Keel laid. 20.12.1976: Launched as KIELDRECHT for Phs.Van Ommeren, Holland. 24.5.1977: Completed for Scheepsvaart Maatschappij 'Kieldrecht' N.V., (Drechtships N.V., managers), Netherlands Antilles. 1986: Sold to Orma Bay Shipping SA, (Van Ommeren Shipping BV, managers), Panama, and renamed COBO BAY. (O.N. 17390-RH). 1987: Transferred to Philippine flag. (O.N. 15972-87). 1988: Sold to Cobo Bay Shipping Company SA, Panama. 1988: Purchased by KS Bulknes, (Jebsens Ship Management AS (JSMA), managers), Norway, and renamed BULKNES. (O.N. 00399). 1989: Transferred to KS Birknes, (Jebsens Ship Management (Bergen) AS, managers), Norway, and renamed BIRKNES. 1992: Sold to Boyanak Nakliyat ve Boya Ticaret AS, (Yardimici Shipping Group, managers), Turkey, for $5.3m. and renamed AYANE. (O.N. 19895). 1999: Sold to Yardimici Denizcilik ve Nakliyat AS, (Moliva Denizcilik AS, managers), Turkey. (O.N. 6299). 2001: Sold to Serdar Denizcilik ve Ticaret Ltd C/O Gayret Denizcilik Sanayii ve Ticaret Ltd., Turkey, and renamed KARADENIZ S. 2003: Sold to Sam International Shipping, Phnom Penh, Cambodia, and renamed HANDY OCEAN, under Cambodia flag.

211. FURUNES (2) (1988 – 1998) see ship No. 109 above.

FURUNES On the Thames November 1988 (World Ship Society Photograph Library)

212. TINNES (3) **(1988 -   )** see ship No. 139 above.

FULLNES in September 1988 (Chriss Reynolds collection)

213. FULLNES	**(1988 – 2001)**	see ship No. 107 above.
214. FREENES	**(1988 – 1992)**	see ship No. 103 above.
215. GENERAL TIRONA	**(1988 – 1989)**	see ship No. 170 above.
216. GENERAL ROMULO	**(1988 – 1989)**	see ship No. 104 above.
217. GENERAL DELGADO	**(1988 – 1989)**	see ship No. 175 above.
218. GENERAL VILLA (2)	**(1988 – 1989)**	see ship No. 179 above.
219. RENKO	**(1988 – 1990)**	see ship No. 102 above.
220. FAIRNES	**(1988 – 1992)**	see ship No. 105 above.
221. FALKNES (2)	**(1988 – 1993)**	see ship No. 140 above.

GENERAL ROMULO leaving Immingham August 1989.

(W.J. Harvey)

GENERAL DELGADO with NYK charter funnel colours.

(World Ship Society Photograph Library)

FAIRNES Passing Maassluis 10 May 1991   (World Ship Society Photograph Library)

SIR CHARLES PARSONS anchored in the Thames Estuary 12 August 1989. (World Ship Society Photograph Library)

8402840
222. SIR CHARLES PARSONS (1989 – 1995) Parsons class
14,201g. 6,275n. 22,530d. 154.87 (BB) x 24.54 x 9.021 metres oa.
8-cyl. 4 S.C.S.A. (400 x 457mm) Mirrlees KMR8MK3 type oil engine made by Mirrlees, Blackstone Ltd., Stockport, geared to a controllable pitch propeller. 5,921 bhp. 12.5 kts. Thwartship thrust, controllable pitch propeller forward and aft.
Gearless bulk carrier.
7.8.1984: Keel laid by Govan Shipbuilders Ltd., Govan (Yard No. 262), for the Central Electricity Generation Board (Stephenson, Clarke Ltd., managers). 7.3.1985: Launched for Bishopgate Colliers Ltd., (Christian Salvesen (Shipping) Ltd., managers), London. 12.7.1985: Completed. 1989: Lease-owner and managers acquired by Atle Jebsen, (Lothian Shipping Ltd., managers), London. (O.N. 709580). 1995: Sold to Powergen Plc., London, (Jebsen Ship Management (London) Ltd., appointed as managers). 1998: Lothian Ship Management (London) Ltd., appointed as managers. 2003: Meridian Marine Management Ltd., Liverpool, appointed as managers 2004: Sold to E.On UK plc., Coventry, (same managers).

LORD CITRINE discharging on the River Medway on 17 June 1989. (World Ship Society Photograph Library)

8402852
223. LORD CITRINE (1989 – 1994) Parsons class
14,201g. 6,275n. 22,447d. 154.87 (BB) x 24.54 x 8.981 metres oa.
8-cyl. 4 S.C.S.A. (400 x 457mm) Mirrlees KMR8MK3 type oil engine made by Mirrlees, Blackstone Ltd., Stockport, geared to a controllable pitch propeller. 5,921 bhp. 12.5 kts. Thwartship thrust, controllable pitch propeller forward and aft.

Gearless bulk carrier.
19.9.1984: Keel laid by Govan Shipbuilders Ltd., Govan (Yard No. 263), for the Central Electricity Generating Board (Stephenson, Clarke Ltd., managers). 5.6.1985: Launched for Bishopgate Colliers Ltd., (Christian Salvesen (Shipping) Ltd., managers), London. 10.2.1986: Completed. (O.N. 709680). 1989: Lease-owner and managers acquired by Atle Jebsen, (Lothian Shipping Ltd., managers), London. 1995: Sold to Powergen Plc., London, (Jebsen Ship Management (London) Ltd., appointed as managers). 1998: Lothian Ship Management (London) Ltd., appointed as managers. 1999: Sold to Unitrack Shipping Company Ltd., (Pacific & Atlantic Corporation, managers), Cyprus, and renamed ATLANTIC LORD. 5.2000: Sold to Malta Bay Ltd., (Italtech Srl, Italy, managers), Malta, and renamed SIDER BAY. 12.2000: Sold to unspecified Republic of China buyers, and renamed JIN BIN. 2004: Sold to Fujian Shipping Company, Fuzhou Fujian, China.

LORD HINTON anchored on the Thames on 10 June 1989. (World Ship Society Photograph Library)

8402864
224. LORD HINTON (1989 – 1994) Parsons class
14,201g. 6,275n. 22,447d.   154.87 (BB) x 24.54 x 8.981 metres oa.
8-cyl. 4 S.C.S.A. (400 x 457mm) Mirrlees KMR8MK3 type oil engine made by Mirrlees, Blackstone Ltd., Stockport, geared to a controllable pitch propeller. 5,921 bhp. 12.5 kts. Thwartship thrust, controllable pitch propeller forward and aft.
Gearless bulk carrier.
2.11.1984: Keel laid by Govan Shipbuilders Ltd., Govan (Yard No. 264), for the Central Electricity Generating Board, (Stephenson, Clarke Ltd., managers). 18.9.1985: Launched for Bishopgate Colliers Ltd., (Christian Salvesen (Shipping) Ltd., managers), London. 28.2.1986: Completed. (O.N. 709736). 1989: Lease-owner and managers acquired by Atle Jebsen, (Lothian Shipping Ltd., managers), London. 1995: Sold to Powergen Plc., London, (Jebsen Ship Management (London) Ltd., appointed as managers). 1998: Lothian Ship Management (London) Ltd., appointed as managers. 2003: Meridian Marine Management Ltd., Liverpool, appointed as managers 2004: Sold to E.On UK plc., Coventry, (same managers).

7616224
225. SUMBURGH HEAD (1989 – 1990) Head class
As built: 4,694g. 2,630n. 7,174d.   110.55 x 17.58 x 7.017 metres oa.
Post 1990: 4,455g. 2,615n. 7,174d.
6-cyl. 2 S.C.S.A. (450 x 800mm) Mitsubishi 6UET45/80D type oil engine made by Kobe Hadsudoki KK, Kobe. 4,500 bhp. 15 kts.
General cargo vessel.

20.10.1976: Keel laid by Hashihama Zosen, Imabari (Yard No. 624), for unspecified Japanese owners and contract subsequently sold to Christian Salvesen Company Ltd., Leith. 11.1.1977: Launched as SUMBURGH HEAD. 9.4.1977: Completed. 1985: Owner restyled as Christian Salvesen Plc, (Christian Salvesen (Shipping) Ltd., managers). 1989: Sold to Trepner International Investment Ltd., (Atle Jebsen Management, managers), Liberia. (O.N. 9231). 1989: Chelston Ship Management Ltd., appointed as managers. 1990: Transferred to Barra Head Shipping Ltd., (same managers), Republic Of Ireland, and renamed HOOK HEAD, (O.N. 402739). 1993: Transferred to Viscaya Shipping Inc., Panama City, (Jebsens Ship Management (London) Ltd., managers), and renamed HOOD HEAD*, then HUSNES under Panama flag. 1998: Sold to Short Sea Shipping, (Wilson Ship Management (Bergen) AS, Bergen, managers), Malta. 2002. Renamed WILSON TANA. 2004: Transferred to Wilson Shipowning AS, Bergen, (same managers), retaining Malta registry.

N.B. * HOOD HEAD was probably an error when quoted in L.R. Supplement, Sept 1993.

SUMBURGH HEAD   (World Ship Society Photograph Library)

BARRA HEAD

(World Ship Society Photograph Library)

7915307
226. BARRA HEAD (1989 – 1996) Head class
As built: 4,691g. 2,691n. 7,162d. 110.55 x 17.56 x 7.016 metres oa.
Post 1994: 4,691g. 2,619n. 7,107d.
Post 1994: 4,913g. 2,531n. 7,107d.
6-cyl. 2 S.C.S.A. (450 x 800mm) Mitsubishi 6UET45/80D type oil engine made by Kobe Hadsudoki KK, Kobe. 4,500 bhp. 12.75 kts.
General cargo vessel.
10.1.1980: Keel laid by Miho Zosensho KK, Shimizu (Yard No. 1151), for Christian Salvesen Company Ltd., Leith. 28.3.1980: Launched. 25.6.6.1980: Completed. 1985: Owner restyled as Christian Salvesen Plc, (Christian Salvesen (Shipping) Ltd., managers). 1989: Sold to Granuaille Shipping Company Ltd., (Atle Jebsen Management, managers), Liberia. (O.N. 9230). 1989: Transferred to L. D. S. Maritime SA, (Jebsens Hamburg GmbH & Company KG, managers), Liberia. 1990: Transferred to Barra Head Shipping Ltd., (Chelston Ship Management Ltd., managers), Republic Of Ireland, (O.N. 402735). 1996: Transferred to Viscaya Shipping Inc., Panama City, (Jebsens Ship Management (London) Ltd., managers), and renamed HORDNES, under Panama flag. 1998: Sold to Short Sea Ltd, (Wilson Ship Management (Bergen) AS, Bergen, managers), Malta. 2003: Renamed WILSON TYNE. 2004: Transferred to Wilson Shipowning AS, Bergen, (same managers), retaining Malta registry.

7926095
227. RORA HEAD (1989 – 1993) Head class
As built: 4,691g. 2,691n. 7,162d. 110.55 x 17.56 x 7.016 metres oa.
Post 1990: 4,924g. 2,651n. 7,160d.
6-cyl. 2 S.C.S.A. (450 x 800mm) Mitsubishi 6UET45/80D type oil engine made by Kobe Hadsudoki KK, Kobe. 4,500 bhp. 13 kts.
General cargo vessel.
12.4.1980: Keel laid by Miho Zosensho KK, Shimizu (Yard No. 1154), for Christian Salvesen Company Ltd., Leith. 8.7.1980: Launched. 30.9.1980: Completed. (O.N. 387792). 1985: Owner restyled as Christian Salvesen PLC., (Christian Salvesen (Shipping) Ltd., managers). 1989: Sold to Altnacraig Shipping Plc, (Atle Jebsen Management, managers), London. 1989: Chelston Ship Management Ltd., appointed as managers. 1993: Transferred to Geralia Two Shipping Company Ltd., Limassol, (Jebsens Ship Management (London) Ltd., managers), and renamed HERNES, under Cyprus flag. 1997: Jebsens (UK) Ltd., appointed as managers. 1998: Osterreichischer Lloyd Ship Management (Cyprus) Ltd., appointed as managers. 2000: Osterreichischer Lloyd Ship Management GmbH., Vienna, appointed as managers. 2004: Renamed WILSON TRENT.

7420273
228. GENERAL CRUZ (2) (1989 – 1990)
As built: 19,264g. 13,689n. 36,937d. 196.07 (BB) x 26.57 x 11.380 metres oa.
Post 1989: 20,986g. 13,552n. 36,937d.
Post 1995: 20,986g. 13,992n. 36,935d.
6-cyl. 2 S.C.S.A. (760 x 1,550mm) Sulzer 6RND76 type oil engine made by H.Cegielski, Poznan. 12,000 bhp. 15 kts.
Bulk carrier with six 16-ton cranes.
1975: Ordered from Hellenic Shipyards, Skaramanga (Yard No. 1109) by I. Alexakis, New York. 31.3.1977: Keel laid as APHRODITE for Olymbos Shipping Corp., Greece. 17.12.1977: Launched. 21.3.1978: Completed. 1985: Sold to Alpro Maritime Agencies Inc., Greece. 1986: Universal Glow Inc., appointed as managers. 1987: Sold to Kamagong Shipping Corporation Panama, and renamed KAMAGONG. (O.N. 18216-

PEXT). 1987: Sold to Phil-Kon Shipping Inc., (Patt, Manfield & Company Ltd., managers), Philippines, and renamed MAHOGANY. 1989: Sold to General Cruz Inc., Phillipines, and renamed GENERAL CRUZ. (O.N. 229575). 1990: Renamed WANI FOREST, (Havtor Management AS, managers), Panama flag, (O.N. 18216-PEXT 3). 1991: Sold to Cemre Deniz Ticaret ve Nakliyat AS, Turkey, and renamed CEMRE II. (O.N.4264). 2002: Sold to Goa Ltd., St Vincent and The Grenadines, and renamed GOA I under the Comoros flag. 2003: Transferred from Comoros to an unknown flag. 2005: Reported as demolished.

WANI HILL 28 September 1989. (World Ship Society Photograph Library)

229. WANI HILL   **(1989 – 1991)** see ship No. 209 above.

230. WANI HUNTER   **(1989 – 1990)** see ship No. 169 above.

WANI LAKE 23 September 1990 (World Ship Society Photograph Library)

231. WANI LAKE   **(1989 – 1993)** see ship No. 171 above.

232. WANI RIVER   **(1989)**   see ship No. 153 above.

233. WANI TIGER   **(1989)**   see ship No. 157 above.

234. WANI SWAN   **(1989 – 1990)** see ship No. 208 above

WANI SWAN After her 1990 conversion to a self-unloading beltship.   (World Ship Society Photograph Library)

235. PEARL PROSPERITY **(1989 – 1993)** see ship No. 100 above.
236. LANKA AMILA   **(1989 – 1992)** see ship No. 170 above.
237. LANKA ARUNA   **(1989 – 1992)** see ship No. 175 above.
238. LANKA ASITHA   **(1989 – 1991)** see ship No. 179 above.
239. BERGNES (3)   **(1989 – 1995)** see ship No. 84 above.
240. FONNES (2)   **(1989 – 2000)** see ship No. 104 above.
241. WANI BIRD   **(1989 – 1991)** see ship No. 144 above.

WANI FALCON 29 December 1989.   (World Ship Society Photograph Library)

242. WANI FALCON   **(1989 – 1991)** see ship No. 143 above.

BIRKNES 3 November 1991.   (World Ship Society Photograph Library)

243. BIRKNES (3)   **(1989 – 1992)** see ship No. 210 above.
244. WANI FOREST   **(1990 – 1991)** see ship No. 228 above.

7528154
245. EOS (1990 - 1999)
As built: 2,875g. 1,677n. 4,979d. 82.38 (BB) x 15.35 x 7.181 metres oa.
Post 1984: 3,963g. 2,035n. 6,189d. 101.96 (BB) x 15.35 x 6.741 metres oa.
Two, 8-cyl. 4 S.C.S.A. (250 x 300mm) Polar F28V-D vee type oil engines made by Ab Bofors Nohab, Trollhattan, geared to twin shafts with controllable pitch propellers. 3,200 bhp. 11.5 kts. Thwartship thrust propeller forward.
Belt-unloading bulk carrier.
7.12.1975: Keel laid as EEMSBORG by A.Vuyk en Zonen Scheepswerven BV, Capelle a/d Ijssel (Yard No. 877), for Wagenborg Scheepvaart BV, Holland. 10.7.1976: Launched. 31.10.1976: Completed. 1984: Purchased by Rederij Thun BV, (Sandfirden Rederij BV, managers), Holland, lengthened, converted into a self unloading bulk carrier, and renamed EOS. 1990: Transferred to Jebsens Thun Beltships (Holland) BV, (Sandfirden BV, managers), Holland. 1992: Transferred to Jebsens Thun Beltships Investments Ltd., Hamilton, Bermuda, and to Norway (NIS) flag, (Jebsens Ship Management (Bergen) AS, Bergen, managers), (O.N. N-01184). 1994: Thunbolaget Shipmanagement Ab, Lidkoping, Sweden, appointed as operators, and removed from management. 1999: Sold to Erik Thun Ab, Lidkoping, Sweden, retaining Norway (NIS) flag.

246. RAFNES   (1990 – 2000) see ship No. 78 above.

247. RISNES (2) (1990 – 2000) see ship No. 73 above.

248. RAMNES   (1990 – 1993) see ship No. 69 above.

249. ALTNES (3) (1990 – 1998) see ship No. 106 above.

250. PEARL LUCK (1990 – 1993) see ship No. 85 above.

251. RADNES   (1990 – 2000) see ship No. 80 above.

HOOK HEAD At the Alcan Terminal, Blyth. (World Ship Society Photograph Library)

252. HOOK HEAD   (1990 – 1993) see ship No. 225 above.

LIDAN   (World Ship Society Photograph Library)

8911841
253. LIDAN (1991 – 1994)
2,490g. 1,395n. 4,050d   88.29 (BB) x 13.21 x 5.741 metres oa.
8-cyl. 4 S.C.S.A. (250 x 300mm) Wartsila 8V25 vee type oil engine made by Wartsila Diesel Ab, Trollhattan, geared to a controllable pitch propeller. 2,298 bhp. 12 kts. Bow jet pump hrusters unit.
Belt-unloading bulk carrier.
1989: Ordered as LIDANES from Scheepswerf "Ferus Smit" BV, Foxhol (Yard No. 280), for Atle Jebsen, Norway. 5.10.1990: Keel laid. 26.6.1991: Launched as LIDAN. 14.9.1991: Completed for Partenrederi for m.v. Lidan, (Erik Thun Ab, managers), Sweden. 1993: Sold to Erik Thun Ab., (Thun Ship Management Ab., managers), Sweden. 1994: Removed from management. 2000: Sold to Partrederiet for m. v. Lidan, (Erik Thun Ab, Lidkoping, managers). 2000: Sold to Tipo Shipping Ab, Lidkoping, Sweden, (Thun Ship Management Ab, Lidkoping, managers), under Cyprus flag. 2001: Sold to Partrederiet for m. v. Lidan, (Erik Thun Ab, Lidkoping, managers), retaining Cyprus flag.   2002: Sold to Tipo Shipping Ab, Lidkoping, Sweden, (Thun Ship Management Ab, Lidkoping, managers), retaining Cyprus flag.

8914128
254. MORNES (2) (1991 – 1999) Mornes class
5,385g. 2,869n. 8,500d.   116.60 (BB) x 15.83 x 7.880 metres oa.
8-cyl. 4 S.C.S.A. (320 x 350mm) Wartsila 8R32E type oil engine made by Oy Wartsila Ab., Vaasa/Vasa, geared to a controllable pitch propeller. 4,461 bhp. 13 kts. Bow jet pump thrusters unit.
Belt-unloading bulk carrier.
21.2.1991: Keel laid by Scheepswerf "Ferus Smit" BV, Foxhol (Yard No. 281), for Atle Jebsen, Norway. 14.9.1991: Launched for Jebsens Thun Beltships Investments Inc. (Jebsens Ship Management (Bergen) AS, managers), Norway (NIS).   5.12.1991: Completed. (O.N. N-01148).   1995: Sold to Norwegian Partners Ltd., Bermuda, (Thunbolaget AS, managers), Norway. 1999: Sold to Thunbolaget AS, Lidkoping, Sweden. 1999: Sold to Erik Thun Ab, Lidkoping, Sweden, retaining Norway (NIS) flag.

MORNES (Jebsens)

255. SEALNES (2) (1991 – 1996) see ship No. 169 above.

GENERAL VILLA (World Ship Society Photograph Library)

256. GENERAL VILLA (2)   (1992 – 2004) see ship No. 179 above.

8129395
257. OSTANHAV (1992 – 1994)
As Built: 2,831g. 1,697n. 4,790d.   88.02 (BB) x 13.09 x 8.851 metres oa.
Post 1987: 3,800g. 2,150n. 5,748d.   108.41 (BB) x 13.09 x 6.871 metres oa.
12-cyl 4 S.C.S.A. (250 x 300mm) Polar SF112VS-F vee type oil engine made by Nohab Diesel Ab, Trollhattan, geared to a controllable pitch propeller. 2,950 bhp. 12.5 kts. Thwartship thrust propeller forward.
Belt-unloading bulk carrier.
5.5.1982: Keel laid by Falkenbergs Varv Ab, Falkenberg (Yard No. 181), for Erik Thun Ab, Sweden. 18.3.1983: Launched. 29.5.1983: Completed for Nordstrom & Thulin Ab,

(Erik Thun Ab, managers). 1985: Sold to Erik Thun Ab. 1987: Lengthened. 1992: Sold to Partenrederi for m.f. Ostanhav, (Erik Thun Ab, managers), Sweden. 1994: Jebsen involvement ceased. 1997: Sold to Helge Kallsson Partenrederi. 2000: Sold to Partrederiet for M.V. Ostanhav, Lidkoping, Sweden, (Erik Thun Ab, Lidkoping, managers).

MOXNES 16 January 1995 (Chriss Reynolds collection.)

8914130
258. MOXNES (1992 – 1996) Moxnes class
5,953g. 3,121n. 9,891d.   126.70 (BB) x 15.87 x 7.680 metres oa.
8-cyl. 4 S.C.S.A. (320 x 350mm) Wartsila 8R32E type oil engine made by Oy Wartsila Ab., Vaasa/Vasa, geared to a controllable pitch propeller. 4,459 bhp. 13 kts. Bow jet pump thrusters unit.
Belt-unloading bulk carrier.
8.8.1991: Keel laid by Scheepswerf "Ferus Smit" BV, Foxhol (Yard No.282), for Atle Jebsen, Norway. 2.5.1992: Launched for Jebsens Thun Beltships Investments Inc., Norway. 6.1992: Completed. 1995: Sold to Erik Thun Ab, and Norwegian Partners Ltd., Hamilton, Bermuda. 1996: Renamed NORDANHAV, under Swedish flag. 1999: Transferred to Netherlands flag, (Marin Ship Management B.V. appointed as managers). 2000: Transferred to Thun II BV, Farmsum, Netherlands, (Thunship Management Holland, Farmsum, managers). 2003: Thun Ship Management Ab, Lidkoping, Sweden, appointed as managers, and transferred to Sweden flag.

259. GARNES (4)   (1992 – 2000) see ship No. 115 above.

260. KORSNES (4)   (1992 – 2000) see ship No. 111 above.

261. REKSNES   (1992 – 2000) see ship No. 93 above.

262. RINGNES   (1992 – 1993) see ship No. 71 above.

263. VIGSNES (4)   (1992 – 2000) see ship No. 108 above.

264. GENERAL TIRONA   (1992 – 2000) see ship No. 170 above.

265. GENERAL DELGADO   (1992 – 2000) see ship No. 175 above.

266. FRINES (2)   (1992 – 2004) see ship No. 103 above.

267. FINNSNES	**(1992 – 2004)**	see ship No. 105 above.
268. RIKNES	**(1992 – 1995)**	see ship No. 75 above.
269. SPRAYNES (2)	**(1992 – 1995)**	see ship No. 157 above.
270. RAKNES (3)	**(1992 – 1995)**	see ship No. 120 above.
271. ROGNES	**(1992 – 2000)**	see ship No. 76 above.

MALMNES outward on the New Waterway   (Chriss Reynolds collection.)

8918631

272. MALMNES (1993 – 1999) Moxnes class
5,883g. 3,103n. 9,891d.   126.75 (BB) x 15.87 x 7.894 metres oa.
8-cyl. 4 S.C.S.A. (320 x 350mm) Wartsila 8R32E type oil engine made by Oy Wartsila Ab., Vaasa/Vasa, geared to a controllable pitch propeller. 4,459 bhp. 13.5 kts. Thwartship thrust propeller in tunnel forward.
Belt-unloading bulk carrier.
8.8.1991: Keel laid by Scheepswerf "Ferus Smit" BV, Foxhol (Yard No. 287), for Atle Jebsen, Norway. 6.3.1993: Launched. 29.5.1993: Completed for Jebsens Thun Beltships Investments Inc., Norway. 1995: Sold to S-Ship SA, Norway. 1995: Sold to Erik Thun Ab, and Norwegian Partners Ltd., Hamilton, Bermuda. 1999: Sold to Erik Thun Ab., Lidkoping, Sweden, retaining Norway flag.

273. HERNES	**(1993 – 2000)**	see ship No. 227 above.
274. HUSNES	**(1993 – 2000)**	see ship No. 225 above.
275. SHEERNES	**(1993 – 1995)**	see ship No. 171 above.

SHEERNES
Port Adelaide 13 April 1995.

(World Ship Society Photograph Library)

ALEXIS at Antwerp 1993

(Chriss Reynolds)

276. ALEXIS   **(1993 – 1998)** see ship No. 72 above.

MARMON

(Chriss Reynolds collection)

277. MARMON   **(1993 – 1998)** see ship No. 71 above.

KARI ARNHILD running acceptance trials (Jebsen)

KARI ARNHILD with replacement discharge boom, on the River Weser January 1998.
(World Ship Society Photograph Library)

9101730
278. KARI ARNHILD (1994 – 2002)
9,855g. 4,502n. 16,073d. 148.00 (BB) x   x 9.521metres oa.
Two, 6-cyl. 4 S.C.S.A. (320 x 350mm) Wartsila 6R32 type oil engines made by Wartsila Diesel Oy, Vaasa/Varna, geared to twin controllable pitch propellers. 6,036 bhp. 14.5 kts. Thwartship thrust propeller forward.
Belt-unloading bulk carrier.
9.11.1993: Keel laid by Kvaerner Kleven Leirvik AS, Leirvik I Sogn (Yard No. 261), for AS Jebsens Assuranceforretning, (Jebsens Ship Management (Bergen) AS, Norway. 23.6.1994: Launched. 29.10.1994: Completed. 1996: Transferred to S. D. Shipping Ltd., (same managers), Panama flag. (O.N. 25185-PEXT). 1997: Sold to Panaka SA, (S. D. Shipping Ltd., managers), Panama. (O.N. 23160-96). (LR-1999 delete owners & managers) Panama. (O.N. 23160-96A). 2.12.1999: Aboitiz, Jebsen Shipmanagement Bergen AS, appointed as managers. 2000: Wilson Shipmanagement Bergen AS, as contact. 8.1.2001: Sold to Partenreederei m.s. Kari Arnhild, Cuxhaven, Germany, (Reederei Frank Dahl, Cuxhaven, managers), under Antigua and Barbuda flag. 3.2002: Renamed SPLITTNES.

9111216
279. RAMON ABOITIZ   (1994 – 2002) Aboitiz class
7,249g. 3,094n. 7,150d.   134.30 x   x 7.118 metres
6-cyl. 4 S.C.S.A. (420 x 1,360mm) B&W 6L42MC type oil engine made by Bryansk Engine Works, Bryansk.   6,933 bhp. 15 kts.
Ice breaking general cargo vessel with two 12-ton cranes and with a container capacity of 336 TEU.
3.4.1991: Keel laid as BRINKNES by Kherson Shipyard, Kherson, (Yard No. 1901), for Aboitiz, Jebsen Bulk Transport Corporation, Philippines. (O.N. 233679). 15.7.1994: Completed as RAMON ABOITIZ. 1996: Owners restyled as W.G. & A. Jebsen Ship Management Inc. 1997: Transferred to Aboitiz, Jebsen Ship Management Inc. 2000: Transferred to Aboitiz, Jebsen Bulk Transport Corporation, Philippines. (O.N. MNLA000452). 2002: Sold to Brinknes SA, Manila, (Aboitiz, Jebsen Bulk Transport Corporation, Manila, managers), and renamed BRINKNES, under Panama flag. 1.2005: Sold to Silver Stream Ltd., Odessa, (Kaalbye Shipping International Ltd., Odessa, managers), and renamed OCEAN SCARLET, under St Vincent and The Grenadines flag.

BRUNTO

(Internet source)

280. BRUNTO (1994 – 2002) see ship No. 177 above.

9111228
281. VIDAL ABOITIZ   (1994 – 1998) Aboitiz class
7,249g. 3,094n. 7,276d.   134.30 x   x 7.118 metres
6-cyl. 4 S.C.S.A. (420 x 1,360mm) B&W 6L42MC type oil engine made by Bryansk Engine Works, Bryansk.   6,933 bhp. 15 kts.
Ice breaking general cargo vessel with two 12-ton cranes and with a container capacity of 336 TEU.
29.4.1992: Keel laid by Kherson Shipyard, Kherson, (Yard No.1902), for Filscan Shipping Inc., (Aboitiz, Jebsen Bulk Transport Corporation, managers), Philippines. (O.N. MNLA000031). 7.11.1994: Completed. 1996: Managers restyled as W.G. & A. Jebsen Ship Management Inc. 1998: Renamed MILLENNIUM EAGLE. 7.2004: Sold to Eagle Navigation Ltd., Athens, (Balthellas Chartering SA, Athens, managers), and

renamed EAGLE SPIRIT, under the Malta flag. 2005: Renamed CECILIA M, retaining Malta flag.

9111230
282. BRINKNES (2) (1995 – 1998) Aboitiz class
7,249g. 3,094n. 7,150d.   134.30 x   x 7.118 metres
6-cyl. 4 S.C.S.A. (420 x 1,360mm) B&W 6DKRN42/136 type oil engine made by Bryansk Engine Works, Bryansk. 6,933 bhp. 15 kts.
Ice breaking general cargo vessel with two 12-ton cranes and with a container capacity of 336 TEU.
27.4.1993: Keel laid by Kherson Shipyard, Kherson, (Yard No. 1903), for Jebsen Short Sea SA, (Aboitiz, Jebsen Bulk Transport Corporation, managers), Philippines. 11.3.1995: Completed. 1996: Managers restyled as W.G. & A. Jebsen Ship Management Inc. 1998: Renamed MILLENNIUM TIGER. (O.N. MNLD009455). 2000: Transferred to Aboitiz, Jebsens Far East Shipping SA, (Aboitiz, Jebsen Bulk Transport Corporation, managers). 2004: Sold to Joss Asian Feeders, Manila, (same managers), retaining Phillipine flag. 20.12.2004: Sold in an unspecific damaged condition to Biendong Shipping, Hanoi, Vietnam, and renamed MY DINH.

NORTHERN LINANES River Trent April 1997 (Chriss Reynolds)

9106924
283. NORTHERN LINANES (1995 – 2000) Linanes class
2,446g.   1,369n   3,680d. 87.90 (BB) x 12.90 x 5.498 metres oa.
8-cyl. 4 S.C.S.A. (240 x 280mm) Deutz SBV8M628 type oil engine made by Motoren Werke Mannheim AG (MWM), Mannheim. 2,039 bhp. 11.75 kts. Thwartship thrust propeller forward.
Ice strengthened general cargo vessel with a container capacity of 176 TEU.
13.4.1993: Keel laid by Slovenske Lodenice AG, Komarno (Yard No. 2922). 8.4.1994: Launched. 7.11.1994: Completed. 3.1.1995: Delivered to Anastasia Ltd., (Jebsens Ship Management (Bergen) AS, managers), Malta. (O.N.4307). 2000: Northern Shipping Company (A/O "Severnoye Morskoye Parokhodstvo"), appointed as managers). 6.2002: Sold to Short Sea Ltd., (Wilson Ship Management AS, Bergen, managers), Malta, and renamed WILSON BORG. 2004: Sold to Wilson Shipowning AS, Bergen, (same managers), retaining Malta flag.

9124419
284. KAPITAN DROBININ (1995 – 2000) Linanes class
2,446g.   957n   3,680d. 87.90 (BB) x 12.90 x 5.498 metres oa.

8-cyl. 4 S.C.S.A. (240 x 280mm) Deutz SBV8M628 type oil engine made by Motoren Werke Mannheim AG (MWM), Mannheim. 2,039 bhp. 11.75 kts. Thwartship thrust propeller forward.
Ice strengthened general cargo vessel with a container capacity of 176 TEU.
23.9.1994: Keel laid by Slovenske Lodenice AG, Komarno (Yard No. 2924). 2.2.1995: Launched. 14.6.1995: Completed for Gee. Em. Shipping Company Ltd., (Jebsens Ship Management (Bergen) AS, managers), Malta. (O.N.4462). 2004: Sold to Wilson Shipowning AS, Bergen, (same managers), and renamed WILSON BLYTH, retaining Malta flag.

KAPITAN DROBININ at Flixborough, River Trent, 12 October 1998. (World Ship Society Photograph Library)

NORTHERN LOFTNES (World Ship Society Photograph Library)

9126687
285. NORTHERN LOFTNES (1995 – 2000) Linanes class
2,446g. 957n 3,700d. 87.90 (BB) x 12.90 x 5.498 metres oa.
8-cyl. 4 S.C.S.A. (240 x 280mm) Deutz SBV8M628 type oil engine made by Kloeckner-Humboldt-Deutz AG, Koeln. 2,039 bhp. 11.75 kts. Thwartship thrust propeller forward.
Ice strengthened general cargo vessel with a container capacity of 176 TEU.

29.9.1994: Keel laid by Slovenske Lodenice AG, Komarno (Yard No. 2926). 18.4.1995: Launched. 20.7.1995: Completed for Margo Shipping Company Ltd., (Jebsens Ship Management (Bergen) AS, managers), Malta. (O.N. 4531). 6.2002: Sold to Short Sea Ltd., (Wilson Ship Management AS, Bergen, managers), Malta, and renamed WILSON GOOLE. 2004: Sold to Wilson Shipowning AS, Bergen, (same managers), retaining Malta flag.

9126900
286. NORTHERN LESNES (1995 – 2000) Linanes class
2,446g. 957n 3,700d. 87.90 (BB) x 12.90 x 5.498 metres oa.
8-cyl. 4 S.C.S.A. (240 x 280mm) Deutz SBV8M628 type oil engine made by Kloeckner-Humboldt-Deutz AG, Koeln. 2,039 bhp. 11.75 kts. Thwartship thrust propeller forward.
Ice strengthened general cargo vessel with a container capacity of 176 TEU.
6.12.1994: Keel laid by Slovenske Lodenice AG, Komarno (Yard No. 2927). 19.5.1995: Launched. 7.9.1995: Completed for Ludmila Shipping Company Ltd., (Jebsens Ship Management (Bergen) AS, managers), Malta. (O.N. 4568). 6.2002: Sold to Short Sea Ltd., (Wilson Ship Management AS, Bergen, managers), Malta, and renamed WILSON BREST. 2004: Sold to Wilson Shipowning AS, Bergen, (same managers), retaining Malta flag.

FOSSNES with J. H. C. on hull, on the Detroit River 1 September 2000.
(World Ship Society Photograph Library)

8908868
287. FOSSNES (3) (1995 – 2002) Fossnes class
11,542g. 5,366n. 16,500d. 149.44 (BB) x 23.16 x 8.50 metres oa.
6-cyl. 2 S.C.S.A. (500 x 1,620mm) B&W 6L50MCE type oil engine made by H. Cegielski Z.P.M., Poznan. 5,182 bhp. 13.5 kts.
Bulk carrier with two 25-ton cranes capable of operating grabs carried aboard.
1989: Ordered as REGA from Stocznia Szczecinska SA, Szczecin (Yard No. B570/04) for Polish Steamship Company (Polska Zegluga Morska), Szczecin, Poland. 3.12.1994: Keel laid. 25.2.1995: Launched as FOSSNES. 8.5.1995: Completed for Rega Shipping

Company Ltd., Nassau, (Jebsens Ship Management (Bergen) AS, managers), under Luxembourg flag. 1996: Jebsens Ship Management Holding AS, Bergen appointed as managers. 1997: Wilson Ship Management (Bergen) AS appointed as managers, and transferred to Norway (NIS) flag. 2000: Aboitiz, Jebsen Bulk Transport Corporation, appointed as managers. 2002: Renamed REGA, (Polish Steamship Company, Szczecin, managers), retaining Bahamas flag.

288. RAMNES (2)   **(1995 – 2000)** see ship No. 120 above.

289. NORNES   **(1995 – 1997)** see ship No. 75 above.

WESTERN CONDOR Port Adelaide 21 February 1996. (World Ship Society Photograph Library)

290. WESTERN CONDOR   **(1995 – 1999)** see ship No. 169 above.

WESTERN EAGLE at Melbourne 13 May 1996. Note Jebsens still on superstructure side – aft. (World Ship Society Photograph Library)

291. WESTERN EAGLE   **(1995 – 1998)** see ship No. 172 above.

292. WESTERN FALCON   **(1995 – 1998)** see ship No. 157 above.

WESTERN FALCON at Port Adelaide 9 March 1997. (World Ship Society Photograph Library)

WESTERN HAWK At Port Adelaide 4 May 1996. (World Ship Society Photograph Library)

293. WESTERN HAWK   **(1995 – 1999)** see ship No. 174 above.

WESTERN OSPREY 17 November 1997. Jebsens has been replaced by Western Bulk on the superstructure side. (World Ship Society Photograph Library)

294. WESTERN OSPREY (1995 – 1998) see ship No. 155 above.

NORTHERN LIFTNES in later life with Wilson on hull. (Chriss Reynolds collection)

9126912
295. NORTHERN LIFTNES (1996 – 2000) Linanes class
2,446g.   957n   3,700d. 87.90 (BB) x 12.90 x 5.498 metres oa.
8-cyl. 4 S.C.S.A. (240 x 280mm) Deutz SBV8M628 type oil engine made by Kloeckner-Humboldt-Deutz AG, Koeln. 2,039 bhp. 11.75 kts.   Thwartship thrust propeller forward.
Ice strengthened general cargo vessel with a container capacity of 176 TEU.
2.6.1995: Keel laid by Slovenske Lodenice AG, Komarno (Yard No. 2928). 11.11.1996: Launched. 26.4.1996: Completed for Fedora Shipping Company Ltd., (Jebsens Ship Management (Bergen) AS, managers), Malta. (O.N. 4818). 6.2002: Sold to Short Sea Ltd., (Wilson Ship Management AS, Bergen, managers), Malta, and renamed WILSON GRIP. 2004: Sold to Wilson Shipowning AS, Bergen, (same managers), retaining Malta flag.

296. HORDNES   (1996 – 2000) see ship No. 226 above.

297. FALKNES (3)   (1996 – 2000) see ship No. 142 above.

298. NORDANHAV   (1996 – 1999) see ship No. 258 above.

9111242
299. LUIS ABOITIZ   (1996 – 1999) Aboitiz class
7,249g. 3,094n. 7,239d.   134.20 x   x 7.118 metres
6-cyl. 4 S.C.S.A. (420 x 1,360mm) B&W 6L42MC type oil engine made by Bryansk Engine Works, Bryansk.   6,933 bhp. 15 kts.
Ice breaking general cargo vessel with two 12-ton cranes and with a container capacity of 336 TEU.

4.6.1995: Keel laid by Kherson Shipyard, Kherson, (Yard No. 1904). 11.4.1996: Launched. 26.6.1996: Completed for Wide Source Maritime Inc., (Aboitiz, Jebsen Shipmanagement, managers), Philippines. (O.N. MNLA000311). 1996: Managers restyled as W.G. & A. Jebsen Ship Management Inc. 1999: Sold to Aboitiz, Jebsens Far East Shipping Company SA, (Aboitiz, Jebsens Bulk Transport Corporation, appointed as managers), and renamed MILLENNIUM DRAGON. 2003: Sold to Arctic Sky Shipping Ltd., Riga, Latvia, (Aquaship Ltd., Riga, managers), and renamed ARCTIC SKY, under Malta flag.

LUIS ABOITIZ at Geelong 21 March 1997. (World Ship Society Photograph Library)

TRIMNES (World Ship Society Photograph Library)

8908583
300. TRIMNES (1996 -   )
14,145g. 4,244n. 17,309d. 149.50 (BB) x   x 8.413 metres oa.
6-cyl. 2 S.C.S.A. (450 x 1,350mm) Mitsubishi 6UEC45LA type oil engine made by Akasaka Tekkosho KK (Akasaka Diesels Ltd.) Yaizu. 5,755 bhp. 14.5 kts. Thwartship tunnel thruster propeller forward and aft.
Belt-unloading bulk carrier.

16.2.1990: Keel laid as EXPRESS by Tsuneishi Zosen KK, Numakuma (Yard No. 635). 8.6.1990: Launched. 30.9.1990: Completed for Howard Smith Industries Proprietry Ltd., Australia. 1996: Sold to Trimnes Shipping SA, Panama (Jebsens Ship Management (Bergen) AS, managers), and renamed TRIMNES. (O.N. 23137-96B) 1997: Transferred to Beltships Shipping KS, (same managers). 1998: Wilson Shipmanagement (Bergen) AS, appointed as managers. 2000: Sold to Trimnes Panama SA, Bergen, and removed from management. 2004: Sold to Vierte Belt Shipping AG., Leer, (AJ Ship Management, Leer, managers), under Panama flag.

ENTERPRISE at Port Adelaide 8 November 1996. (World Ship Society Photograph Library)

301. ENTERPRISE (1996 -   ) see ship No. 171 above.

8918459
302. LANGENES (1996 – 1998) Langenes class
4,197g. 2,033n. 6,250d. 112.70 x   x 6.558 metres oa.
12-cyl. 4 S.C.S.A. (280 x 320mm) Alpha 12V28 / 32A type oil engine made by MAN B&W Diesel AS, Alpha Diesel, Frederikshavn. 3,589 bhp. 12.5 kts. Thwartship thrust propeller forward.
Ice strengthened bulk carrier.
31.3.1990: Keel laid by "Apatin" Brodogradaliste, Apatin (Yard No. 1103), for Patria I AS, (Jebsens Ship Management (Bergen) AS, managers), Norway. 14.2.1991: Launched. Due to internal Yugoslavian Ethnic conflict work was suspended. 15.7.1996: Completed for Rederiet Nordavind DA, (Bergen Shipping SA, managers) Bahamas. (O.N. 729587). 1998: Sold to Elianna AS, (Bships Management AS managers), and renamed ELIANNA. 2000: Sold to Unisky Shipping Company Ltd., Bergen, (Bergen Shipping AS, managers). 2002: Sold to Wilson Shipping AS, (Wilson Ship Management (Bergen) AS, managers), and renamed WILSON SKAW.

NORTHERN LOKNES At Gunness Wharf, River Trent 8 September 1998. (World Ship Society Photograph Library)

9150236
303. NORTHERN LARSNES /
NORTHERN LOKNES (1996 – 2000) Linanes class
2,446g. 1,369n 3,694d. 87.90 (BB) x 12.90 x 5.498 metres oa.
8-cyl. 4 S.C.S.A. (240 x 280mm) Deutz SBV8M628 type oil engine made by Motorenwerke Mannheim A.G. (MWM). 2,039 bhp. 11.75 kts. Thwartship thrust propeller forward.
Ice strengthened general cargo vessel with a container capacity of 176 TEU.
17.10.1995: Keel laid as NORTHERN LARSNES by Slovenske Lodenice AG, Komarno (Yard No. 2930). 10.6.1996: Launched as NORTHERN LOKNES. 7.8.1996: Completed for Fedora Shipping Company Ltd., (Jebsens Ship Management (Bergen) AS, managers), Malta. (O.N. 5028). 2004: Sold to Wilson Shipowning AS, Bergen, (Wilson Ship Management (Bergen) AS, managers), and renamed WILSON GHENT, retaining Malta flag.

NORTHERN LANGNES (World Ship Society Photograph Library)

9150482
304. NORTHERN LAUNES /
NORTHERN LANGNES (1996 – 2000) Linanes class
2,446g. 1,369n 3,695d. 87.90 (BB) x 12.90 x 5.498 metres oa.
8-cyl. 4 S.C.S.A. (240 x 280mm) Deutz SBV8M628 type oil engine made by Motorenwerke Mannheim A.G. (MWM). 2,039 bhp. 11.75 kts. Thwartship thrust propeller forward.
Ice strengthened general cargo vessel with a container capacity of 176 TEU.

14.2.1996: Keel laid as NORTHERN LAUNES by Slovenske Lodenice AG, Komarno (Yard No. 2931). 7.9.1996: Launched as NORTHERN LANGNES. 7.11.1996: Completed for Fedora Shipping Company Ltd., (Jebsens Ship Management (Bergen) AS, managers), Malta. (O.N. 5177). 6.2002: Sold to Short Sea Ltd., (Wilson Ship Management AS, Bergen, managers), Malta, and renamed WILSON LEER. 2004: Sold to Wilson Shipowning AS, Bergen, (same managers), retaining Malta flag.

9150494
305. NORTHERN LINDNES /
NORTHERN LARSNES (1996 – 2000) Linanes class
2,446g. 957n 3,700d. 87.90 (BB) x 12.90 x 5.498 metres oa.
8-cyl. 4 S.C.S.A. (240 x 280mm) Deutz SBV8M628 type oil engine made by Motorenwerke Mannheim A.G. (MWM). 2,039 bhp. 11.75 kts. Thwartship thrust propeller forward.
Ice strengthened general cargo vessel with a container capacity of 176 TEU.
14.6.1996: Keel laid as NORTHERN LINDNES by Slovenske Lodenice AG, Komarno (Yard No. 2932). 7.9.1996: Launched as NORTHERN LARSNES. 2.11.1996: Completed for Emary Shipping Company Ltd., (Jebsens Ship Management (Bergen) AS, managers), Malta. (O.N. 5290). 2004: Renamed WILSON BRUGGE, (Wilson Ship Management (Bergen) AS, managers), retaining Malta flag.

NORTHERN LAUNES at Immingham 30 May 2000. (World Ship Society Photograph Library)

9150509
306. NORTHERN LURNES /
NORTHERN LAUNES (1997 – 2000) Linanes class
2,446g. 1,369n 3,700d. 88.00 (BB) x 12.80 x 4.45 metres oa.
8-cyl. 4 S.C.S.A. (240 x 280mm) Deutz SBV8M628 type oil engine made by KHD Industriemotoren GmbH, Koeln. 2,041 bhp. 11.75 kts. Thwartship thrust propeller forward tunnel thrusters unit.
Ice strengthened general cargo vessel with a container capacity of 176 TEU.
7.8.1996: Keel laid as NORTHERN LURNES by Slovenske Lodenice AG, Komarno (Yard No. 2933). 8.6.1997: Launched as NORTHERN LAUNES. 11.4.1997: Completed for

Nataly Shipping Company Ltd., (Jebsens Ship Management (Bergen) AS, managers), Malta. (O.N. 5417). 6.2002: Sold to Short Sea Ltd., (Wilson Ship Management AS, Bergen, managers), Malta, and renamed WILSON LEITH. 2004: Sold to Wilson Shipowning AS, Bergen, (same managers), retaining Malta flag.

NORTHERN LINDNES 15 April 1999 (World Ship Society Photograph Library)

9150511
307. NORTHERN LAKENES /
NORTHERN LINDNES (1997 – 2000) Linanes class
2,446g. 1,300n. 3,700d. 87.90 (BB) x 12.90 x 5.498 metres oa.
8-cyl. 4 S.C.S.A. (240 x 280mm) Deutz SBV8M628 type oil engine made by KHD Industriemotoren GmbH, Koeln. 2,039 bhp. 11.75 kts. Thwartship thrust propeller forward.
Ice strengthened general cargo vessel with a container capacity of 176 TEU.
10.9.1996: Keel laid as NORTHERN LAKENES by Slovenske Lodenice AG, Komarno (Yard No. 2934). 2.3.1997: Launched as NORTHERN LINDNES. 27.5.1997: Completed for Olga Shipping Company Ltd., (Jebsens Ship Management (Bergen) AS, managers), Malta. (O.N. 5473). 2004: Renamed WILSON BRAKE, (Wilson Ship Management (Bergen) AS, managers), retaining Malta flag.

9150535
308. NORTHERN LURNES (1997 – 2000) Linanes class
2,446g. 1,369n. 3,695d. 88.00 (BB) x 12.80 x 4.45 metres oa.
8-cyl. 4 S.C.S.A. (240 x 280mm) Deutz SBV8M628 type oil engine made by Motorenwerke Mannheim A.G. (MWM). 2,039 bhp. 11.75 kts. Thwartship thrust propeller forward.
Ice strengthened general cargo vessel with a container capacity of 176 TEU.
7.10.1996: Keel laid by Slovenske Lodenice AG, Komarno (Yard No. 2936). 7.4.1997: Launched. 9.6.1997: Completed for Love Shipping Company Ltd., (Jebsens Ship Management (Bergen) AS, managers), Malta. (O.N. 5529). 6.2002: Sold to Short Sea Ltd., (Wilson Ship Management AS, Bergen, managers), Malta, and renamed WILSON TEES. 2004: Sold to Wilson Shipowning AS, Bergen, (same managers), retaining Malta flag.

*From this point please see also the Jebsen – Hartmann Carriers fleet section in parallel with this fleet listing.

8918461

309. BOREALNES   (1998 – 2000) Langenes class
4,197g. 2,033n. 6,250d.   112.70 x   x 6.547 metres oa.
12-cyl. 4 S.C.S.A. (280 x 320mm) Alpha 12V28 / 32A type oil engine made by MAN B&W Diesel AS, Alpha Diesel, Frederikshavn. 3,589 bhp. 12.5 kts. Thwartship thrust propeller forward.
Ice strengthened general cargo vessel.
3.9.1990: Keel laid by "Apatin" Brodogradaliste, Apatin (Yard No. 1104), for Patria II AS, (Jebsens Ship Management (Bergen) AS, managers), Norway. Due to internal Yugoslavian Ethnic conflict work was suspended. 30.6.1996: Launched as BOREAL. 9.3.1998: Completed as BOREALNES for Borealnes AS, (Bships Management AS managers), Bahamas. (O.N. 731004). 2000: Sold to Unicoast Shipping Company Ltd., Bergen, (Bergen Shipping AS, managers), under Cyprus flag. 2003: Renamed WILSON SAGA. 2004: Sold to Boreal Shipping & Industrier AS, Nordnes, Norway, (Wilson Ship Management AS, Bergen, managers).

310. FROMNES	**(1998 – 2003)**	see ship No. 98 above.
311. ROCKNES	**(1998 – 2000)**	see ship No. 72 above.
312. ALCEM GALACA	**(1998 – 2002)**	see ship No. 109 above.
313. ALCEM LUGAIT	**(1998 – 2000)**	see ship No. 153 above.
314. MILLENNIUM EAGLE	**(1998 – 2004)**	see ship No. 280 above.
315. MILLENNIUM TIGER	**(1998 – 2004)**	see ship No. 281 above.

EAGLE At Port Adelaide 4 April 1999.   (World Ship Society Photograph Library)

316. EAGLE	**(1998 – 2001)**	see ship No. 172 above.
317. HAWK	**(1999)**	see ship No. 174 above.
318. CONDOR	**(1999)**	see ship No. 169 above.

319. MILLENNIUM DRAGON (1999 – 2003) see ship No. 297 above.

320. SURENES (2) (1999 – 2004) see ship No. 174 above.

321. SEALNES (2) (1999 – 2004) see ship No. 169 above.

8918473
322. ISNES (3)   (1999 – 2000) Langenes class
4,200g. 2,144n. 6,000d.   112.70 x 15.50 x 6.260 metres oa.
12-cyl. 4 S.C.S.A. (280 x 320mm) Alpha 12V28 / 32A type oil engine made by MAN B&W Diesel AS, Alpha Diesel, Frederikshavn. 3,589 bhp. 12.5 kts. Thwartship thrust propeller forward.
Ice strengthened general cargo vessel.
1.11.1990: Keel laid by "Apatin" Brodogradaliste, Apatin (Yard No. 1105), for AS A. J. Marine Services, (Jebsens Ship Management (Bergen) AS, managers), Norway. Due to internal Yugoslavian Ethnic conflict work was suspended. 11.5.1998: Launched. 25.2.1999: Completed for Borealvik AS, (Bships Management A S managers) 2000: Sold to Unimoon Shipping Company Ltd., Bergen, (Bergen Shipping AS, managers), under Cyprus flag.

8918485
323. LINDNES (2) / LINITO (2000) Langenes class
4,500g. 2,144n. 6,000d.   112.64 x 15.50 x 6.684   metres oa.
12-cyl. 4 S.C.S.A. (280 x 330mm) Alpha 12V28 / 32A type oil engine made by MAN B&W Diesel AS, Frederikshavn. 3,589 bhp. 12.5 kts. Thwartship thrust propeller forward.
Ice strengthened general cargo vessel.
1.2.1991: Keel laid as LINDNES by "Apatin" Brodogradaliste, Apatin (Yard No. 1106), for Patria III AS, (Jebsens Ship Management (Bergen) AS, managers), Norway. Due to internal Yugoslavian Ethnic conflict work was suspended. 10.12.1999: Launched. 24.11.2000: Completed as LINITO for Linito Shipping Company Ltd., Bergen (Wilson Ship Management (Bergen) AS, Bergen, managers), under Cyprus flag.

8918497
. **DELAYED NES (-)**   Langenes class
Proposed. 4,500g. 2,144n. 6,000d.   112.64 x 15.50 x 6.684 metres oa.
12-cyl. 4 S.C.S.A. (280 x 330mm) Alpha 12V28 / 32A type oil engine made by MAN B&W Diesel AS, Alpha Diesel, Frederikshavn. 3,589 bhp. 12.5 kts. Thwartship thrust propeller forward.
Ice strengthened general cargo vessel.
3.1991: Keel laid by "Apatin" Brodogradaliste, Apatin (Yard No. 1107), for AS A. J. Marine Services, (Jebsens Ship Management (Bergen) AS, managers), Norway. Due to internal Yugoslavian Ethnic conflict work was suspended. 10.2002: Still recorded as being "under construction". 5.2005: Bergen Management AS, quoted as manager for unknown owners "In Build" on Equasis website.

324. WILLIAM OLDENDORFF (2000 – 2002) see ship No. 171 above.

WILLIAM OLDENDORFF at Singapore 10 August 2000. (World Ship Society Photograph Library)

FREDERIKE OLDENDORFF at Singapore 3 July 2000. (World Ship Society Photograph Library)

325. FREDERIKE OLDENDORFF (2000 – 2002) see ship No. 176 above.

326. TABA **(2000 – 2002)** see ship No. 156 above.

327. REFSNES **(2000 – 2000)** see ship No. 67 above.

SANDNES (Courtesy of David Calvert)

9306029
336. SANDNES (3)   (2005 -   )
17,357g. 5,748n. 27,711d. 166.7 (BB) x 24.75 x 10.5 metres oa.
8-cyl. 4 S.C.S.A. (430 x 610mm) MaK 8M43 type oil engine made by Caterpillar Mororen Rostock GmbH, Rostock, reduction geared to a controllable pitch propeller. 9,942 bhp. 14 kts. Thwartship controllable pitch propeller forward and aft.
Belt-unloading bulk carrier.
19.12.2003: Sub-contracted hull keel laid by Daewoo-Mangalia Heavy Industries SA, Mangalia (Yard No. 1044) for J. J. Sietas Schiffswerft Gmbh & Company KG, Hamburg. 26.9.2004: Launched and subsequently towed to Hamburg for completion. 6.4.2005: Completed by J. J. Sietas Schiffswerft Gmbh & Company KG, Hamburg (Yard No. 1219), for Hans Jurgen Hartman, m.s. Sandnes, Manila, Philippines, (Aboitiz, Jebsen Bulk Transport, Manila, managers), for the Antigua and Barbuda flag. 4.2005: Cuxships Management GmbH, Cuxhaven, appointed as managers.

7812220
337. IRON STURT   (2005 -   )
14,785g. 6,141n. 22,093d. 161.93 (BB) x 22.92 x 10.040 metres oa.
6-cyl. 2 S.C.S.A. (680 X 1,250mm) Sulzer 6RND68 type oil engine made by Ishikawajima – Harima Heavy Industry Company Ltd., (IHI), Aioi. 9,000 bhp. 15 kts. Thwartship thrust propeller forward.
Gearless bulk carier.
5.12.1978: Keel laid by Ishikawajima – Harima Heavy Industry Company Ltd., (IHI), Kure (Yard No.2728), for Bulkships Finance Pty. Ltd., Australia. 9.2.1979: Launched. 27.4.1979: Completed. 1987: Broken Hill Propriety Company Ltd., appointed as managers. 1988: BHP Transport Ltd., appointed as managers. 1989: Sold to BHP Transport Ltd. 1990: Sold to Broken Hill Propriety Company Ltd. 1993: Sold to BHP Transport Propriety Ltd. 2000: Sold to BHP Transport & Logistics Pty.Ltd. 2002: Teekay Shipping (Australia) Pty Ltd, appointed as managers. 15.2.2005: Sold to

Jebsens Coastal Shipping Services Pty Ltd., Melbourne (ASP Ship Management Pty Ltd., managers).

IRON STURT (Internet source)

CLYDENES 17 July 2005, arriving at Kilroot on maiden voyage for work-up trials and familiarisation after conversion, before entering onto her charter work. (Courtesy Trevor Kidd)

9101546
338. CLYDENES (2)   (2005 -   )
4,783g. 2,519n. 7,184d.   99.95 x 17.06 x 6.764 metres.
6-cyl. 4 S.C.S.A. (320 x 480mm) MaK 6M32 type oil engine by Krupp MaK Maschinenbau GmbH, Kiel, single reduction reverse geared to screw shaft with controllable pitch propeller.   3,589 bhp.   12.5 kts. Thwartship thrust propeller forward.
17.5.1995: Keel laid as ARKLOW BRIDGE by Appledore Shipbuilders Ltd., Appledore, (Yard No. 161), for Arklow Shipping Ltd. 4.11.1995: Launched for Devon Line, Dorchester, (Arklow Shipping Ltd., managers), Arklow. 3.1.1996: Completed. 3.2005: Sold to Capstan Shipping Ltd., (same managers), Arklow. 4.2005: Purchased by Clydenes Shipping Ltd., Bergen, (Beltships Shipping AS, Bergen, managers), and renamed CLYDENES, under Norway NIS flag, and converted into a self-discharging vessel in Poland. Chartered for 5-year contract to Clydeport for shipment of coal from Hunterston on the Clyde to Manisty Wharf on the Manchester Ship Canal.

339. NORDNES **(2005 -   )** see ship No. 329 above.

Jebsen – Hartmann Carriers

The funnel markings remained the same as the original fleet with the exception of the white band that became pale yellow. Hulls were amended to brick red, with buff superstructure and cargo handling equipment, as were some vessels in the main fleet. J.H.C. was subsequently added to ship sides.

Following the purchase of Jebsens 50% shareholding by Hartmann Group the operation was
on the
1 April 2001
restyled as
United Bulk Carriers
NZ Lumber website (12/02) states UBC as Philadelphia based.
The funnel henceforth was blue with a red band 2/3 up from the base.

BRUNES (Chriss Reynolds collection)

9107033
JH.1. BRUNES (4)   (1995 – 2001) B class
13,695g. 7,737n. 22,056d. 157.60 (BB) x 26.00 x 9.110 metres oa.
6-cyl. 2 S.C.S.A. (450 x 1,350mm) Mitsubishi 6UEC45LA type oil engine made by Akasaka Tekkosho KK, (Akasaka Diesels Ltd.), Yaizu. 6,458 bhp. 14 kts.
Bulk carrier with four 30-ton cranes capable of operating grabs carried aboard.
1991: Ordered as MEGAWAVE from Saiki Jukoggo K.K., Saiki (Yard No. 1050), by Megawave Shipping Company Ltd., (Athena Marine Company Ltd., managers), Cyprus. 23.12.1994: Keel laid. 18.2.1995: Launched as BRUNES. 14.4.1995: Completed. (O.N. 710376). 1996: Transferred to Megawave Two Navigation Company Ltd., Cyprus,

(same managers). 2001: Transferred to Atlas Trampship m.v. "Wega Reeder" (Hartman Schiffahrtges mbH & Co. KG, Leer, Germany, managers), Cyprus, and renamed UBC BEAUMONT. 2005: Sold to Vierte Cooper Schiffahrts GmbH, Leer, Germany, (same managers), and renamed BEAUMONT.

9107045
JH.2. BERNES (3) (1995 – 2001) B class
13,695g. 7,737n. 22,056d. 157.60 (BB) x 26.00 x 9.107 metres oa.
6-cyl. 2 S.C.S.A. (450 x 1,350mm) Mitsubishi 6UEC45LA type oil engine made by Akasaka Tekkosho KK, (Akasaka Diesels Ltd.), Yaizu. 6,458 bhp. 14 kts.
Bulk carrier with four 30-ton cranes capable of operating grabs carried aboard.
1991: Ordered as POINT FORTUNE from Saiki Jukoggo KK, Saiki (Yard No. 1051), for Point Fortune Shipping Company Ltd., (Athena Marine Company Ltd., managers), Cyprus. 18.2.1995: Keel laid. 15.4.1995: Launched as BERNES. 9.6.1995: Completed. (O.N.710377). 2001: Renamed UBC BARRANQUILLA. 2005: Sold to Vierte Cooper Schiffahrts GmbH, Leer, Germany, (same managers), and renamed BARRANQUILLA.

BRIMNES arriving at Naantali 19 September 1998. (World Ship Society Photograph Library)

9152478
JH.3. BRIMNES (3) (1997 - 2001) B class
14,661g. 8,088n. 23,250d. 154.35 x 26.00 x 9.518 metres oa.
6-cyl. 2 S.C.S.A. (450 x 1,350mm) Mitsubishi 6UEC45LA type oil engine made by Akasaka Tekkosho KK, (Akasaka Diesels Ltd.), Yaizu. 6,458 bhp. 14.5 kts.
Bulk carrier with four 30-ton cranes capable of operating grabs carried aboard.
1991: Ordered as OCEAN LEADER by Saiki Jukogyo KK, Saiki (Yard No. 1070) for Ocean Leader Shipping Company, (Athena Marine Company Ltd., manager), Cyprus. 26.3.1997: Keel laid. 13.5.1997: Launched as BRIMNES. 27.6.1997: Completed. 2001: Renamed UBC BOSTON.

9152466
JH.4. BROOKNES (3) (1998 – 2001) B class
14,700g. 7,900n. 23,250d. 154.35 x   x 9.518 metres oa.

6-cyl. 2 S.C.S.A. (450 x 1,350mm) Mitsubishi 6UEC45LA type oil engine made by Akasaka Tekkosho KK, (Akasaka Diesels Ltd.), Yaizu. 6,458 bhp. 14.5 kts.
Bulk carrier with four 30-ton cranes capable of operating grabs carried aboard.
1991: Ordered as OCEAN GIANT from Saiki Jukogyo KK, Sakai (Yard No. 1068) for Ocean Giant Shipping Company (Athena Marine Company Ltd., manager), Cyprus. 10.2.1997: Keel laid. 26.3.1997: Launched. 12.5.1997: Completed. 1998: Renamed BROOKNES. 2001: Renamed UBC BALBOA.

BROOKNES at Port Adelaide 2 August 1999. (World Ship Society Photograph Library)

BIRKNES arriving at Port Jackson, Sydney 27 September 1998. (World Ship Society Photograph Library)

9177961
JH.5. BIRKNES (4) (1998 – 2001) B class
14,706g. 8,385n. 24,072d. 154.35 (BB) x x 9.650 metres oa.
6-cyl. 2 S.C.S.A. (450 x 1,350mm) Mitsubishi 6UEC45LA type oil engine made by Akasaka Tekkosho KK, (Akasaka Diesels Ltd.), Yaizu. 6,458 bhp. 14.5 kts.
Bulk carrier with four 30-ton cranes capable of operating grabs carried aboard.

1991: Ordered as LADY V from Saiki Jukoggo KK, Saiki (Yard No. 1077), for Lady V Shipping Company Ltd., (Athena Marine Company Ltd., managers), Cyprus. 23.1.1998: Keel laid. 26.3.1998: Launched as BIRKNES. 15.5.1998: Completed. 2001: Renamed UBC BREMEN.

BAYNES at Port Adelaide 15 August 1998. (World Ship Society Photograph Library)

9177973
JH.6. BAYNES (3) (1998 – 2001) B class
14,706g. 8,385n. 24,034d. 154.35 (BB) x   x 9.650 metres oa.
6-cyl. 2 S.C.S.A. (450 x 1,350mm) Mitsubishi 6UEC45LA type oil engine made by Akasaka Tekkosho KK, (Akasaka Diesels Ltd.), Yaizu. 6,458 bhp. 14.5 kts.
Bulk carrier with four 30-ton cranes capable of operating grabs carried aboard.
1991: Ordered as BAYSHORE from Saiki Jukoggo KK, Saiki (Yard No. 1078), for Bayshore Shipping Company Ltd., (Athena Marine Company Ltd., managers), Cyprus. 26.3.1998: Keel laid. 14.5.1998: Launched as BAYNES. 30.6.1998: Completed. 2001: Renamed UBC BATON ROUGE.

SWIFTNES departing Newcastle N.S.W. 9 May 2000. (World Ship Society Photograph Library)

9189665
JH.7. SWIFTNES (3) (1999 – 2001) S Class
19,743g. 10,718n. 31,828d. 171.59 (BB) x   x   9.550 metres oa.
6-cyl. 2 S.C.S.A. (520 x 1,600mm) Mitsubishi 6UEC52LA type oil engine made by Akasaka Tekkosho KK, (Akasaka Diesels Ltd.), Yaizu. 9,599 bhp. 14.5 kts.
Bulk carrier with four 30-ton cranes capable of operating grabs carried aboard.
Ordered as OCEAN SPRING from Saiki Jukoggo KK, Saiki (Yard No. 1085), for Ocean Spring Navigation Company Ltd., (Athena Marine Company Ltd., managers), Cyprus. 1.12.1998: Keel laid. 6.2.1999: Launched as SWIFTNES. 5.4.1999: Completed. 2001: Renamed UBC SALVADOR.

SIRNES arriving Port Adelaide 3 September 1999. (World Ship Society Photograph Library)

9189677
JH.8. SIRNES (1999 – 2001) S Class
19,743g. 10,718n. 31,828d. 171.59 (BB) x   x   9.550 metres oa.
6-cyl. 2 S.C.S.A. (520 x 1,600mm) Mitsubishi 6UEC52LA type oil engine made by Akasaka Tekkosho KK, (Akasaka Diesels Ltd.), Yaizu. 9,599 bhp. 14.5 kts.
Bulk carrier with four 30-ton cranes capable of operating grabs carried aboard.
Ordered as OCEAN GUARD from Saiki Jukoggo KK, Saiki (Yard No. 1086), for Ocean Guard Navigation Company Ltd., (Athena Marine Company Ltd., managers), Cyprus. 6.2.1999: Keel laid. 6.4.1999: Launched as SIRNES. 5.4.1999: Completed. 28.10.2001: Renamed UBC SVEA at Lisahally, Londonderry, N. Ireland.

9190080
JH.9. ATLANTIC PIONEER (1999 – 2001) A Class
12,993g. 5,894n. 17,451d. 143.15 (BB) x 22.80 x 9.710 metres oa.
7-cyl. 2 S.C.S.A. (420 x 1,360mm) B&W 7L42MC type oil engine made by Hudong Shipyard, Shanghai. 9,469 bhp. 16 kts. Thwartship thrust controllable pitch propeller forward.
Ice strengthened general cargo vessel with two 45-ton cranes and a container capacity of 1080 TEU.
25.8.1998: Keel laid by Jingiang Shipyard, Jingiang (Yard No. Js98-010) for Aspire Navigation Company Ltd., (Athena Marine Company Ltd., managers), Cyprus. (Jebsen – Hartmann Carriers). 16.4.1999: Launched. 22.5.1999: Completed. 2001: Renamed SEABOARD PIONEER.

ATLANTIC PIONEER (Jebsens)

ATLANTIC PATROLLER (Internet source)

9190092
JH.10. ATLANTIC PATROLLER   (2000 – 2001) A Class
12,993g. 5,894n. 17,800d. 143.15 (BB) x 22.80 x 8.300 metres oa.
7-cyl. 2 S.C.S.A. (420 x 1,360mm) B&W 7L42MC type oil engine made by Hudong Shipyard, Shanghai. 9,517 bhp. 16 kts. Thwartship thrust controllable pitch propeller forward.
Ice strengthened general cargo vessel with two 45-ton cranes and a container capacity of 1080 TEU.
25.9.1998: Keel laid by Jingiang Shipyard, Jingiang (Yard No. Js98-011) for Pendium Navigation Company Ltd., (Athena Marine Company Ltd., managers), Cyprus. (Jebsen – Hartmann Carriers). 16.4.1999: Launched 5.1.2000: Completed. 2001: Renamed FOREST PATROLLER.

9190107
JH.11. ATLANTIC PRIDE   (2000 – 2001) A Class
12,993g. 5,894n. 17471d. 143.15 (BB) x 22.80 x 9.710 metres oa.
7-cyl. 2 S.C.S.A. (420 x 1,360mm) B&W 7L42MC type oil engine made by Hudong Shipyard, Shanghai. 8,523 bhp. 15 kts. Thwartship thrust controllable pitch propeller forward.

Ice strengthened general cargo vessel with two 45-ton cranes and a container capacity of 974 TEU.
30.3.1998: Keel laid by Jingiang Shipyard, Jingiang (Yard No. Js98-012) for Pentium Pro Navigation Company Ltd., (Athena Marine Company Ltd., managers), Cyprus. (Jebsen – Hartmann Carriers). 21.9.1999: Launched. 8.4.2000: Completed. 2001: Renamed SEABOARD ROVER. 2002: Renamed ATLANTIC PRIDE. 2005: Transferred to Carbonia Shipping Ltd., (same managers), and renamed SEABOARD CHILE II.

9190119
JH.12. ATLANTIC POWER (2000 – 2001) A Class
12,993g. 5,894n. 17451d. 143.15 (BB) x 22.80 x 8.300 metres oa.
7-cyl. 2 S.C.S.A. (420 x 1,360mm) B&W 7L42MC type oil engine made by Hudong Shipyard, Shanghai. 8,523 bhp. 15 kts. Thwartship thrust controllable pitch propeller forward.
Ice strengthened general cargo vessel with two 45-ton cranes and a container capacity of 1080 TEU.
17.4.1998: Keel laid by Jingiang Shipyard, Jingiang (Yard No. Js98-013) for Acer Pro Navigation Company Ltd., (Athena Marine Company Ltd., managers), Cyprus. (Jebsen – Hartmann Carriers). 22.10.1999: Launched. 11.5.2000: Completed. 2001: Renamed SEABOARD POWER.

9220976
JH.13. SANDNES (2) (2000 – 2001) S Class
19,743g. 10,718n. 31,300d. 171.59 (BB) x x 9.550 metres oa.
6-cyl. 2 S.C.S.A. (520 x 1,600mm) Mitsubishi 6UEC52LA type oil engine made by Akasaka Tekkosho KK, (Akasaka Diesels Ltd.), Yaizu. 9,599 bhp. 14.5 kts.
Bulk carrier with four 30-ton cranes capable of operating grabs carried aboard.
Ordered from Saiki Jukoggo KK, Saiki (Yard No. 1107), for Groupero Shipping Inc., (Athena Marine Company Ltd., managers), Cyprus. 1.6.2000: Keel laid. 10.3.2000: Launched. 19.10.2000: Completed. 2001: Renamed UBC SAVANNAH.

STORNES arriving Port Adelaide 22 June 2001.   (World Ship Society Photograph Library)

9220988
JH.14. STORNES (2001) S Class
19,743g. 10,718n. 31,923d. 171.60 (BB) x   x   10.400 metres oa.
6-cyl. 2 S.C.S.A. (520 x 1,600mm) Mitsubishi 6UEC52LA type oil engine made by Akasaka Tekkosho KK, (Akasaka Diesels Ltd.), Yaizu. 9,599 bhp. 14.5 kts.
Bulk carrier with four 30-ton cranes capable of operating grabs carried aboard.
Ordered from Saiki Jukoggo KK, Saiki (Yard No. 1108), for Mundi Shipping Inc, (Athena Marine Company Ltd., managers), Cyprus.   10.8.2000: Keel laid. 20.10.2000: Launched. 10.12.2001: Completed. 2001: Renamed UBC SEATTLE. 2005: Sold to Mundi Shipping Company Ltd., Limassol, Cyprus, (same managers), and renamed SEATTLE.

9236078
JH.15. SPRAYNES (3) (2001) S Class
19,743g. 10,718n. 31,828d. 171.59 (BB) x   x   9.550 metres oa.
6-cyl. 2 S.C.S.A. (520 x 1,600mm) Mitsubishi 6UEC52LA type oil engine made by Akasaka Tekkosho KK, (Akasaka Diesels Ltd.), Yaizu. 9,599 bhp. 14.5 kts.
Bulk carrier with four 30-ton cranes capable of operating grabs carried aboard.
Ordered from Saiki Jukoggo KK, Saiki (Yard No. 1111), for Southern King Shipping.Ltd., (Athena Marine Company Ltd., managers), Cyprus. 26.4.2001: Keel laid. 27.6.2001: Launched. 28.8.2001: Completed as SPRAYNES.   11.2001: Renamed UBC SYDNEY.

9236080
JH.16. STEMNES (2001) S Class
19,743g. 10,718n. 31,828d. 171.59 (BB) x   x   9.550 metres oa.
6-cyl. 2 S.C.S.A. (520 x 1,600mm) Mitsubishi 6UEC52LA type oil engine made by Akasaka Tekkosho KK, (Akasaka Diesels Ltd.), Yaizu. 9,599 bhp. 14.5 kts.
Bulk carrier with four 30-ton cranes capable of operating grabs carried aboard.
Ordered from Saiki Jukoggo KK, Saiki (Yard No. 1112), for Karlin Navigation Inc., (Athena Marine Company Ltd., managers), Cyprus. 17.6.2001: Keel laid. 23.8.2001: Launched. 24.10.2001: Completed. 11.2001: Renamed UBC SACRAMENTO.

PART 2

Time- Charters

The following are representative of a much larger charter-fleet.

FRIBORG   (World Ship Society Photograph Library)

5418006
C.1. FRIBORG   (1965 - 1970)
As built: 1,890g.   989n.   255.9 x 41.0 x 19.9 feet
Post 1960: 2,039g.   1,191n.   3,100d.   299' 2" x 41' 2" x 17' 3¾" oa.
Post 1978: 1,998g.   1,162n.   3,201d.
Post 1980: 1,567g.   1,181n.   3,201d.
As built: Four, 6-cyl. 2 S.C.S.A. (220 x 320mm) oil engines made by the shipbuilder, with hydraulic coupling and gearing to a single screw shaft.
Post 1963: 8-cyl. 4 S.C.S.A. (400 x 580mm) Deutz type oil engine made by Klockner-Humbildt-Deutz AG, Koeln. 2,300 bhp. 11 kts.
Ice strengthened, general cargo vessel with eight 3-ton derricks.
1949: Completed as TRUDVANG by Bergens Mekaniske Verksteder AS, Bergen (Yard No. 383), for Albert Schjelderups Rederi AS, (Albert Schjelderup, manager), Norway. 1959: Sold to Skibsrederi AS Star Shipping, (Per Waaler, manager), Norway, and renamed STARFIGHTER. 1960: Lengthened. 1963: Sold to O. H. Melling, Norway, re-engined and renamed STAVBORG. 1965: Sold to Skibsrederi AS Venborg, (Frimann Skeie, manager), Norway, and renamed FRIBORG. 1970: Sold to L'ami Shipping & Investment Company SA, Greece, and renamed UTE. (O.N. 3815). 1975: Sold to Pidaliou Tessera Shipping Company Ltd., Greece, and renamed SPYROS II 1980: Sold to Pantelis Matarangas, Panama. (O.N. 9978-PEXT). 4.5.1981: Arrived at Gadani Beach for demolition. 22.5.1981: Rashid Ltd., commenced work.

6719902
C.2. FIDUCIA (1) (1967 - 1969)
As built: 2,447g.   1,641n. 3,800d.   312' 5½" x 44' 0¼" x 19' 2¼"oa.
Post 1994:   2,451g.   1,416n.   3,780d.
6-cyl. 4 S.C.S.A. (450 x 550mm) MaK type oil engine made by Atlas-Mak Maschinenbau, Kiel. 2,300 bhp. 13.5 kts.
Ice strengthened general cargo vessel with two 10-ton and two 3½-ton derricks.
20.4.1967: Launched by Werft Nobiskrug GmbH, Rendsburg (Yard No. 654), for J. Jost, Flensburg, W. Germany.1967: Completed for Fiducia Schiffahrts Gesellschaft m.b.H., (J. Jost, manager), Flensburg. 1969: J. Jost, as managing owners acquired by Atle Jebsen. 1975: Sold to Helmsing Schiffahrts Betrieb GmbH, Singapore, and

renamed JOHN C. HELMSING. 1983: Sold to Euroafrican Shipping Ltd., (Helmsing and Grimm (GmbH & Company), managers), Cyprus.

6802216
C.3. GRATIA (1967 - 1969)
As built: 2,377g. 1,615n. 3,770d. 312' 6¼" x 43' 11¼" x 19' 2"oa.
Post 2000: 2,521g. 1,416n. 3,770d.
6-cyl. 4 S.C.S.A. (450 x 550mm) MaK type oil engine made by Atlas-Mak Maschinenbau, Kiel. 2,300 bhp. 13.5 kts.
Ice strengthened general cargo vessel with two 10-ton and two 3½-ton derricks.
21.9.1967: Launched by Werft Nobiskrug GmbH, Rendsburg (Yard No. 652), for J. Jost, Flensburg, W. Germany. 1967: Completed for Bremer Schiffahrtskontor Brink & Company, (J. Jost, manager), Flensburg. 1969: J. Jost, as managing owners acquired by Atle Jebsen. 1977: Sold to Hainsworth, Watson (UK) Ltd., Liverpool, and renamed ABDUL RAZAAK SANUSI. 1979: John Helmsing Tramp Seeschiffahrtsbetrieb GmbH, (Helmsing and Grimm GmbH & Company, managers), Panama, and renamed FIONE. 1994: Sold to Fione Panama Inc., (same managers).

LAETITIA in the Kiel Canal, 18 June 1973, with black funnel (World Ship Society Photograph Library)

6819403
C.4. LAETITIA (1968 - 1969)
2,389g. 1,607n. 3,770d. 312' 6¼" x 43' 11¼" x 19' 2½"oa.
6-cyl. 4 S.C.S.A. (450 x 550mm) MaK type oil engine made by Atlas-Mak Maschinenbau, Kiel. 2,300 bhp. 13.5 kts.
Ice strengthened general cargo vessel with two 10-ton and two 3½-ton derricks.
26.4.1968: Launched by Werft Nobiskrug GmbH, Rendsburg (Yard No. 658), for Laetitia Schiffahrtskontor Brink & Company, (J. Jost, manager), Flensburg, W. Germany. 1968: Completed. 1969: J. Jost, as managing owners acquired by Atle Jebsen.1975: Sold to Societe Bretonne di Armement Maritime, France, and renamed POINTE DU MINOU. 1975: Sold to Condor Shipping Corp., Panama, and renamed FIRST FLIGHT. 1979: Sold to Nevada Shipping Corp., Panama, and renamed DANIE. 1981: Sold to Trans-ship Corp. Inc., Panama, and renamed BOUNTY. 1995: Demolished.

C.5. SATYA PADAM   (1973 – 1978) see ship No. 29 in owned fleet.

SATYA PADAM

(Author's collection / M.R. Dippy)

GALLIC MINCH outward from the Manchester Ship Canal.

(World Ship Society Photograph Library)

C.6. GALLIC MINCH   (1974 – 1981) see ship No. 42 in owned fleet.

GALLIC STREAM

(W. J. Harvey)

C.7. GALLIC STREAM   (1974 – 1975) see ship No. 45 in owned fleet.

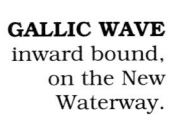

GALLIC WAVE inward bound, on the New Waterway.

(W.J. Harvey)

7421875
C.8. GALLIC WAVE (1976 – 1981)

1,599g. 1,187n. 3,076d.   83.52 x 14.13 x 5.188 metres oa.
8-cyl. 4 S.C.S.A. (320 x 450mm) MaK 8M452AK type oil engine made by MaK Maschinenbau GmbH, Kiel. 2,400 bhp. 12.5 kts.
Gearless bulk carrier. Subsequently fitted with midship mounted mast and derricks.
4.1976: Completed by Scheepsbouw en Repariebedrijf Gebrouder Sander BV, Foxhol (Yard No. 272), for Gallic Shipping Ltd., (Denholm, Maclay Company Ltd., managers), London. (O.N. 366091). 1981: Managers restyled as Denmac Ltd. 1983: Sold to North Bay Shipping Ltd., (Gallic Shipping group), (Denholm (I.O.M.)Ltd., managers), and renamed ALL STATE. (O.N. 402241), under Republic of Ireland flag. 1987: Transferred to Philippines flag, (Denholm Ship Management (UK) Ltd., appointed as managers). 1989: Renamed GLENTROOL. 1989: Sold to Blue Moon Shipping Ltd., (Blumared SA, managers), Malta, and renamed COVA DA IRIA. (O.N. 2335). 1992: Sold to Gabrielle Shipping Company Ltd, (Mata Galpa SA, managers), Malta, and renamed VALDA IR. 1994: Sold to Chahaya Selaji Inc., (Chahaya Shipping & Trading Compant Private Ltd., managers), Panama, and renamed CHAHAYA SEJATI. (O.N. 23241-PEXT). 1999: Sold to Korea Wasan Shipping Company, Nampo, North Korea, and renamed MISAN. 1.4.2003: Demolition commenced at an unspecified location.

N.B. The above vessel, as ALL STATE, was chartered for a further period as yet unidentified other than including 1989 (see below).

ALL STATE - 21 March 1989 on the River Tees. This photograph has been placed in this position to illustrate the midship conversion that had been undertaken. Similar work was also carried out on MARY ANDERSON below. (Chriss Reynolds collection)

MARY ANDERSON inward to the Manchester Ship Canal. (J. K. Byass)

7421887
C.9. MARY ANDERSON (1976 – 1981)
As built: 1,599g. 1,187n 3,100d. 83.52 x 14.13 x 5.188 metres oa.
Post 1988: 2,492g. 988n. 3,100d. 93.95 x 14.13 x 5.350 metres oa.
8-cyl. 4 S.C.S.A. (320 x 450mm) MaK 8M452AK type oil engine made by MaK Maschinenbau GmbH, Kiel. 2,400 bhp. 12.5 kts.
Gearless bulk carrier. Subsequently fitted with midship mounted mast and derricks.
6.1976: Completed by E. J. Smit & Zoon's Scheepwerven BV, Westerbroek (Yard No. 809), Gallic Shipping Ltd., (Denholm, Maclay Company Ltd., managers), London. (O.N. 366201). 1981: Managers restyled as Denmac Ltd. 1982: Sold to North Bay Shipping Ltd., (Gallic Shipping group), and renamed ARGO ISLAND. 1982: Denholm (I.O.M.) Ltd., appointed as managers, renamed MARYLANDER under Republic of Ireland, flag. (O.N. 402240). 1987: Transferred to Philippines flag, (Denholm Ship Management (UK) Ltd., appointed as managers). 1988: Sold to Transinsular – Transportes Maritimos Insulares S.a.r.L., Portugal, and lengthened and converted into a bulk cement carrier. 1989: Renamed TI OUTAO. (O.N. J-384). 1989: Sold to Branda Marine Company Ltd., (Naviera Marine America, managers), Cyprus, and renamed BRANDA. 3.10.2001: Demolition commenced at an unspecified location.

LESLIE GAULT outward from Blyth April 1981. Her funnel was still blue but the white band had been altered.
(World Ship Society Photograph Library)

7614692
C.10. LESLIE GAULT (1977 – 1981)
As built: 1,592g. 1,240n. 3,256d. 91.52 (BB) x 13.31 x 5.140 metres oa.
Post 1994: 1,991g. 1,119n. 3,256d.
16-cyl. 4 S.C.S.A. (222 x 292mm) Blackstone ESL16MRG type oil engine made by Mirrlees Blackstone (Stamford) Ltd., Stamford. 2,440 bhp. 12.5 kts.
Gearless bulk carrier.
7.1977: Completed by Appledore Shipbuilders Ltd., Appledore (Yard No. A.S. 116), for Gallic Shipping Ltd., (Denholm, Maclay Company Ltd., managers), London. (O.N. 377334). 1981: Managers restyled as Denmac Ltd. 1983: Transferred to Isle of Man flag, (Denholm (I.O.M.) Ltd., appointed as managers. Transferred to Republic of Ireland flag. (O.N. 402420). 1986: Sold to North Bay Shipping Ltd., (Gallic Shipping group),

(Denholm Ship Management (UK) Ltd., appointed as managers). 1989: Seascot Shiptrading Ltd., appointed as managers. 1992: Transferred to Gdynia, Poland flag and renamed LESZEK G, (Seascot Shipmanagement Ltd., appointed as managers). 2000: Sold to J. T. M. Shipping Ltd., Beirut, (Wilhelm Tietjen Befrachtungsges.mbH, Hamburg, managers), and renamed JAMAL, under St Vincent & The Grenadines flag. 2003: Sold to Dahani N M, Beirut, (Mody Shipping, Beirut, managers), and renamed MARUF.

GALLIC FJORD (World Ship Society Photograph Library)

7614707
C.11. GALLIC FJORD (1977 – 1981)
As built: 1,592g. 1,240n. 3,256d.   91.52 (BB) x 13.31 x 5.119 metres oa.
Post 1994: 1,991g. 1,119n. 3,256d.
16-cyl. 4 S.C.S.A. (222 x 292mm) Blackstone ESL16MRG type oil engine made by Mirrlees Blackstone (Stockport) Ltd., Stockport. 2,440 bhp. 12.5 kts.
Gearless bulk carrier.
9.1977: Completed by Appledore Shipbuilders Ltd., Appledore (Yard No. A.S. 117), for Gallic Shipping Ltd., (Denholm Maclay Company Ltd., managers), London. (O.N. 377397). 1981: Managers restyled as Denmac Ltd. 1983: Transferred to Isle of Man flag, (Denholm (I.O.M.) Ltd., appointed as managers. 1985: Sold to North Bay Shipping Ltd., (Gallic Shipping group), (Denholm (I.O.M.) Ltd., managers), Dublin, Republic of Ireland. (O.N. 402413). 1987: Transferred to Philippines flag. (O.N. 266), (Denholm Ship Management (UK) Ltd., appointed as managers). 1989: Transferred to Isle of Man flag (O.N. 377397), (Seascot Shiptrading Ltd., appointed as managers). 1993: Sold to Gallic Shipping Ltd., (Seascot Shipmanagement Ltd., managers), and renamed GAUSS F, under Vanuatu flag. (O.N. 803). 1996: Sold to Harbour Ltd., (Gerassimos P. Kavados, Greece, manager), and renamed ZOIS, under St Vincent & the Grenadines flag. 2003: Sold to Friendship Shipping, Thessaloniki (Thalatta Shinning Management, Thessaloniki, managers), and renamed FRIENDSHIP.

C.12. HITTEEN   (1983 – 1990) see ship No. 54 in owned fleet.

HITTEEN (W. J. Harvey)

KARAMEH (W. J. Harvey)

C.13. KARAMEH (1983 – 1990) see ship No. 57 in owned fleet.

8321644
C.14. JEBSEN SOUTHLAND (1984 - 1988)
As built;   10,615g. 5,694n. 14,160d. 151.01 (BB) x 22.97 x 8.302 metres oa.
Post 1994: 10,615g. 5,694n. 14,265d.
8-cyl. 4 S.C.S.A. (580 x 600mm) MaK 8M601AK type oil engine made by Krupp, MaK Maschinenbau GmbH, Kiel, geared to a controllable pitch propeller. 10,876 bhp. 16.25 kts. Thwartship thrust propeller forward.
Ice strengthened general cargo vessel with two 40-ton cranes and a fixed guide container capacity of 907 TEU. Subsequently 1080 TEU without guides.
14.11.1983: Keel laid as KARIN S by Werft Nobiskrug GmbH, Rendsburg (Yard No. 719), for Schepers & Company KG, m.s. "Karin S", W. Germany. 31.3.1984: Launched. 14.6.1984: Completed as JEBSEN SOUTHLAND. 1987: Heinrich und Rudolf Schepers GmbH, appointed as managers. 31.8.1988: Renamed KARIN S. 10.1.1989: Renamed EMCOL CARRIER. 21.12.1991: Renamed ATLANTA. 1992: Sold to West Cape Marine Company Ltd., Liberia, and renamed CCNI VALPARAISO. (O.N. 9790). 8.1994: Sold to Egon Oldendorff (Liberia) Inc. 1995: Herrera y Compania Las Palmas SA, appointed as managers, transferred to Spanish flag and renamed FRANCOLI. 1998: Sold to Mint Express Shipping SA, (Moliva Denizcilik AS, managers), Liberia, and renamed ISABELA B. 1999: Sold to Egon Oldendorff (Liberia) Inc., (Egon Oldendorff, manager),

and renamed ELSA OLDENDORFF. (O.N. 9790). 3.2000: Renamed EWL COLOMBIA. 2000: Sold to Adria Maritime Srl, Trieste, Italy, and renamed ADRIA VERDE. 2005: Renamed LT VERDE

JEBSEN AUCKLAND at Auckland 29 January 1988. Funnel repainted and Jebsen partly removed from bow
(World Ship Society Photograph Library)

7600134
C.15. JEBSEN AUCKLAND (1986 - 1988)
As built: 15,777g. 9,466n. 20,750d. 193.02 (BB) x 26.67 x 10.0 metres oa.
Post 1995:   17,379g. 8,383n. 20,754d.
7-cyl. 2 S.C.S.A. (760 x 1,550) Sulzer 7RND76M type oil engine made by the shipbuilder at Kobe. 16,800 bhp. 12.75 kts.
General cargo vessel with three 25-ton cranes, one 150-ton derrick and four 10-ton derricks and a fixed guide container capacity of 642 TEU.
8.11.1976: Keel laid as EIFFEL by Mitsubishi Heavy Industries Ltd., Yokohama (Yard No. 982), for Compagnie Generale Maritime et Financiere (C.G.M.F.), France. 17.3.1977: Launched. 23.6.1977: Completed. 1985: Sold to Compania Naviera Independencia SA, Philippines, and renamed ELMA DIEZ. (O.N. 228338). 1986: Renamed JEBSEN AUCKLAND, (Jebsens Ship Management AS (JSMA), appointed managers), under Panama flag. (O.N. 15930-86C). 1.1988: Renamed AUCKLAND. 1988: Renamed SEAS EIFFEL. 1990: Sold to Compagnie de Navigation d'Orbigny and Compania Naviera Independencia SA, (Jebsens Hamburg GmbH & Company KG, managers). 1992: Compagnie Generale Maritime (C.G.M.) appointed as managers. 1993: Renamed EIFFEL, (Compagnie de Navigation d'Orbigny, appointed as managers). 1994: Renamed CSAV RAPEL. 2000: Sold to Mrs Viking 1, and renamed SEABOARD VALPARAISO, under Bahamas flag. 2001: Renamed EIFFEL. 6.7.2001: Demolition commenced at Alang by T. D. D. Breakers. 26.10.2001: Completed.

7116872
C.16. THALASSA (1986 - 1988)
1,589g. 1,118n. 3,038d. 259' 10½" (BB) x 46' 5½" x 17' 3¾" oa.
6-cyl. 4 S.C.S.A. (400 x 580mm) Deutz RBV6M358 type oil engine made by Kloeckner-Humboldt-Deutz AG, Koeln, geared to a controllable pitch propeller. 2,000 bhp. 12.75 kts.
Ice strengthened general cargo vessel with four 5-ton Velle type derricks capable of operating grabs.
2.7.1971: Launched as RONDANE by Batservice Vaerft AS Mandal (Yard No. 573), Odd K. Mortensen, Norway. 12.12.1971: Completed for RA Almora, (Odd K. Mortensen,

Oslo, manager), Norway. 1978: Sold to Partenrederi Thalassa, Sweden, and renamed THALASSA. 1993: Sold to J. R. Shipping Ab, Sweden. 1999: Sea Partner AS, appointed as managers. 2000: Sold to Serenade Shipping Ltd., (Strand Shipping AS, managers), and renamed RONDANE, under Gibraltar flag. 2002: Sea Partner AS, appointed as managers. 2003: Sold to Newhaven Shipping Ltd., (Sea Glory Navigation Ltd., managers), and renamed LIBERO. 2004: Sold to Brookes & Partners Ltd., (Eestinova Ltd., managers), and renamed FAIRPLAY, under the Dominica flag. 2.2005: Sold to unspecified owners, retaining Dominica flag.

THALASSA although having different main machinery, was an almost identical product of the same shipbuilder as the "Tornes class" of the early 1970's and indeed was the missing yard No. in that sequence.
(World Ship Society Photograph Library)

HVALNES 5 September 1992. (World Ship Society Photograph Library)

7023805
C.17. HVALNES (1988 - 1993)
As built;   1,926g. 1,103n. 4,481d.   102.88 x 14.64 x 5.811 metres oa.
Post 1995: 2,904g. 1,333n. 4,481d.
Post 1996: 3,133g. 1,367n. 4,481d.
8-cyl. 4 S.C.S.A. (450 x 550mm) MaK 8M551AK type oil engine made by Atlas-MaK Maschinenbau, Kiel. 3,000 bhp. 13 kts.
Ice strengthened general cargo vessel.
1970: Completed as SAMBA by VEB Schiffswerft "Neptun", Rostock (Yard No. 458/1282), for Brunvall Schiffarts-Ges., W. Germany. 1972: Transferred to Singapore flag, and renamed MAMBO. 1975: Sold to Vikur h/f, Iceland, and renamed HVALVIK. (O.N. 1422). 1988: Sold to Glacier Maritime Company Ltd., (Jebsens Ship Management (Bergen) AS, managers), Cyprus, and renamed HVALNES. (O.N. 708677). 1992: Speed rating reduced to 10kts. 1993: Sold to Linz Shipping Corporation, (Osterreichischer Lloyd Ship Management GmbH, managers), Austria, and renamed LINZ. 2003: Sold to Argo Shipping Ltd., Varna, and transferred to St Vincent and The Grenadines flag.

LAURA HELENA at Terneuzen 1988, with Jebsen wave markings on bridge wing end.
(World Ship Society Photograph Library)

8411695
C.18. LAURA HELENA (1) (1988 - 1992)
1,861g. 1,024n. 3,030d.   91.01 x 11.41 x 4.700 metres oa.
6-cyl. 4 S.C.S.A. (230 x 320mm) MWM TBD444-6 type oil engine made by Motoren Werke Mannheim AG (MWM), Mannheim, geared to a controllable pitch propeller. 1,170 bhp. 10 kts. Thwartship thrust propeller forward.
General cargo vessel with a capacity for 72 TEU containers.
28.11.1984: Launched as IERSEZEE by BV Scheepswerf "Waterhuizen" J. Pattje, Waterhuizen (Yard No. 358), for Noordlijn BV, Holland. 1985: Completed as KAAP HOORN for Kustvaartrederij CV, (Scheepvaartbedrijf "Poseidon" BV, managers), Holland. (O.N. 21844). 1988: Sold to Supership Maritime Company Ltd., (Reederei Alfred Hartmann KG, Leer, managers), Cyprus, and renamed LAURA HELENA. (O.N. 708458). 1990: Hartmann Schiffarhtsges mbH & Company KG., appointed as managers. 1992: Sold to Coral Springs Shipping Company Ltd., (Hansel Schiffahrtsges mbH, Leer, managers), Cyprus, and renamed KARLA D. 1997: Sold to Afran Zenith Shipping Company Ltd., (Hartmann Schiffarhtsges mbH & Company KG, Leer, managers), Cyprus, and renamed LOFOU. 2002: Intership Navigation Company Ltd., Limassol, appointed as managers. 2004: Sold to Eastern Progress Inc, Istanbul,

(Naiboglu Denizcilik Ticaret Kollektif Sirketi Hacsanpasa Tugfacibasi, Istanbul, managers), and renamed HATICE C, under St Vincent and The Grenadines flag.

SAVA LAKE (Internet source)

8719073
C.19. SAVA LAKE (1990 – 1995)
2,030g. 888n. 3,050d. 74.65 (BB) x 12.70 x 6.020 metres oa.
8-cyl. 4 S.C.S.A. (250 x 300mm) Normo KRM-8 type oil engine made by BMV Bergen Diesel AS, Bergen, geared to a controllable pitch propeller. 1,801 bhp. 12 kts. Thwartship thrust controllable pitch propeller in tunnel forward.
Ice strengthened gearless bulk carrier, with a container capacity of 98 TEU.
16.8.1989: Launched by Brodogradaliste Sava Macvanska, Mitrovica (Yard No. 297) for Fonnbulk AS, (Mikkal Myklebusthaug, manager), Norway. (O.N. N00978). 7.1990: Completed. 1992: Sold to Partenrederi Mons K. Mellingen og Nils Olav Mellingen (Nils Olav Melingen, manager), Panama. (O.N. 22185-PEXT). 1993: Sold to AS Sava Lake (same manager), Panama. (O.N. 20855-93A). 1997: (O.N. altered to 20855-93B). 1999: (O.N. altered to 20855-93C). 12.2002: Sold to Fri Sava AS, Kopervik, (Kopervik Ship Management AS, managers), and transferred to Bahamas flag.

8719085
C.20. SAVA RIVER (1990 – 1995)
2,030g. 888n. 3,050d. 74.65 (BB) x 12.70 x 6.020 metres oa.
8-cyl. 4 S.C.S.A. (250 x 300mm) Normo KRM-8 type oil engine made by BMV Bergen Diesel AS, Bergen, geared to a controllable pitch propeller. 1,801 bhp. 12 kts. Thwartship thrust controllable pitch propeller in tunnel forward.
Ice strengthened gearless bulk carrier, with a container capacity of 98 TEU.
16.12.1989: Launched by Brodogradaliste Sava Macvanska, Mitrovica (Yard No. 298) for Fonnbulk AS, (Mikkal Myklebusthaug, manager), Norway, (NIS). (O.N. 20670). 10.1990: Completed. 1992: Sold to Myklebusthaug Shipping AS., (Haugship AS, managers), Panama. (O.N. 22184-PEXT). 1993: (O.N. 20830-93). 2000: Sold to Nes HF Skipafelag, Iceland, and renamed HAUKUR under Norway NIS flag.

SAVA RIVER At Falmouth 15 August 1997   (Chriss Reynolds collection)

SAVA HILL At Rochefort 1993. Note the travelling deck crane – not recorded in Lloyds Register.
(Chriss Reynolds collection)

8719097
C.21. SAVA HILL   (1991 – 1996)
2,026g. 885n. 3,080d. 74.65 (BB) x 12.70 x 6.020 metres oa.
8-cyl. 4 S.C.S.A. (250 x 300mm) Normo KRM-8 type oil engine made by BMV Bergen Diesel AS, Bergen, geared to a controllable pitch propeller. 1,801 bhp. 12 kts. Thwartship thrust controllable pitch propeller in tunnel forward.
Ice strengthened bulk carrier, with a mobile gantry crane and a container capacity of 98 TEU.
11.6.1990: Launched by Brodogradaliste Sava Macvanska, Mitrovica (Yard No. 299) for Fonnbulk AS, (Mikkal Myklebusthaug, manager), Norway, (NIS). (O.N. 20700). 2.1991: Completed. 1992: Sold to Toromi AS., (Haugship AS, managers), Panama. (O.N. altered to 22186-PEXT). 1994: (O.N. altered to 22186-PEXT3). 1995: (O.N. altered to 20821-93A). 1996: (O.N. altered to 20821-93B). 2000: Sold to Mikkal Myklebusthaug Rederi. (O.N. altered to 20821-93C).

SAVA STAR   (Chriss Reynolds collection)

8719102
C.22. SAVA STAR   (1992 – 1997)
2,026g. 885n. 3,080d. 74.65 (BB) x 12.70 x 6.020 metres oa.
8-cyl. 4 S.C.S.A. (250 x 300mm) Normo KRM-8 type oil engine made by BMV Bergen Diesel AS, Bergen, geared to a controllable pitch propeller. 1,801 bhp. 12 kts. Thwartship thrust controllable pitch propeller in tunnel forward.
Ice strengthened gearless bulk carrier, with a container capacity of 98 TEU.
7.10.1991: Launched by Brodogradaliste Sava Macvanska, Mitrovica (Yard No. 300) for PR Gard Gullaksen & Sonner, (Gard Gallaksen, manager), Panama, (O.N. 22183-PEXT). 5.1992: Completed. 1993: Sold to Fonnship AS, (O.N. 20832-93A). 1997: (O.N. altered to 20832-93B). 1999: Tripan ship Management AS appointed as managers. (O.N. altered to 20832-93C). 12.2000: Gullfonn Management AS, Fonnes, managers), converted into a tanker, and renamed ORASTAR, under Norway NIS flag.

8901585
C.23. WISLANES   (1992 - 1999)
As built: 9,815g.   4,799n.   13,790d.   143.70 (BB) x 20.99 x 8.420 metres oa.
Post 1995: 9,815g.   4,798n.   11,700d.

6-cyl. 2 S.C.S.A. (500 x 1,620mm) B&W 6L50MCE type oil engine made by H. Cegielski Z.P.M., Poznan. 5,182 bhp. 13.5 kts.

Ice strengthened general cargo vessel with one 12.5 ton and four 16-ton cranes capable of operating grabs carried aboard. The 16-ton cranes can work in tandem to provide a 32-ton lift.

1989: Ordered as WISLA from Stocznia Szczecinska SA, Szczecin (Yard No. B567/01), by Polish Steamship Company (Polska Zegluga Morska), Szczecin, Poland. 19.12.1990: Keel laid. 27.6.1991: Launched for Wisla Shipping Company Ltd., Szczecin, (Polish Steamship Company (Polska Zegluga Morska), Szczecin, managers), under the Vanuatu flag.. 23.4.1992: Completed as WISLANES. 1995: Polsteam Shorttramp Ltd., appointed as managers. 1999: Renamed WISLA, (Polish Steamship Company, Szczecin, managers), retaining Vanuatu flag.

WISLANES (Internet source)

8901597
C.24. ODRANES (1992 - 1999)
9,818g. 4,798n. 13,790d. 143.70 (BB) x 20.92 x 8.429 metres oa.

6-cyl. 2 S.C.S.A. (500 x 1,620mm) B&W 6L50MCE type oil engine made by H.Cegielski Z.P.M., Poznan. 5,180 bhp. 13.5 kts.

Ice strengthened general cargo vessel with one 12.5 ton and four 16-ton cranes capable of operating grabs carried aboard. The 16-ton cranes can work in tandem to provide a 32-ton lift.

1989: Ordered as ODRA from Stocznia Szczecinska SA, Szczecin (Yard No. B567/02), by Polish Steamship Company (Polska Zegluga Morska), Szczecin, Poland. 5.7.1991: Keel laid. 11.12.1991: Launched for Odra Shipping Company Ltd., Szczecin, (Polish Steamship Company (Polska Zegluga Morska), Szczecin, managers), under the Bahamas flag. (O.N. 720800). 14.8.1992: Completed as ODRANES. 1995: Polsteam Shorttramp Ltd., appointed as managers. 1999: Renamed ODRA, (Polish Steamship Company, Szczecin, managers), retaining Bahamas flag.

WARTANES (Chriss Reynolds collection)

8902929
C.25. WARTANES (1992 - 1999)
9,815g. 4,798n. 13,790d.   143.70 (BB) x 20.92 x 8.400 metres oa.
6-cyl. 2 S.C.S.A. (500 x 1,620mm) B&W 6L50MCE type oil engine made by H. Cegielski Z.P.M., Poznan.   5,182 bhp.   13.5 kts.
Ice strengthened general cargo vessel with one 12.5 ton and four 16-ton cranes capable of operating grabs carried aboard. The 16-ton cranes can work in tandem to provide a 32-ton lift.
1989: Ordered as WARTA from Stocznia Szczecinska SA, Szczecin (Yard No. B567/03), by Polish Steamship Company (Polska Zegluga Morska), Szczecin, Poland. 27.9.1991: Keel laid. 20.3.1992: Launched for Warta Shipping Company Ltd., Szczecin, (Polish Steamship Company (Polska Zegluga Morska), Szczecin, managers), under the Bahamas flag. (O.N. 723128). 11.10.1992: Completed as WARTANES. 1995: Polsteam Shorttramp Ltd., appointed as managers. 1999: Renamed WARTA, (Polish Steamship Company, Szczecin, managers), retaining Bahamas flag.

DUBROVNIK (Chriss Reynolds Collection)

8023254
C.26. DUBROVNIK (1992-1997)
As built: 32,499g. 24,701n. 61,318d. 224.01 (BB) x 32.57 x 12.845 metres oa.
Post 1991: 35,055g. 19,173n. 61,318d.

6-cyl. 2 S.C.S.A. (760 x 1,550mm) Sulzer 6RND76M type oil engine made by the shipbuilder at Manises Works, Valencia. 14,400 bhp. 14 kts.
Gearless bulk carrier.
24.4.1983: Launched as EREAGA by Astilleros Espanoles SA, (AESA), Factoria de Puerto Real, Cadiz (Yard No. 34), for Naviera Galea SA, Bilbao, Spain. 1983: Completed. (O.N. 979). 1989: Sold to unspecified buyers, and renamed LUX WARRIOR. 1989: Sold to unspecified buyers, and renamed BIG GEORGE. 1989: Sold to Atlantic Conbulk Maritime Corporation, (Atlantska Plovidba, managers), Dubrovnik, Yugoslavia, and renamed DUBROVNIK. (O.N. 312). 1991: Sold to Dubrovnik Shipping Company Ltd., (same managers), under Malta flag. (O.N. 2900). 1997: Sold to Atlant Adria Corporation, (Atlantska Plovidba d.d., managers), Croatia, and renamed CITY OF DUBROVNIK. 1.2003: Sold to Filonos Maritime SA, Piraeus, (Arion Shipping SA, Piraeus, managers), and renamed MIGHTY MICHALIS, under Malta flag.

NIDANES at Sydney 19 July 1993. (World Ship Society Photograph Library)

8902931
C.27. NIDANES   (1993 - 1999)
9,815g. 4,798n. 13,790d. 143.70 (BB) x 20.92 x 8.440 metres oa.
6-cyl. 2 S.C.S.A. (500 x 1,620mm) B&W 6L50MCE type oil engine made by H. Cegielski Z.P.M., Poznan. 5,182 bhp. 13.5 kts.
Ice strengthened general cargo vessel with one 12.5 ton and four 16-ton cranes capable of operating grabs carried aboard. The 16-ton cranes can work in tandem to provide a 32-ton lift.
1989: Ordered as NIDA from Stocznia Szczecinska SA, Szczecin (Yard No. B567/04), by Polish Steamship Company (Polska Zegluga Morska), Szczecin, Poland. 27.2.1992: Keel laid. 31.7.1992: Launched for Nida Shipping Company Ltd., Szczecin, (Polish Steamship Company (Polska Zegluga Morska), Szczecin, managers), under the Bahamas flag. (O.N. 723153). 1.2.1993: Completed as NIDANES. 1995: Polsteam Shorttramp Ltd., appointed as managers. 1999: Renamed NIDA, (Polish Steamship Company, Szczecin, Szczecin, managers), retaining Bahamas flag.

8719114
C.28. SAVA OCEAN (1993 – 199)
2,030g. 888n. 3,050d. 74.65 (BB) x 12.70 x 6.020 metres oa.
8-cyl. 4 S.C.S.A. (250 x 300mm) Normo KRM-8 type oil engine made by BMV Bergen Diesel AS, Bergen, geared to a controllable pitch propeller. 1,801 bhp. 12 kts. Thwartship thrust controllable pitch propeller in tunnel forward.
Ice strengthened gearless bulk carrier, with a container capacity of 98 TEU.
7.1993: Completed by Brodogradaliste Sava Macvanska, Mitrovica (Yard No. 301) for Sava Ocean AS, (Bergen Ship Management AS, managers), Panama. (O.N. 20960-93A). 1998: Managers restyled as Bship Management AS. (O.N. altered to 20960-93A). 2000: Sold to Multibulk AS, (same managers). 10.2003: Sold to Fri Ocean AS, Kopervik, (Kopervik Ship Management AS, managers), and transferred to Bahamas flag.

LAURA HELENA at Gunness Wharf, R. Trent 14 June 1994. (World Ship Society Photograph Library)

9064891
C.29. LAURA HELENA (2) (1993 -   )
2,811g. 1,688n. 4,206d. 91.20 (BB) x 13.85 x 5.753 metres oa.
6-cyl. 4 S.C.S.A. (320 x 420mm) MaK 6M453C type oil engine made by Krupp MaK Maschinenbau, Kiel, geared to a controllable pitch propeller. 2,991 bhp. 13.5 kts. Thwartship Thrust propeller forward.
Ice strengthened general cargo vessel with a container capacity of 190 TEU
7.1.1993: Keel laid by BV Scheepswerf "Waterhuizen" J. Pattje, Waterhuizen (Yard No. 384). 3.6.1993: Launched for Arctic Sea Shipping Company Ltd., Cyprus, for operation by Jebsen, Wilson Eurocarriers Ltd. 7.7.1993: Completed. (O.N. 709872). 1996: Sold to Florino Shipping Company Ltd., (Intership Navigation Company Ltd., Limassol, managers), Cyprus. 2000: Hartmann Schiffsfahrtsges mbH & Company KG, Leer, Germany, appointed as managers. 2002: Sold to Atlas Trampship Reedeerei GmbH & Company ms Sirius KG, Leer, (same managers). 2003: (Reederei Hesse GmbH & Company KG, Leer, managers).

9100164
C.30. LEKNES (3) (1994 - 1999)
2,901g. 1,693n. 4,223d. 91.09 (BB) x 13.86 x 5.748 metres oa.

6-cyl. 4 S.C.S.A. (320 x 420mm) MaK 6M453C type oil engine made by Krupp MaK Maschinenbau, Kiel, geared to a controllable pitch propeller. 2,991 bhp. 13.5 kts. Thwartship Thrust propeller forward.
Ice strengthened general cargo vessel with a container capacity of 188 TEU
7.1.1994: Keel laid as WILKE by BV Scheepswerf "Waterhuizen" J. Pattje, Waterhuizen (Yard No. 386). 22.4.1994: Launched for Briese Schiffahrts KG m.s. "Wilke", (Briese Schiffahrtsges mbH & Company KG, managers,) Germany. 4.6.1994: Completed as LEKNES under Cyprus flag. (O.N. P278). 1999: Released from charter and reverted to WILKE. 2003: Renamed WANI WILKE.

LEKNES (Author's collection / Jebsens)

FJORDNES (Jebsens)

8908856
C.31. FJORDNES (3) (1995 - 1997) Fossnes class
As Built: 11,542g. 5366n. 16,880d. 149.44 (BB) x 23.16 x 8.50 metres oa.

Post 1997: 11,829g. 3,548n. 16,880d.
6-cyl. 2 S.C.S.A. (500 x 1,620mm) B&W 6L50MCE type oil engine made by H. Cegielski Z.P.M., Poznan. 5,182 bhp. 13.5 kts.
Bulk carrier with two 25-ton cranes capable of operating grabs carried aboard.
1989: Ordered as DRAWA from Stocznia Szczecinska SA, Szczecin (Yard No. B570/03) for Polish Steamship Company (Polska Zegluga Morska), Szczecin, Poland. 19.9.1994: Keel laid. 26.11.1994: Launched as FJORDNES. 9.2.1995: Completed for Drawa Shipping Company Ltd., Nassau, (Jebsens Ship Management (Bergen) AS, managers), under the Luxembourg flag. 1996: Jebsens Ship Management Holding AS, Bergen appointed as managers. 1997: Converted into a chemical tanker and renamed KALIOPE (Polsteam Tankers Ltd., Szczecin, managers), under the Bahamas flag.

8908870
C.32. FONDNES (1995 proposed) Fossnes class
As launched:- 11,542g. 5,366n. 16,500d. 149.44 (BB) x 23.16 x 8.50 metres oa.
As completed:- 11,829g. 3,584n. 15,329d.
6-cyl. 2 S.C.S.A. (500 x 1,620mm) B&W 6L50MCE type oil engine made by H. Cegielski Z.P.M., Poznan. 5,182 bhp. 13.5 kts.
Bulk carrier with two 25-ton cranes capable of operating grabs carried aboard.
1989: Ordered as INA from Stocznia Szczecinska SA, Szczecin (Yard No. B570/05) for Ina Shipping Company Ltd., Nassau, by Polish Steamship Company (Polska Zegluga Morska), Szczecin, Poland. 5.5.1995: Keel laid as FONDNES for Jebsen pool operation (Polish Steamship Company (Polska Zegluga Morska), Szczecin, under the Luxembourg flag. 1995: Contract transferred to Ina Shipping Ltd., Nassau, under the Bahamas flag. 1.7.1995: Launched and renamed PENELOPE for completion, thence for conversion into a chemical tanker at Gdansk. 4.9.1995: Arrived at Gdansk. 20.3.1996: Completed, Polsteam Tankers Ltd., Poland, appointed as managers.

9008079
C.33. TRADENES (1996 - 2004)
4,860g. 2,196n. 6,280d. 111.60 (BB) x 18.04 x 5.813 metres oa.
6-cyl. 4 S.C.S.A. (400 x 740mm) Hanshin 6LF46 type oil engine made by Hanshin Diesel Works Ltd., Japan. 2,976 bhp. 12.75 kts.
General cargo vessel with two 25-ton cranes.
15.11.1991: Keel laid as SOCOFL TRADE by Kyokuyo Zosen KK, Chofu (Yard No. 373). 19.3.1992: Launched. 20.5.1992: Completed for Aurora Nav S. A. Panama, (Unicom Management Services (Cyprus) Ltd., managers). 1993: Transferred to Kamchalka Shipping Company, Russia. 1994: Transferred to Aurora Nav SA, (Kamchalka Shipping Company Ltd, managers), Russia. 1995: Transferred to Kamchalka Shipping Company Ltd., Russia. 1996: Transferred to Aurora Navigation SA, Panama 1997: Kamchalka Shipping Company Ltd., appointed as managers and transferred to Russia flag. 1999: Unicom Management Services (Cyprus) Ltd., appointed as managers, and transferred to Panama flag. (O.N. 20221-92C). 2.2004: Sold to Navemar Srl, Naples, and renamed TRADEN, under Italian flag.

9008081
C.34. TIDENES (1996 - 2004)
4,860g. 2,196n. 6,280d. 111.60 (BB) x 18.04 x 5.813 metres oa.
6-cyl. 4 S.C.S.A. (400 x 740mm) Hanshin 6LF46 type oil engine made by Hanshin Diesel Works Ltd., Japan. 2,976 bhp. 12.75 kts.
General cargo vessel with two 25-ton cranes.

26.1.1992: Keel laid as SOCOFL TIDE by Kyokuyo Zosen KK, Chofu (Yard No. 375). 7.5.1992: Launched. 18.7.1992: Completed for Aurora Nav S.A. Panama, (Unicom Management Services (Cyprus) Ltd., managers). 1993: Transferred to Kamchalka Shipping Company Ltd., Russia. 1996: Transferred to Aurora Navigation SA, Panama 1997: Kamchalka Shipping Company Ltd., appointed as managers and transferred to Russia flag 1999: Unicom Management Services (Cyprus) Ltd., appointed as managers, and transferred to Panama flag. (O.N. 20324-92B). 1.2004: Sold to Romeo Shipping Srl, Livorno, (Italtech, managers), and renamed SIDER TIDE, under Italian flag.

9008134
C.35. WAVENES (1996 - 2004)
4,860g. 2,196n. 6,280d. 111.30 (BB) x 18.05 x 5.800 metres oa.
6-cyl. 4 S.C.S.A. (400 x 740mm) Hanshin 6LF46 type oil engine made by Hanshin Diesel Works Ltd., Japan. 2,976 bhp. 12.75 kts.
General cargo vessel with two 25-ton cranes.
12.12.1991: Launched as SOCOFL TRUST by Yamanishi Zosen KK, Ishinomaki (Yard No.994) for Aurora Nav S. A. Panama, (Unicom Management Services (Cyprus) Ltd., managers). 9.3.1992: Launched. 9.6.1992: Completed as SOCOFL WAVE. 1993: Transferred to Kamchalka Shipping Company Ltd., Russia. 1996: Transferred to Aurora Nav S. A. Panama and renamed WAVENES. 1997: Kamchalka Shipping Company Ltd., appointed as managers and transferred to Russia flag. 1998: Unicom Management Services (Cyprus) Ltd., appointed as managers, and transferred to Panama flag. (O.N. 20245-92C). 2.2004: Sold to Euronavi Srl, Naples, and renamed ALESSANDRA, under Italian flag.

9008146
C.36. STARNES (1996 - 2004)
4,860g. 2,196n. 6,280d. 111.30 (BB) x 18.05 x 5.800 metres oa.
6-cyl. 4 S.C.S.A. (400 x 740mm) Hanshin 6LF46 type oil engine made by Hanshin Diesel Works Ltd., Japan. 2,976 bhp. 12.75 kts.
General cargo vessel with two 25-ton cranes.
12.3.1991: Keel laid as SOCOFL STAR by Yamanishi Zosen KK, Ishinomaki (Yard No.995). 9.6.1992: Launched. 6.9.1992: Completed for Aurora Nav S. A. Panama, (Unicom Management Services (Cyprus) Ltd., managers). 1996: Renamed STARNES. 1997: Kamchalka Shipping Company Ltd., appointed as managers and transferred to Russia flag. 1999: Unicom Management Services (Cyprus) Ltd., appointed as managers, and transferred to Panama flag. (O.N. 20397-92B). 4.2004: Sold to CIC Breves Shipping AS, (Clipper International Carriers), Svendborg, (CEC Shipmanagement AS, managers), and renamed CIC BREVES, under the Bahamas flag.

9127045
C.38. SALTNES (4) (1997 - 1999)
11,474g. 6,343n. 18,596d. 144.75 x   x 9.050 metres oa.
8-cyl. 2 S.C.S.A. (350 x 1400mm) B&W 8S35MC type oil engine made by Hyundai Heavy Industries, Engine & Machinery Division, Ulsan. 7,600 bhp. 13.5 kts.
Bulk carrier with four 30-ton cranes.
25.10.1995: Keel laid as APISARA NAREE by Chunggu Marine Industry Company, Ulsan (Yard No. 1096). 22.7.1996: Launched. 22.11.1996: Completed for Precious Lagoons Ltd., Bangkok, (Great Circle Shipping Agency Ltd., managers), Thailand. (O.N. 391000371). 1997: Renamed SALTNES. 1999: Released early from 5-year charter and

reverted to APISARA NAREE. 2000: Precious Shipping Public Ltd., Bangkok, appointed as managers.

9127057
C.38. SOLNES (1) (1997 - 1999)
11,474g. 6,343n. 18,596d. 144.75 x x 9.650 metres oa.
8-cyl. 2 S.C.S.A. (350 x 1400mm) B&W 8S35MC type oil engine made by Hyundai Heavy Industries, Engine & Machinery Division, Ulsan. 7,600 bhp. 13.5 kts.
Bulk carrier with four 30-ton cranes.
27.5.1996: Keel laid as BUSSARA NAREE by Chunggu Marine Industry Company, Ulsan (Yard No. 1097). 5.12.1996: Launched. 26.3.1997: Completed for Precious Cliffs Ltd., Bangkok, (Great Circle Shipping Agency Ltd., managers), Thailand. (O.N. 391001636). 1997: Renamed SOLNES. 1999: Released early from 5-year from charter and reverted to BUSSARA NAREE. 2000: Precious Shipping Public Ltd., Bangkok, appointed as managers.

ARTNES (Internet source)

9008055
C.39. ARTNES (1997 - 2004)
4,860g. 2,196n. 6,262d. 111.60 (BB) x 18.04 x 5.813 metres oa.
6-cyl. 4 S.C.S.A. (400 x 740mm) Hanshin 6LF46 type oil engine made by Hanshin Diesel Works Ltd., Akashi, Japan. 2,976 bhp. 12.75kts.
General cargo vessel with two 25-ton cranes.
23.7.1991: Keel laid as ARTEM by Kyokuyo Zosen KK, Chofu (Yard No. 371). 12.11.1991: Launched. 14.1.1992: Completed for Kamchalka Shipping Company Ltd., Russia. 1997: Transferred to Aurora Nav S. A. Panama, (Unicom Management Services (Cyprus) Ltd., managers), and renamed ARTNES. (O.N. 20171-92C). 1.2004: Sold to Navemar Srl, Naples, and renamed ARTNE, under Italian flag.

A Selection Of General Arrangement Plans

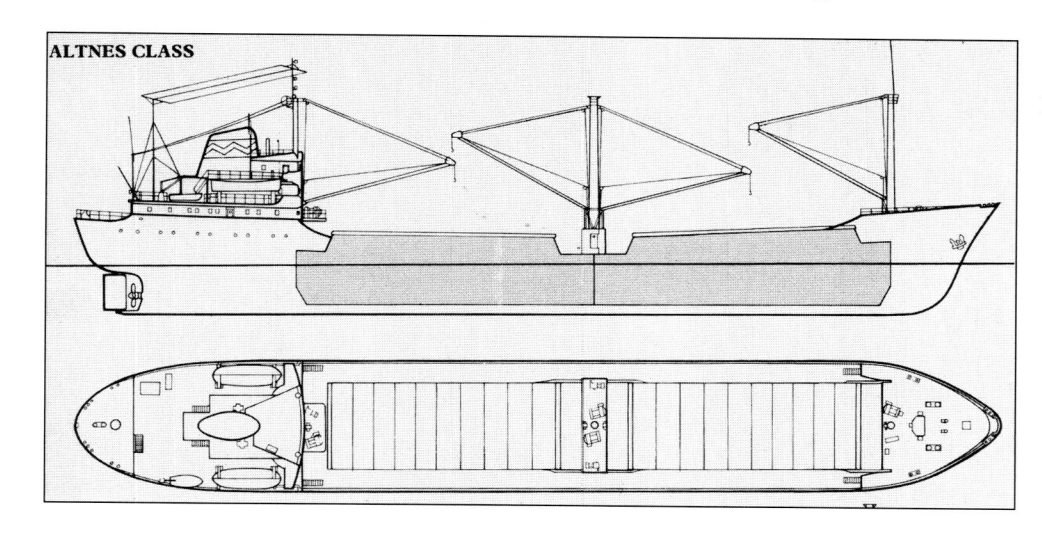

Fr. Lürssen Werft GmbH & Company, Bremen-Vegesak

ALTNES (Yd. No. 13366)
KORSNES (Yd. No. 13367)
GARNES (Yd. No. 13368)
TELNES (Yd. No. 13399)

Werft Nobiskrug GmbH, Rendsburg.

GRATIA (Yd. No. 652)
FIDUCIA (Yd. No. 654)
LAETITIA (Yd. No. 658)

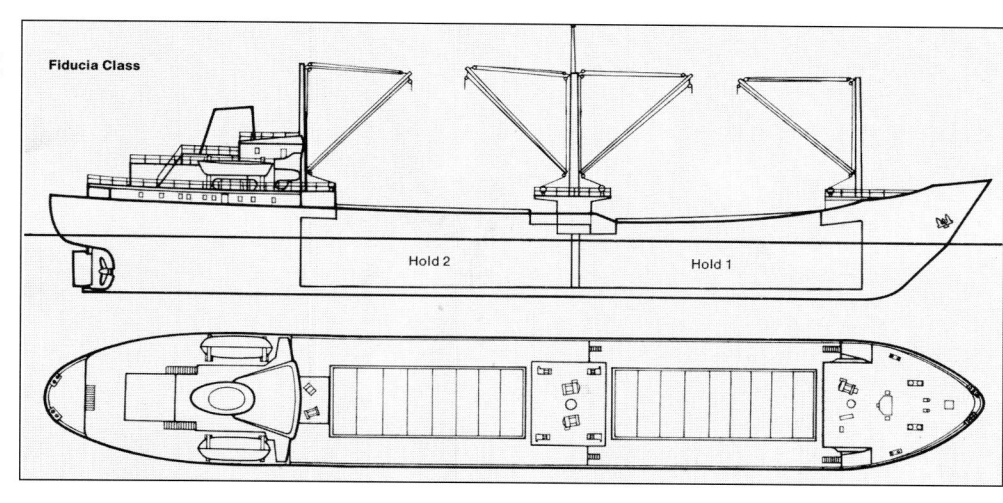

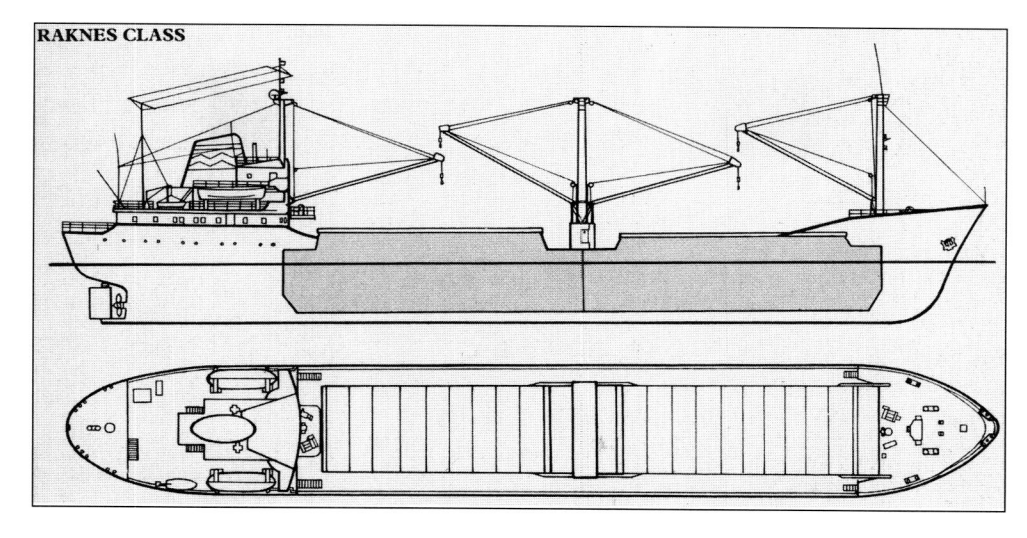

Fr. Lürssen Werft GmbH & Company, Bremen-Vegesak

RAKNES (Yd. No. 13369)
LEKNES (Yd. No. 13388)
VIGSNES (Yd. No. 13390)
TINNES (Yd. No. 13396)

Fr. Lürssen Werft GmbH & Company, Bremen-Vegesak

FRINES
(Yd. No. 13385)

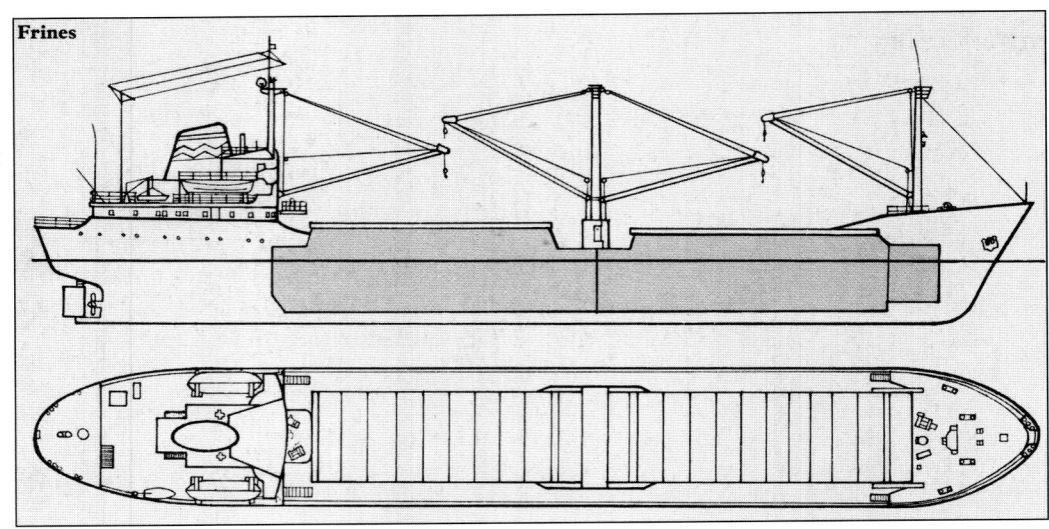

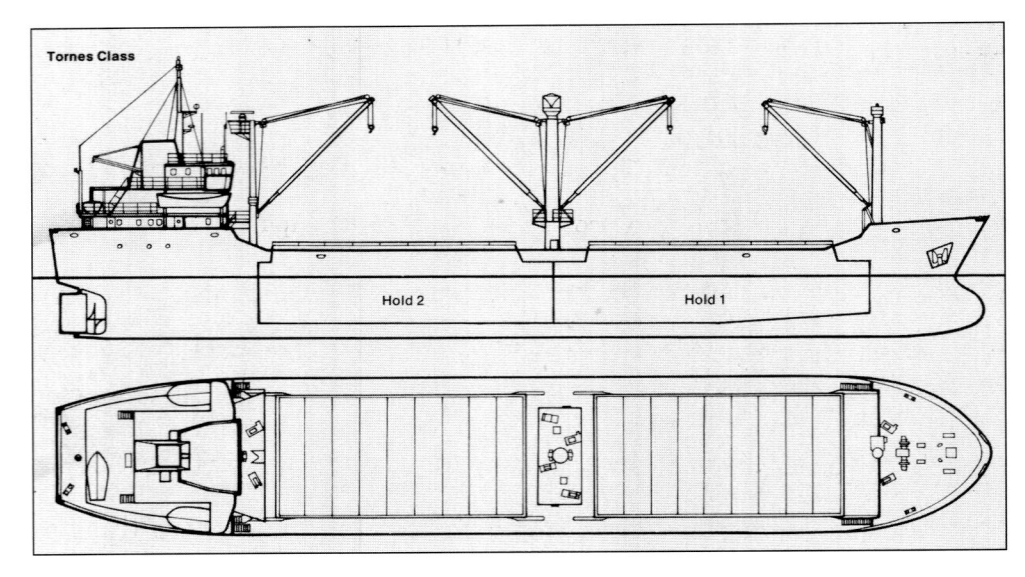

Baatservice Vaerft AS. Mandal.

TORNES
(Yd. No. 571)

FONNES
(Yd. No. 572)

THALASSA
(Yd. No. 573)

MORNES
(Yd. No. 574)

Fr. Lürssen Werft GmbH & Company, Bremen-Vegesak

JENNES
(Yd. No. 13397)

BRINKNES
(Yd. No. 13398)

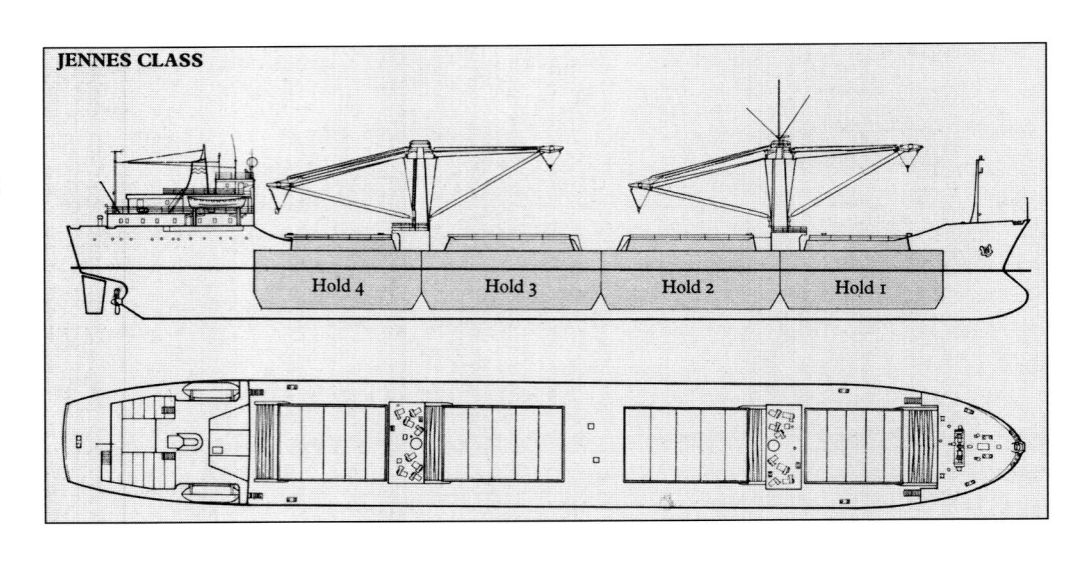

BAUGNES CLASS

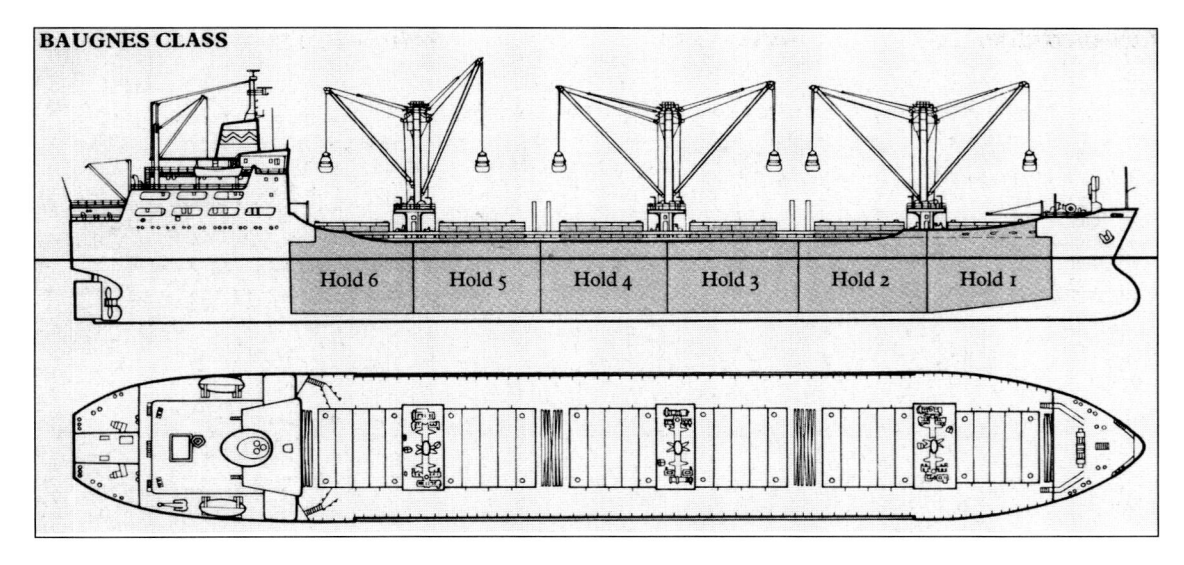

Hold 6 Hold 5 Hold 4 Hold 3 Hold 2 Hold 1

Lithgows Ltd., Port Glasgow.

       BRUNES   (Yd. No. 1172)

Lithgows (1969) Ltd., East Yard, Port Glasgow.

       BAUGNES   (Yd. No. 1173)
       BRISKNES   (Yd. No. 1174)
BAKNES   (Yd. No. 1175) sub-contracted to Scott's Shipbuilding Company (1969) Ltd. Greenock
BULKNES   (Yd. No. 1176) sub-contracted to Scott's Shipbuilding Company (1969) Ltd. Greenock
       BROOKNES (Yd. No. 1177)
       BLIDNES   (Yd. No. 1178)
BINSNES   (Yd. No. 1179) sub-contracted to Scott's Shipbuilding Company (1969) Ltd. Greenock

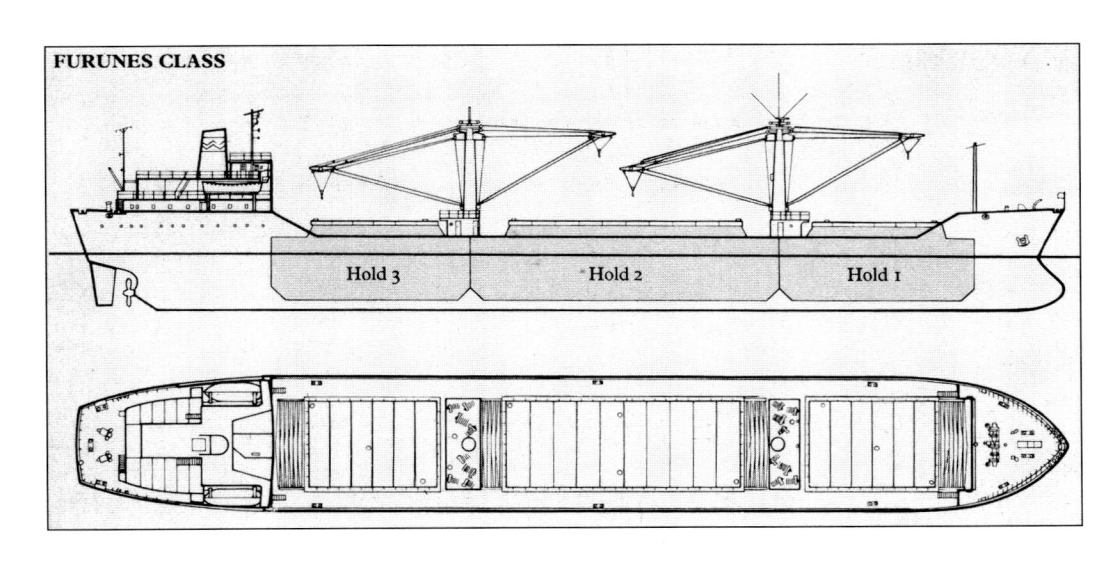

FURUNES CLASS

Hold 3 Hold 2 Hold 1

Fr. Lürssen Werft GmbH & Company, Bremen-Vegesak

       FURUNES   (Yd. No. 13400)
       FJORDNES   (Yd. No. 13420)
       FALKNES   (Yd. No. 13425)

SWIFTNES CLASS

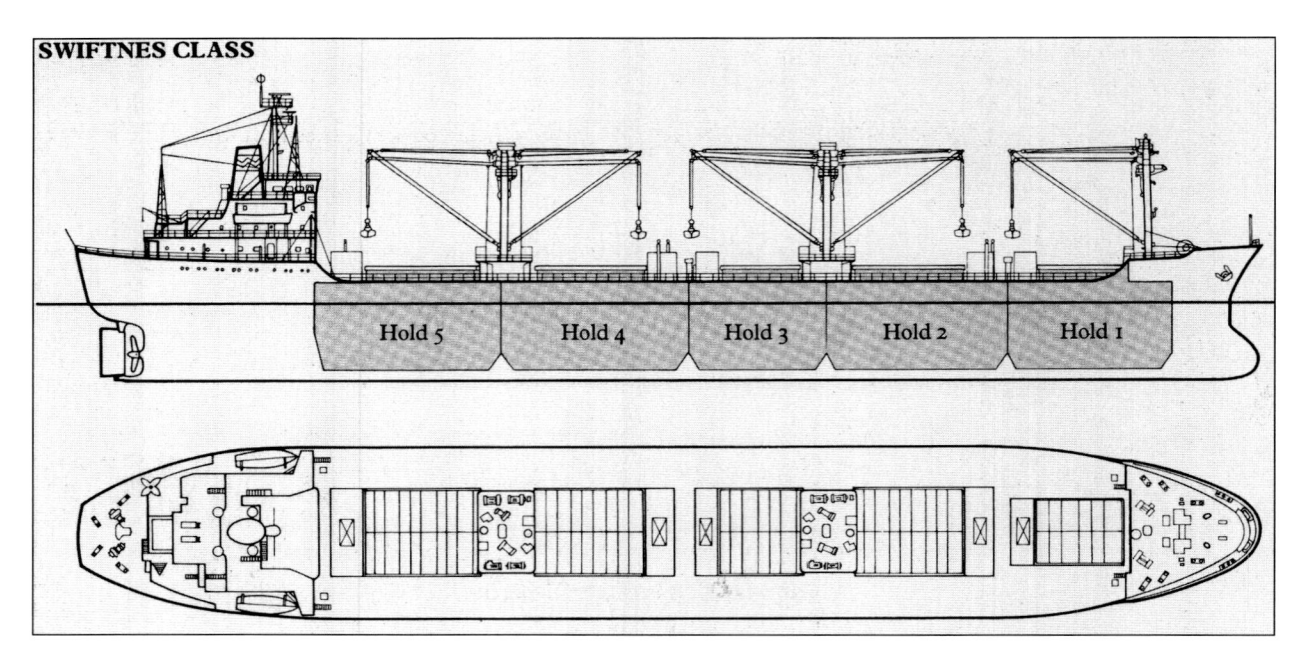

Nippon Kokan K. K., Shimizu

SALTNES (Yd. No. 306)
SEALNES (Yd. No. 307)
SHARPNES (Yd. No. 308)
SURENES (Yd. No. 312)
SWIFTNES (Yd. No. 315)
SPRAYNES (Yd. No. 316)

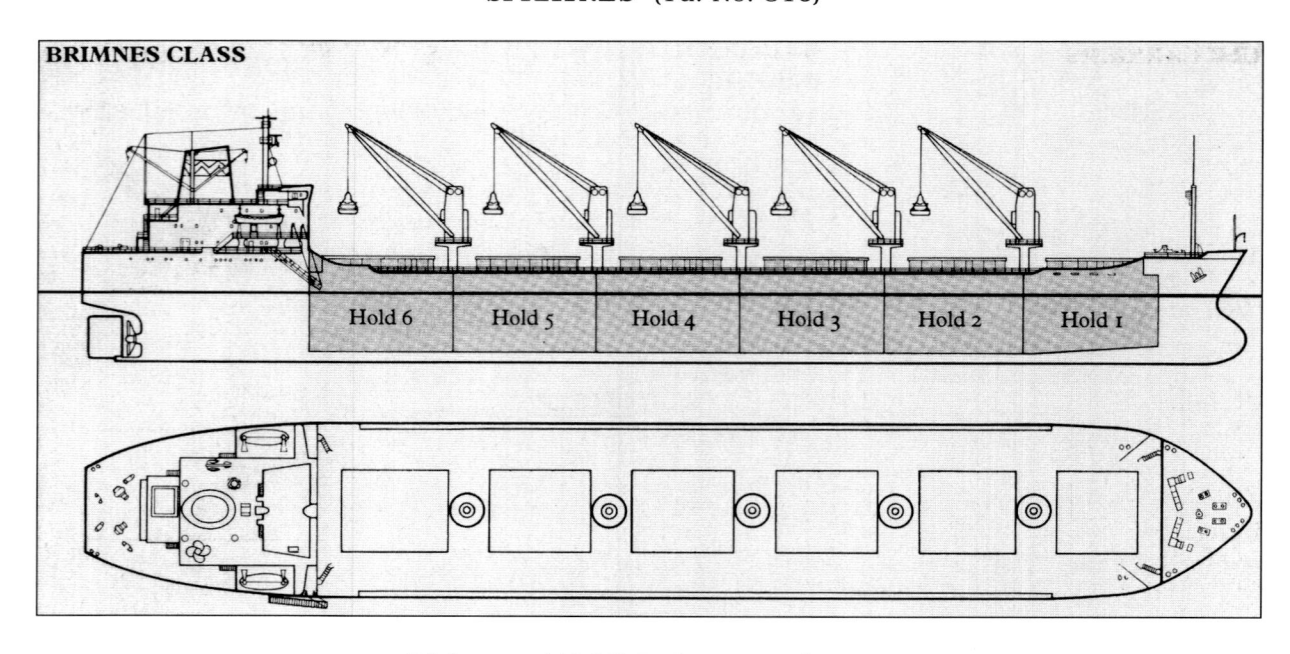

BRIMNES CLASS

Lithgows (1969) Ltd., Port Glasgow

BRIMNES (Yd. No. 1184)
BERNES (Yd. No. 1185)
BRAVENES (Yd. No. 1186)

ROSSNES CLASS

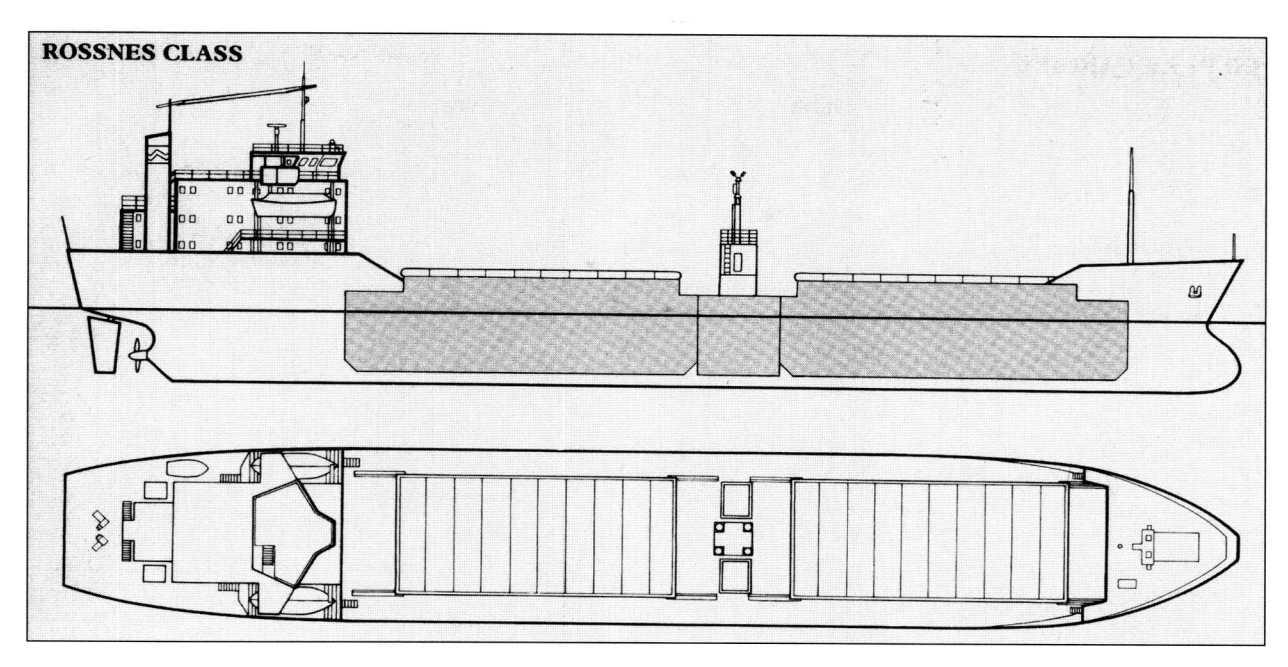

Kleven Mekaniske Verksteder AS, Ulsteinvik	G. Eides, Sonner AS, Hoylandsbygd.	Brodrene Lothe AS, Haugesund.
REFSNES (Yd. No. 26)	**ROSSNES** (Yd. No. 100)	**RAMNES** (Yd. No. 34)
RIKNES (Yd. No. 27)	**RONNES** (Yd. No. 101)	**ROGNES** (Yd. No. 35)
RAFNES (Yd. No. 28)	**RADNES** (Yd. No. 102)	**REKSNES** (Yd. No. 36)

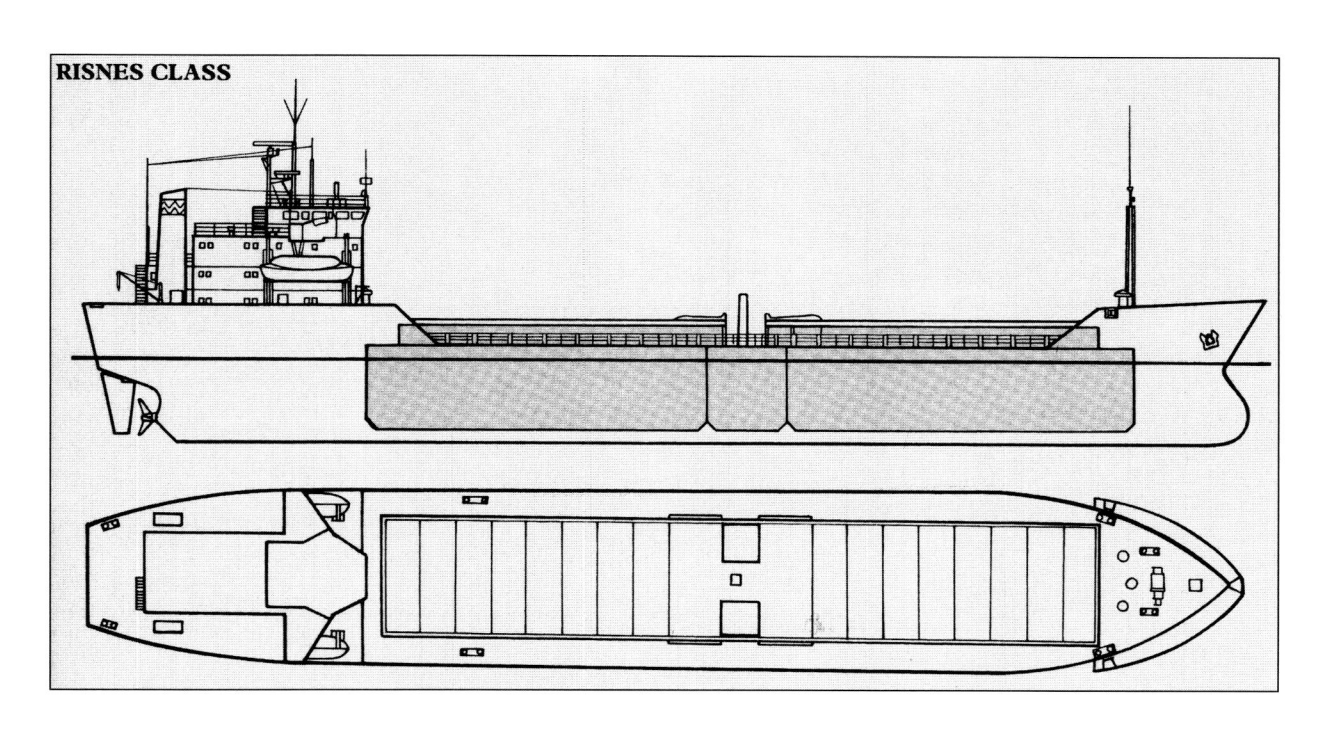

RISNES CLASS

Appledore Shipbuilders Ltd., Appledore

RISNES (Yd. No. A.S. 105)	**OPTION 1** (Yd. No. A.S. 109) **contract sold**.
RINGNES (Yd. No. A.S. 106)	**OPTION 2** (Yd. No. A.S. 110) **contract sold**.
ROCKNES (Yd. No. A.S. 107)	**OPTION 3** (Yd. No. A.S. 111) **contract sold**.
ROLLNES (Yd. No. A.S. 108)	

BIRKNES CLASS

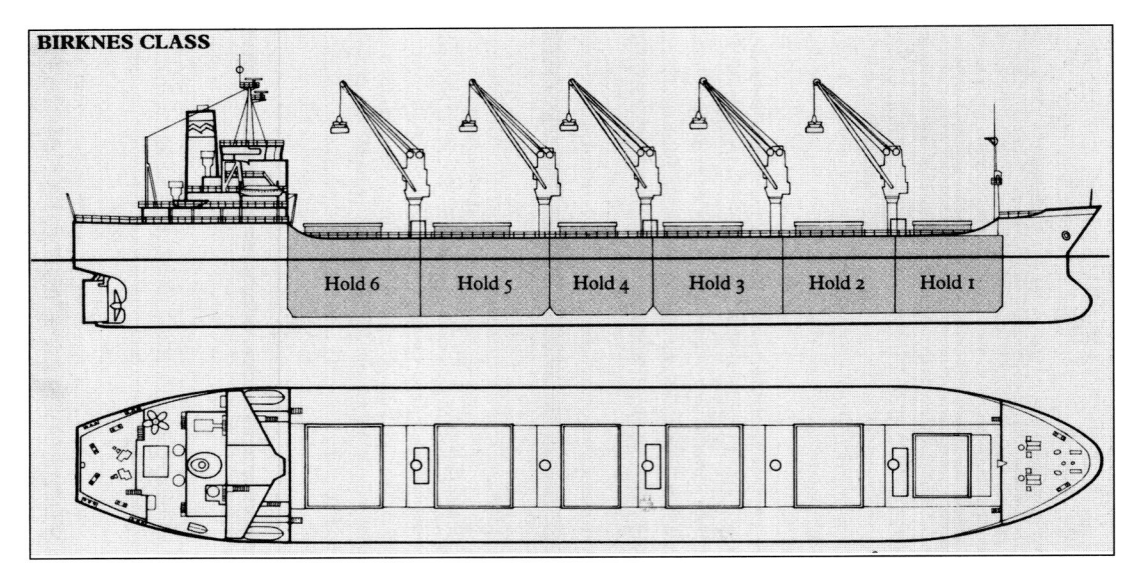

Hold 6 | Hold 5 | Hold 4 | Hold 3 | Hold 2 | Hold 1

Nippon Kokan K. K., Shimizu

BIRKNES (Yd. No. 331)
BERGNES (Yd. No. 332)
BELLNES (Yd. No. 335)
BRAVENES (Yd. No. 340)
BOLNES (Yd. No. 351)
BROOKNES (Yd. No. 352)
CANCELLED (Yd. No. 353)
   BULKNES proposed.
BECKNES (Yd. No. 354)

BRISKNES (Yd. No. 355)
CANCELLED (Yd. No. 356)
   BARNES proposed.
CANCELLED (Yd. No. 357)
   BRINKNES proposed.
CANCELLED (Yd. No. 358)
   BAUGNES proposed.
BORGNES (Yd. No. 359)

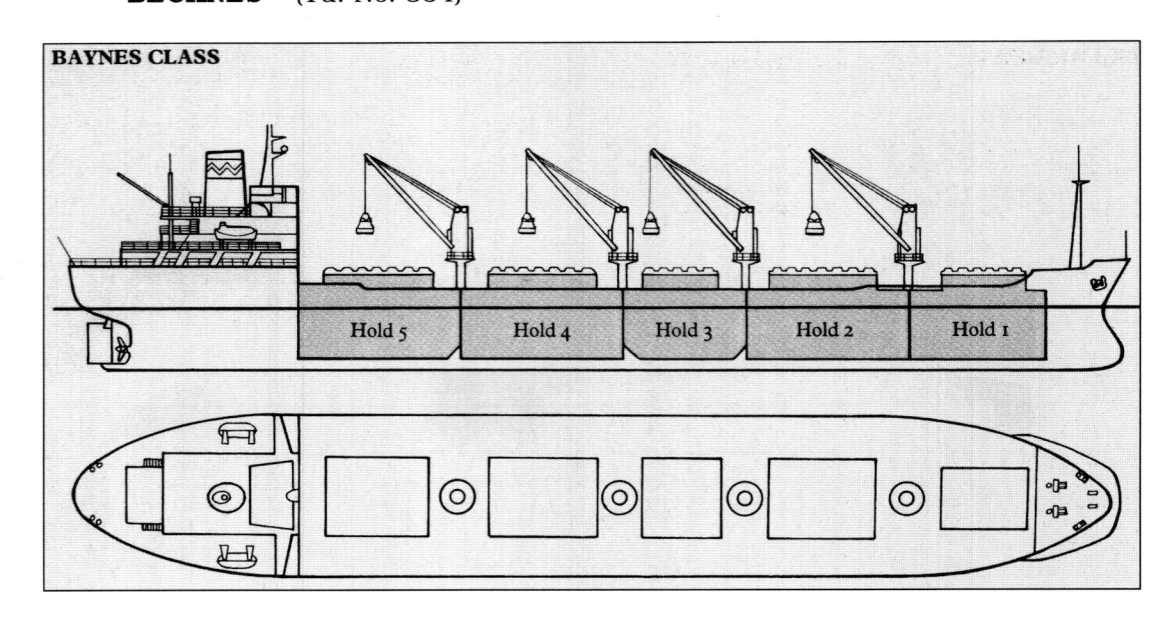

BAYNES CLASS

Hold 5 | Hold 4 | Hold 3 | Hold 2 | Hold 1

Sumitomo Heavy Industries Ltd., Uraga

CANCELLED (Yd. No. 985)
   BLIDNES proposed.
BINSNES (Yd. No. 986)
BESSNES (Yd. No. 987)
BARKNES (Yd. No. 988)

BAYNES (Yd. No. 989)
CANCELLED (Yd. No. 990)
   BOLDNES proposed.
BERGNES (Yd. No. 1000)
BRUNES (Yd. No. 1047)

FONNES CLASS

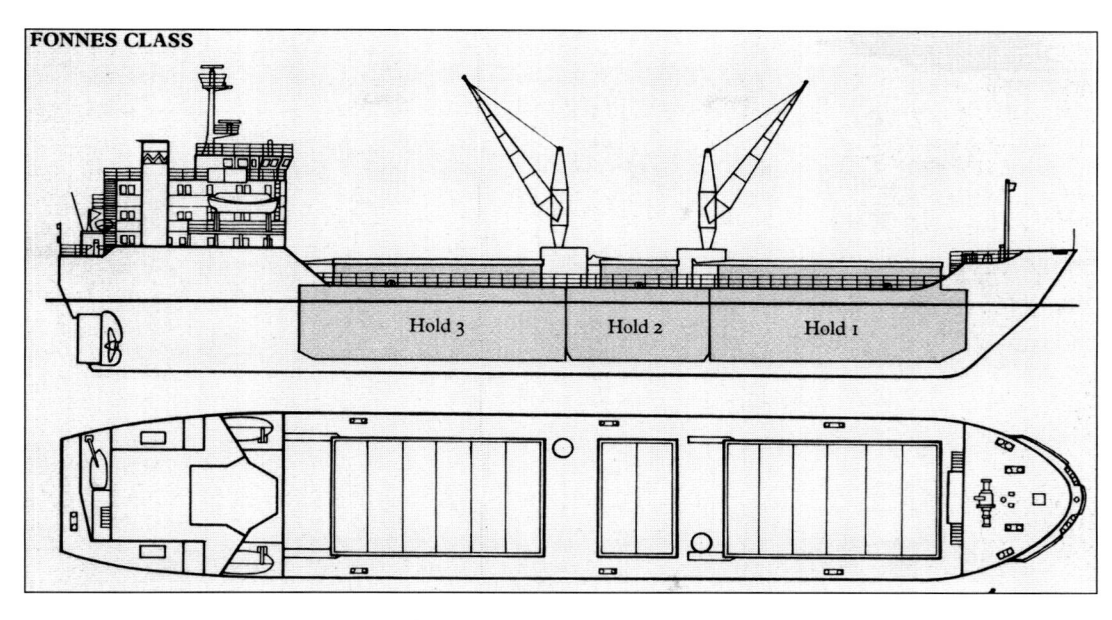

Fr. Lürssen Werft GmbH & Company, Bremen-Vegesak

	FONNES	(Yd. No. 13454)
	FRAMNES	(Yd. No. 13455)
CANCELLED	(Yd. No. 13456) - **FAIRNES** proposed
CANCELLED	(Yd. No. 13457) - **FULLNES** proposed

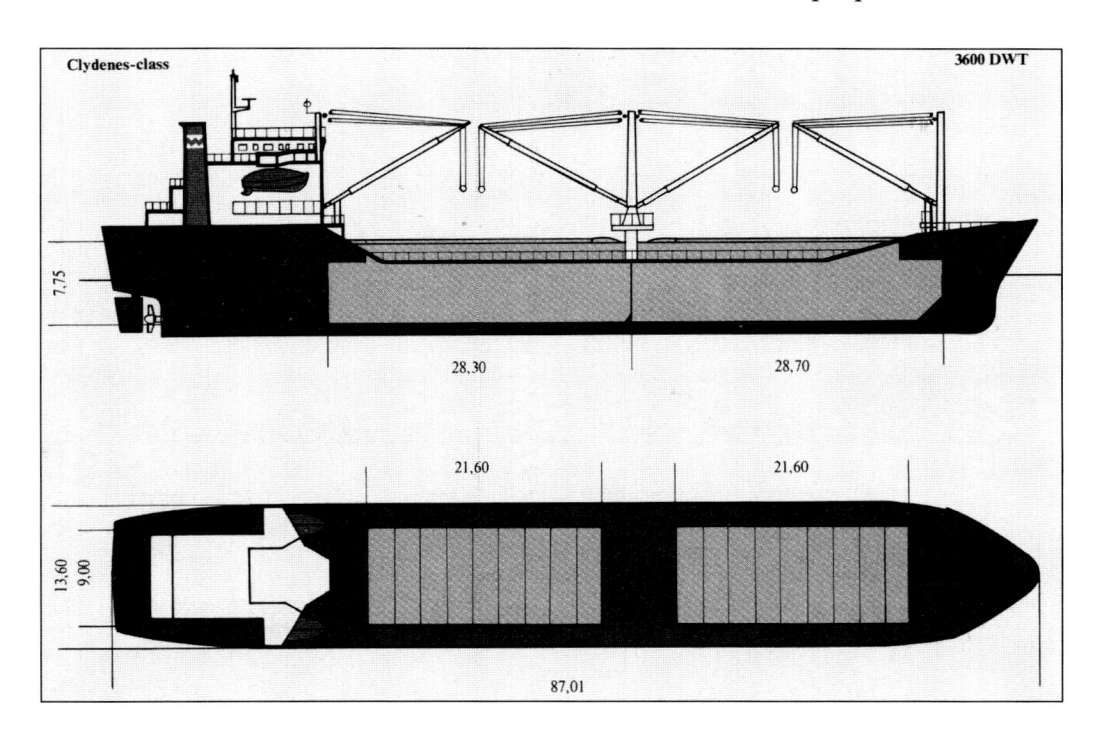

Ferguson Brother (Port Glasgow) Ltd., Port Glasgow.

CLARKNES (Yd. No. 474)

CLYDENES (Yd. No. 475) subcontracted to Scotts Shipbuilding Company Ltd., Greenock as their (Yd. No. 748)

CANCELLED	(Yd. No. 476) - **CHARTNES** proposed.
CANCELLED	(Yd. No. 477) - **CLEARNES** proposed.

213

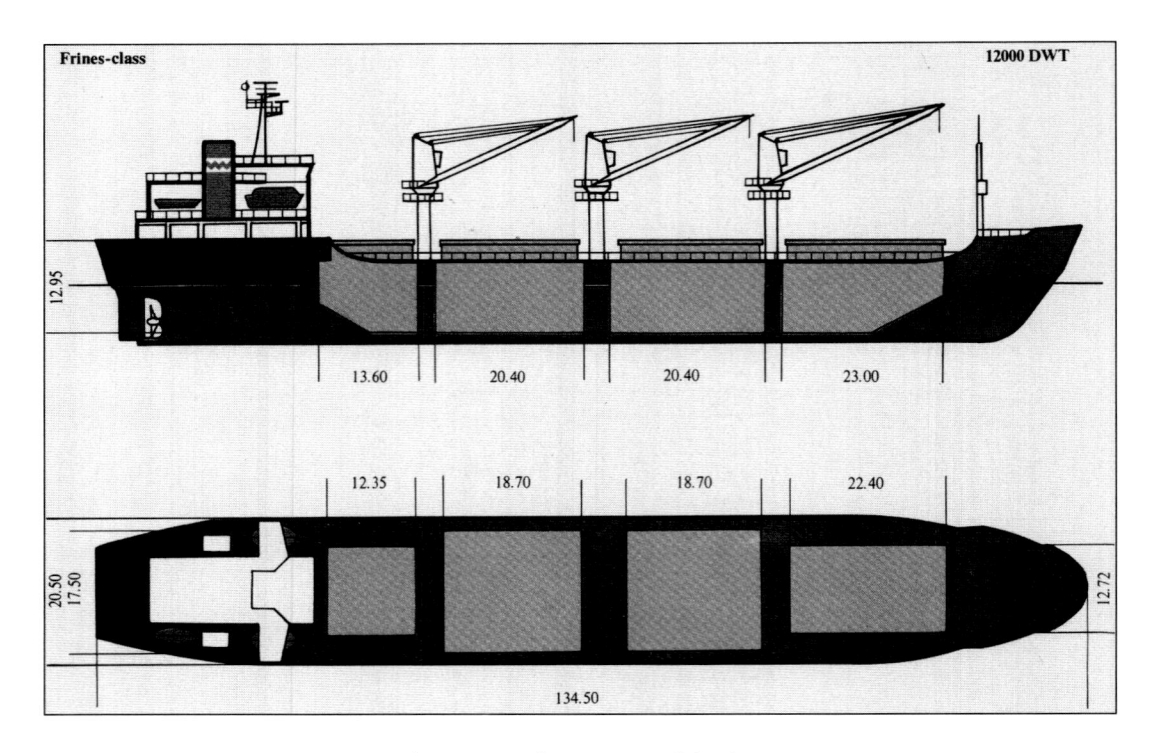

Nippon Kokan KK, Shimizu.

FRINES (Yd. No. 371)
FINNSNES (Yd. No. 372)

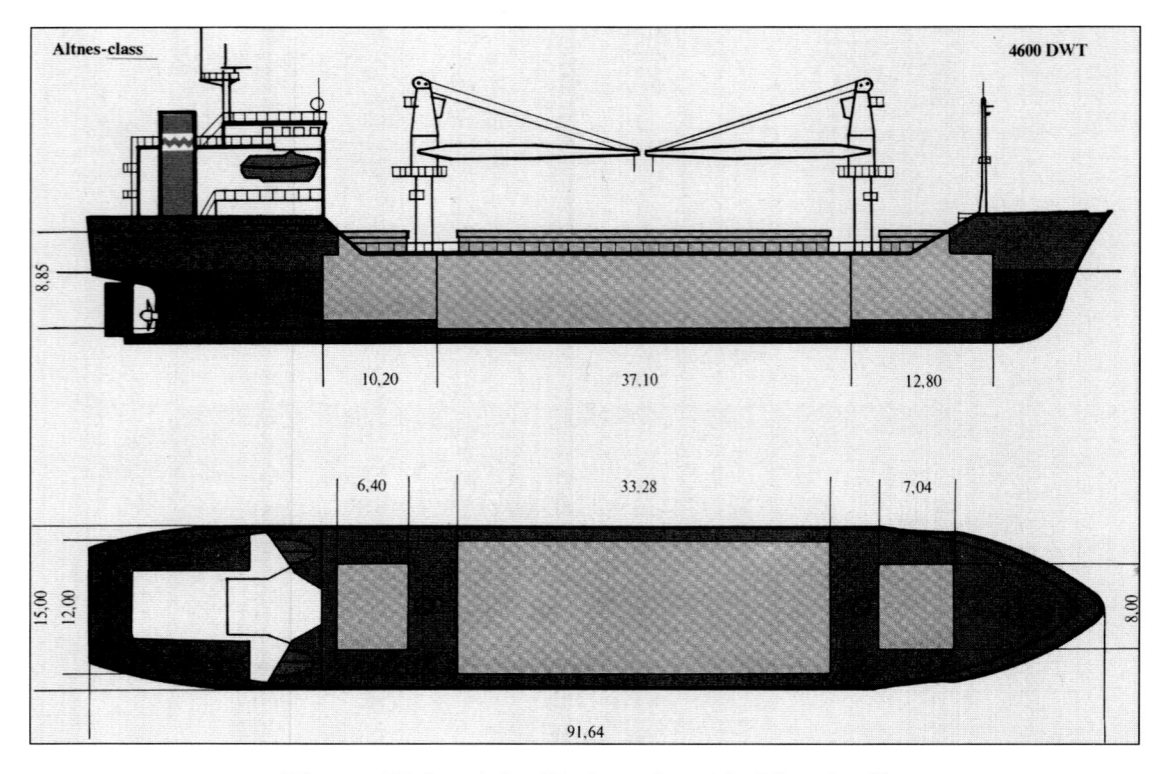

Kleven Mekaniske Verksteder AS, Ulsteinvik

ALTNES (Yd. No. 32)
VIGSNES (Yd. No. 33)

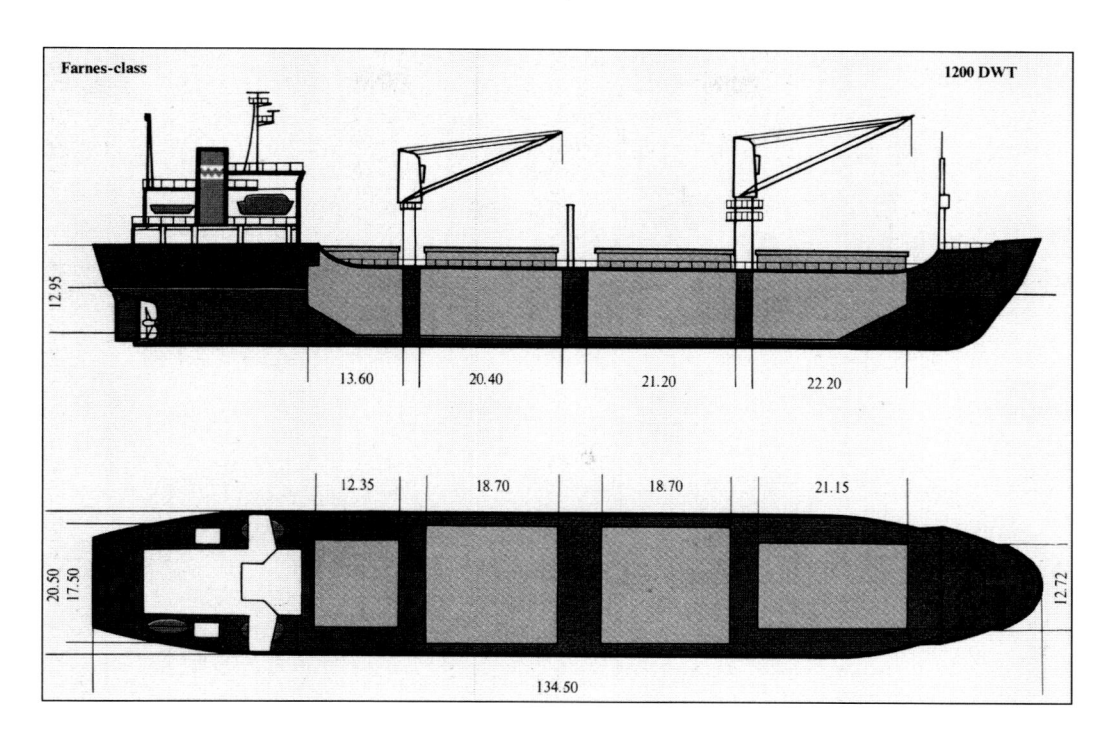

Nippon Kokan KK, Shimizu.

FARNES (Yd. No. 379)
FIRMNES (Yd. No. 380)

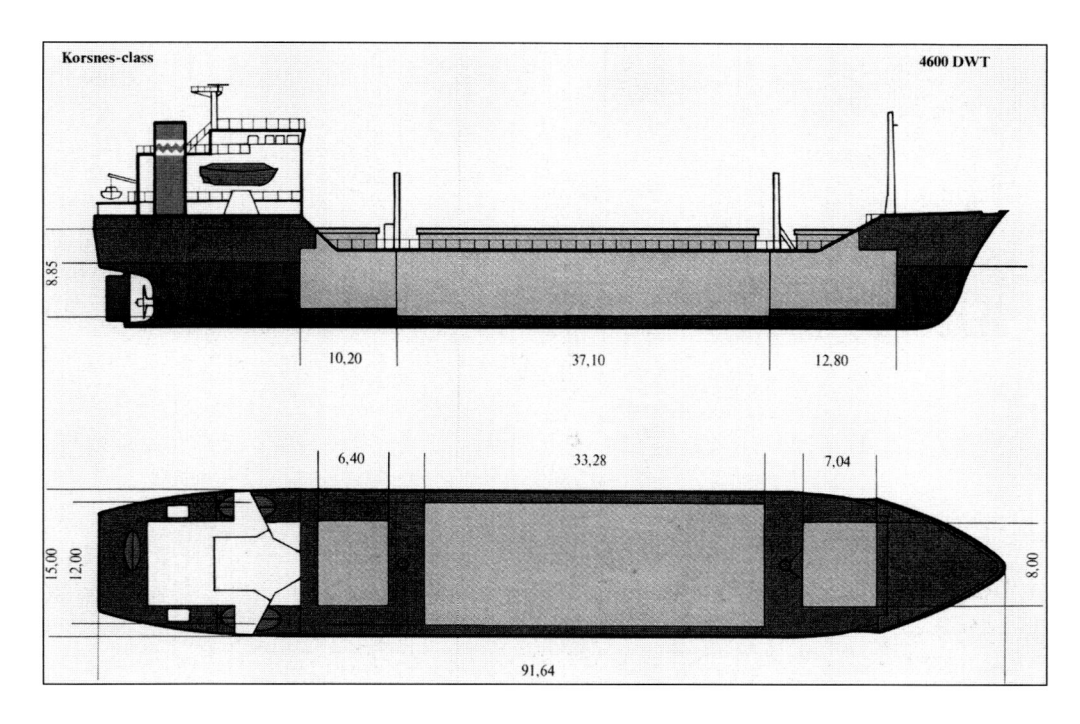

Storviks Mekaniske Verksteder AS, Kristiansand.

KORSNES (Yd. No. 90)
GARNES (Yd. No. 91)
RAKNES (Yd. No. 92)

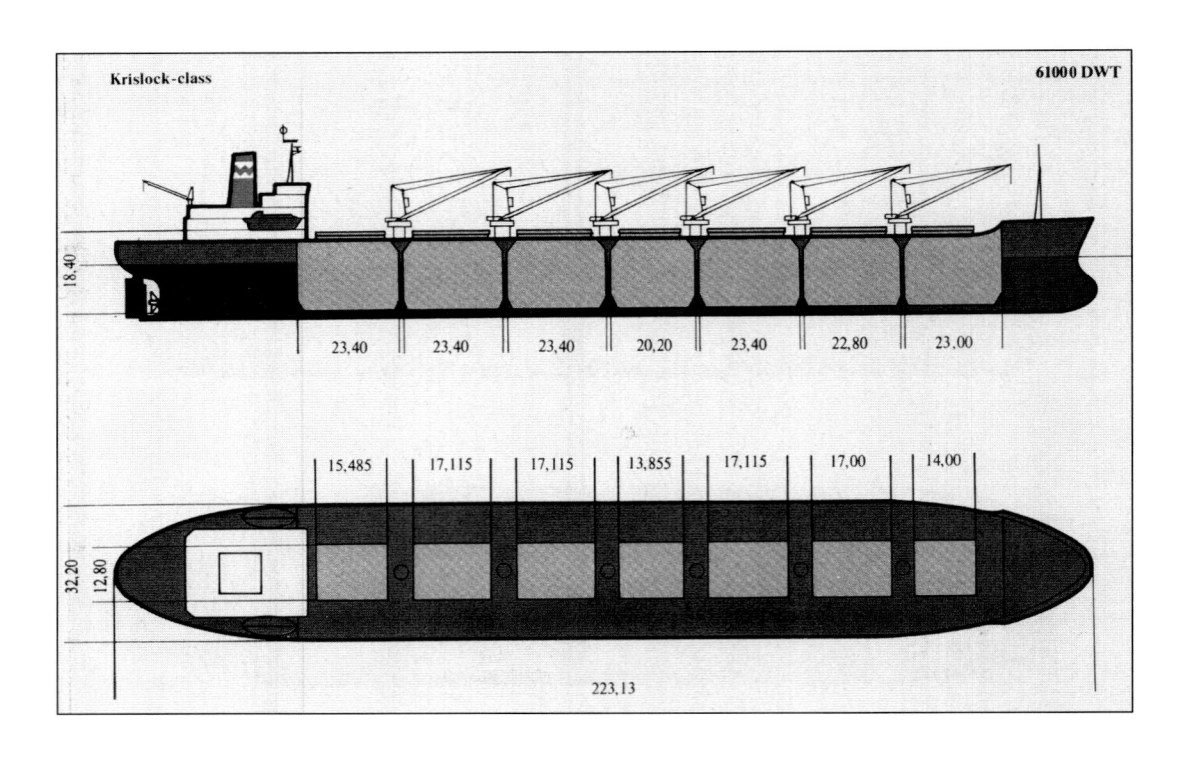

Koyo Dockyard Company Ltd., Mihara

KRISLOCK	(Yd. No. 1013)
CANCELLED	(Yd. No. 1014)

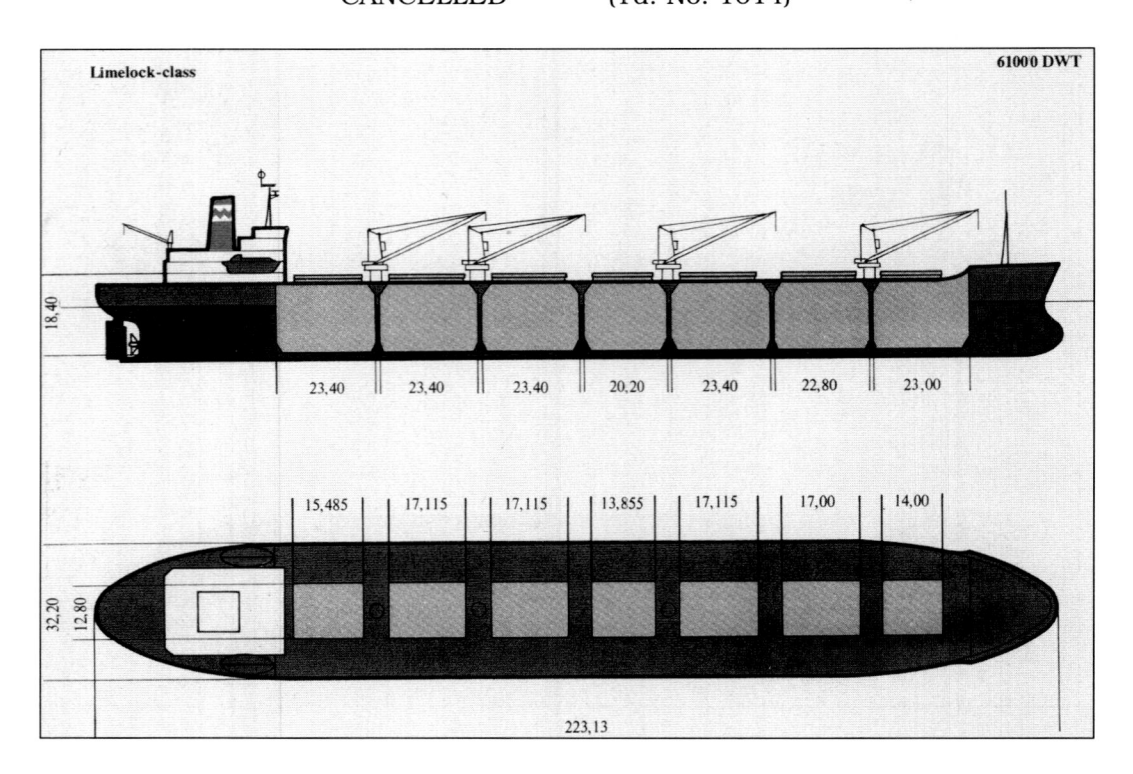

Koyo Dockyard Company Ltd., Mihara

LIMELOCK	(Yd. No. 1015)
NORSELOCK	(Yd. No. 1025)
CANCELLED	(Yd. No. 1026)

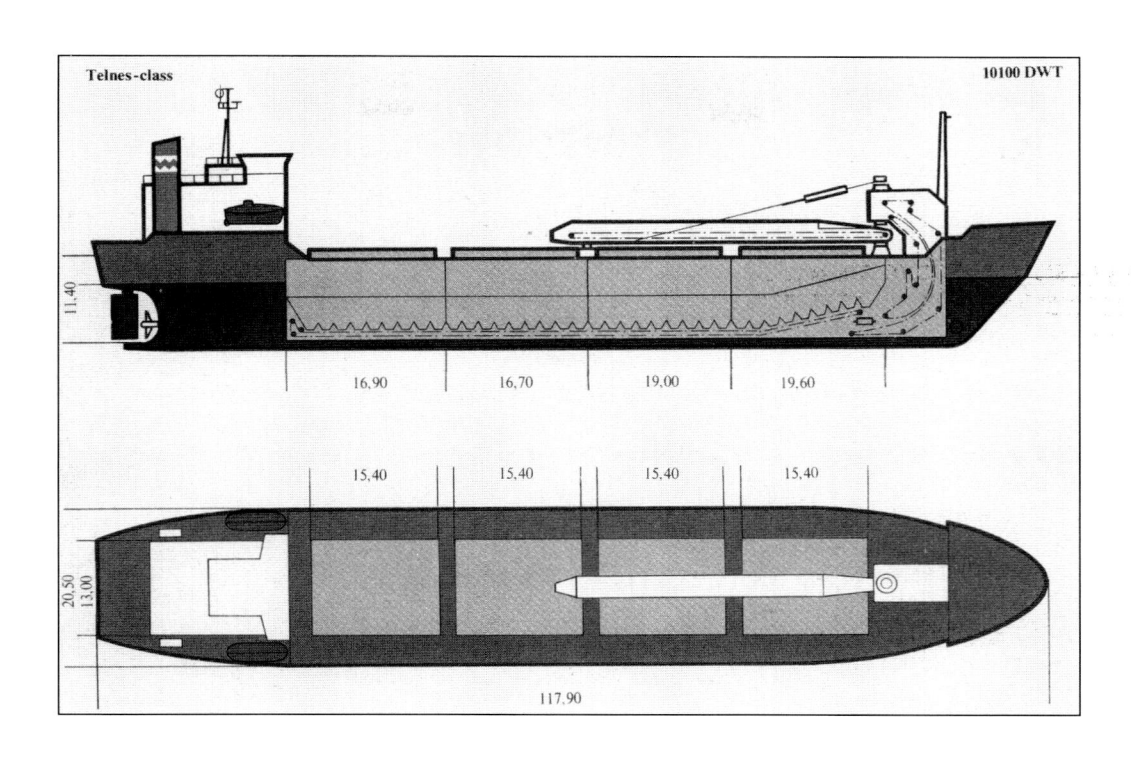

Kleven Mekaniske Verksteder AS, Ulsteinvik

TELNES (Yd. No. 38)
TINNES (Yd. No. 39)

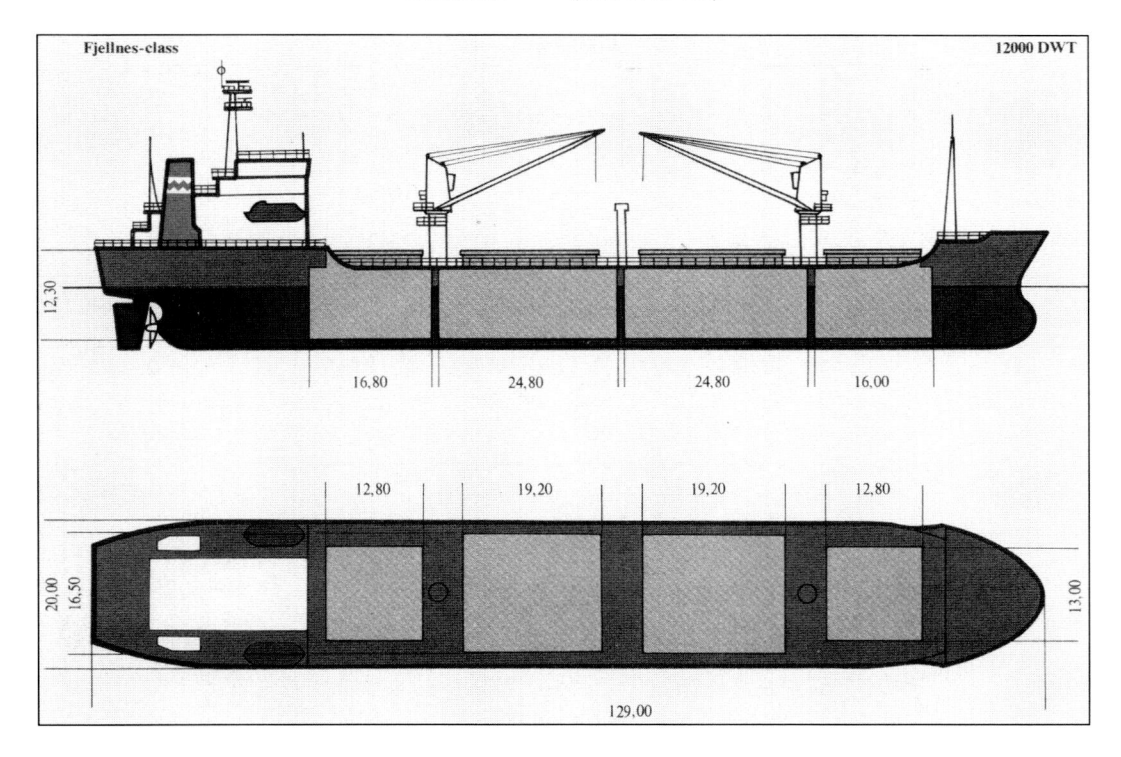

Miho Zosensho KK, Shimizu.

FJELLNES (Yd. No. 1209)
FOSSNES (Yd. No. 1210)
FALKNES (Yd. No. 1211)
FJORDNES (Yd. No. 1212)

Bibliography

Dick & Kentwell **Sold East**
Rohwer, Jurgen, **Axis Submarine Successes 1939-1945**

Other publications and periodicals consulted:

Fairplay, Lloyd's Casualty Returns, Lloyd's Confidential Indices, Lloyd's Register of Shipping – register books for the appropriate period, Lloyd's Register of Shipping - shipbuilding records, Lloyd's Register of Shipping - wreck books, Marine News, journal of the World Ship Society, Mercantile Navy Lists, The Motor Ship, Jebsen Bladet (Company house magazine), Jebsens marketing literature, Shipbuilding & Shipping Record.

Key to Funnels On Back Cover

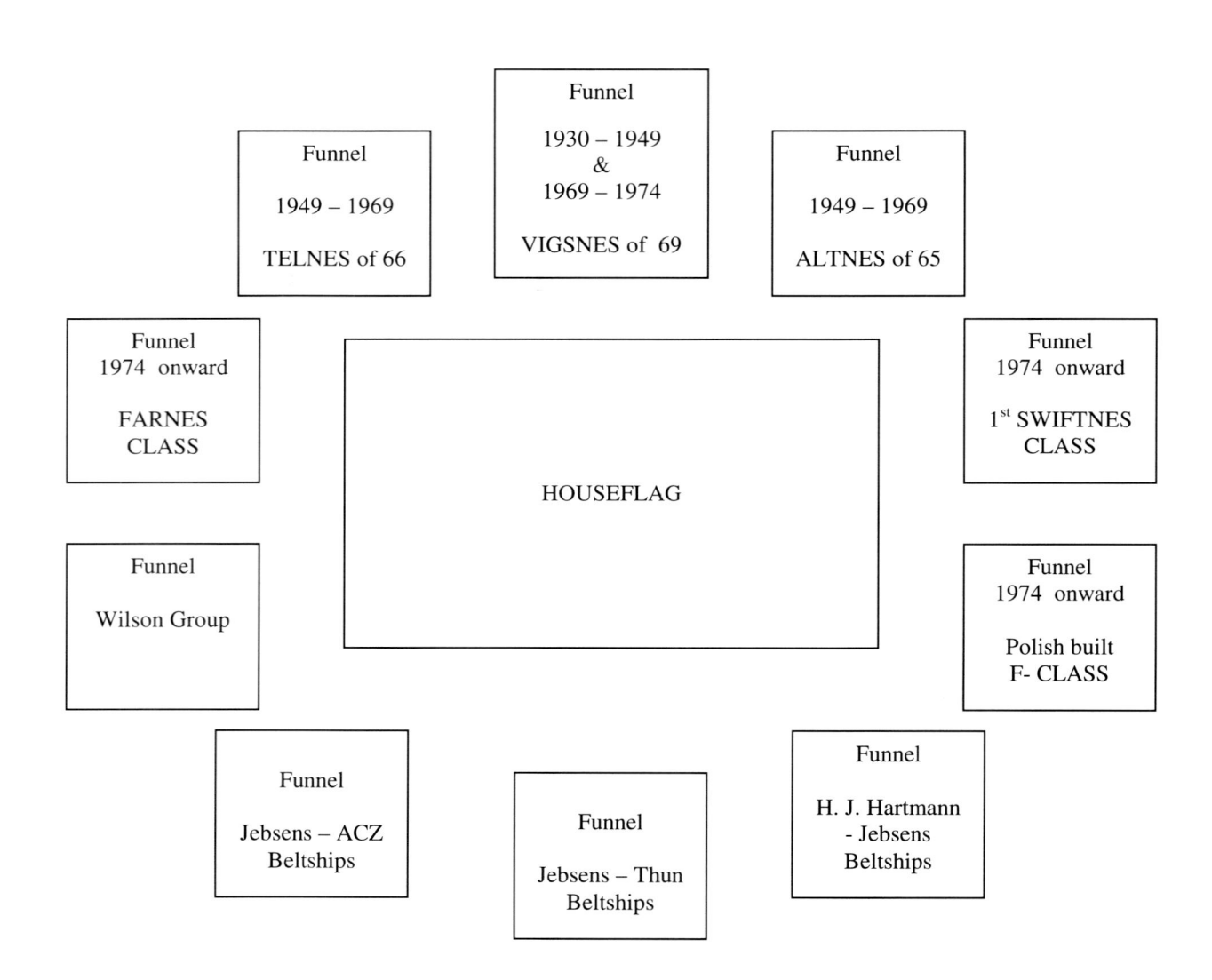

	Funnel 1930 – 1949 & 1969 – 1974 VIGSNES of 69	
Funnel 1949 – 1969 TELNES of 66		Funnel 1949 – 1969 ALTNES of 65
Funnel 1974 onward FARNES CLASS	HOUSEFLAG	Funnel 1974 onward 1st SWIFTNES CLASS
Funnel Wilson Group		Funnel 1974 onward Polish built F- CLASS
Funnel Jebsens – ACZ Beltships	Funnel Jebsens – Thun Beltships	Funnel H. J. Hartmann - Jebsens Beltships

Ship Index

BOLD TYPE defines names of vessel during Company involvement. Non-bold defines names before and / or after Company involvement. The number indicates the page containing the relevant entry.

A

Abdul Razaak Sanusi 187
ABOITIZ SUPERCONCARRIER 1 140
Adria Verde 193
Agios Vissarion 63
Ahmad S 111
AKRANES 108
Al Mujeer 92
ALADDIN 83
Albaforth 52
Alberto Dormio 71
ALCEM GALACA 171
ALCEM LUGAIT 171
Aldora 57
Alessandra 205
Alexander 72
Alexander I 92
Alexandros S 100
ALEXIS 157
Algosea 60
ALI BABA 106
ALL STATE 189
Ally II 86
Alpha 92
ALTNES (1) 39
ALTNES (2) 45
ALTNES (3) 98
Alycia 95
Amalia 88
Amalija 53
Amatista 90
Amir Ahmad 79
An Anne 44
Anis 47
Antonis 119
Aphrodite 149
Apiliotis 45
Apisara Naree 205
Aquila 61
Arcadia Progress 72
Arctic Sky 166
Argo Island 190
Argo Spray 60
Argoclyde 55
Argotweed 58
Aristi 143
Aristi D 143
Arklow Bridge 177
Arklow Dawn 114
Arklow Day 110
Artem 206
Artne 206
ARTNES 206
Aspen Arrow 127
Asterix 106
Astra 63
Atlanta 192
Atlantic Lord 147
ATLANTIC PATROLLER 183
ATLANTIC PIONEER 182
ATLANTIC POWER 184
ATLANTIC PRIDE .. 183
Auckland 193
AUN (1) 38
AUN (2) 40
Ayane 143

B

Bago 45
BAKNES 55
Balsa 117
Bamia 116
Banak 116
Barkald 122
BARKNES 96
BARRA HEAD 149
Barranquilla 179
BAUGNES 54
BAYNES (1) 50
BAYNES (2) 80
BAYNES (3) 181
Bayshore 181
BEAGLE 108
Beatrice 47
Beaumont 179
BEAVER 125
BECKNES 94
Bekir Kalkavan 73
BELLNES (1) 52
BELLNES (2) 75
BERGNES (1) 71
BERGNES (2) 85
BERGNES (3) 151
BERNES (1) 44
BERNES (2) 67
BERNES (3) 179
BESSNES 90
Bibi M 123
Big George 201
BINSNES (1) 46
BINSNES (2) 58
BINSNES (3) 87
BINSNES (4) 116
BIRKNES (1) 49
BIRKNES (2) 71
BIRKNES (3) 151
BIRKNES (4) 180
BLIDNES 61
Boem 67
BOLNES (1) 48
BOLNES (2) 82
BOLNES (3) 116
Bomin 43
Boreal 171
BOREALNES 171
BORGNES (1) 51
BORGNES (2) 88
Bosut 50
Bounty 187
Branda 190
BRAVENES (1) 69
BRAVENES (2) 72
Brazilian Confidence 130
Brenda 54
BRIMNES (1) 44
BRIMNES (2) 64
BRIMNES (3) 179
BRINKNES (1) 57
BRINKNES (2) 160
BRINKNES (3) 175
BRISKNES (1) 61
BRISKNES (2) 95
BROOKNES (1) 59
BROOKNES (2) 86
BROOKNES (3) 179
Brother Star 61
BRUNES (1) 44
BRUNES (2) 53

BRUNES (3) 87	Danie 187	**FAIRNES** 144
BRUNES (4) 178	Demi Green 115	**FALKNES (1)** 68
Bruni 133	Denizati 72	**FALKNES (2)** 113
Brunto 133	Dennis Carrier 58	**FALKNES (3)** 165
BRUNTO 159	Dewi Umayi 106	Fanling 111
BULKNES (1) 56	Diane Green 110	**FARNES** 99
BULKNES (2) 143	Dimitrios 54	**FASTNES** 137
Bussara Naree 206	Dixie 76	Fei Cui Hai 69
	Dneproges 87	Fenix 128
C	Dollart 141	Feyza 124
C. Aydin 133	Don Antonio 92	Fidility Trust 55
Calatagan 124	**DON ANTONIO**	**FIDUCIA (1)** 55, 186
Callian S 71	**BOTELHO** 91	**FIDUCIA (2)** 105
Capitaine Cook II ... 97	Dragonland 71	**FINNSNES** 97
Captain Daniel 80	Drawa 204	Fione 187
Captain Frank 57	**DUBROVNIK** 200	**FIRMNES** 101
Captain Pandelis S.	Dyvi Oceanic 128	First Flight 187
Lyras 49		**FITNES** 138
Caribbean Dreams 44	**E**	**FJELLNES (1)** 88
Carpo 39	**EAGLE** 171	**FJELLNES (2)** 110
Castor 110	**EASTERN ALLIANCE**	**FJORDNES (1)** 65
CCNI Valparaiso ... 192	 108	**FJORDNES (2)** 115
Cecilia M 160	Ecuador 68	**FJORDNES (3)** 203
Celtic Spirit 142	**EDCO** 104	**FONDNES** 204
Cem K 99	**EEMNES** 139	**FONNES (1)** 62
Cemre II 150	Eemsborg 152	**FONNES (2)** 97
Chahaya Sejati 189	Efthalia 61	Forest Patroller 183
Chang Hai 51	Eiffel 193	Formosabulk No. 3
Chang Tong 143	**EL ARISH** 103	 110
Charlie B 76	El Arish – El Tor ... 105	Fortune 48
Chian Mariner 71	**EL TOR** 105	**FOSSNES (1)** 89
China Progress 120	El-Arish 105	**FOSSNES (2)** 110
Chios Captain 58	Elianna 167	**FOSSNES (3)** 162
Chios Pilot 55	Elpida 47	Fotinoula 71
Christos 94	Elpida I 47	**FRAMNES** 93
CIC Breves 205	Elpis 42, 97, 115	Francesca B 77
Ciclope 131	Elsa Oldendorff 193	Francoli 192
Cikola 54	Eltem 58	**FREDERIKE**
City Of Dubrovnik 201	Emcol Carrier 192	**OLDENDORFF** 173
CLARKNES 94	Emerald Producer 107	**FREENES** 144
CLYDENES (1) 92	**ENTERPRISE** 167	**FRIBORG** 186
CLYDENES (2) **177**	**EOS** 152	**FRIBOURG** 112
Cobo Bay 143	Ereaga 201	Friendship 191
Comoros 94	Eurobulker 68	**FRINES (1)** 71
CONDOR 171	Europa Point 65	**FRINES (2)** 96
Cova Da Iria 189	European 75	Fritre 71
CSAV Rapel 193	European I 75	**FROMNES** 171
	EWL Colombia 193	**FULLNES** 144
D	Excellus 57	**FURUNES (1)** 64
Daisy Green 114	Express 167	**FURUNES (2)** 143
Dakis 1 48	Express Rebel 143	
Dan Baroness 83		**G**
Dan Countess 85	**F**	Galatic Dolphin 92
Dania Marine 103	Faethon 119	**GALLIC FJORD** 191
		GALLIC MINCH 188
		GALLIC STREAM 188
		GALLIC WAVE 189

Gardsky 142
GARNES (1) 37
GARNES (2) 39
GARNES (3) 47
GARNES (4) 104
Gauss F 191
GENERAL AGUINALDO 111
GENERAL AQUINO 140
GENERAL BONIFACIO 139
GENERAL CAMPOS 137
GENERAL CAPINPIN 111
GENERAL CRUZ (1) 135
GENERAL CRUZ (2) 149
GENERAL DELGADO 144
GENERAL DUQUE . 136
GENERAL ESTRELLA 139
GENERAL FITNES . 138
GENERAL GARCIA 140
GENERAL HIZON ... 124
GENERAL JACINTO 138
GENERAL LACUNA 125
GENERAL LAPUS ... 139
GENERAL LIM (1) .. 105
GENERAL LIM (2) .. 138
GENERAL LIM (3) .. 142
GENERAL LUKBAN 139
GENERAL LUNA (1) 107
GENERAL LUNA (2) 137
GENERAL MALVAR 118
GENERAL MASCARDO (1) ... 118
GENERAL MASCARDO (2) ... 142
GENERAL MATA 130
GENERAL MOJICA 135
GENERAL PAPA 141
GENERAL PERALTA 141
GENERAL RICARTE 138
GENERAL ROMULO 144
GENERAL ROXAS (1) 111
GENERAL ROXAS (2) 139
GENERAL SANTOS 123
GENERAL SEGUNDO 111
GENERAL TINIO 125
GENERAL TIRONA 144
GENERAL VALDEZ 114
GENERAL VALERIANO 140
GENERAL VARGAS 133
GENERAL VILLA (1) 139
GENERAL VILLA (2) 144
Geneva I 65
Georgios 67
Georgios I 67
Georgios X. II 92
Georgios XII 92
Gini I 65
Giorgos 125
Glentrool 189
Glory Bon 142
Goa I 150
Gold I 48
Granton 47
GRATIA 55, 187
Great Sky 109
Grumant 123
Guang Shun 67

H

Hai Neng 129
Hai Nun 129
Handy Ocean 143
Hatice C 196
Haukur 196
Havtjeld 120
HAWK 171
Hea 111
HERNES 156
HITTEEN 191
Hood Head 148
HOOK HEAD 153
HORDNES 165
Huaxinghai 120
Humanitas 43
HUSNES 156
HVALNES 195
Hvalvik 195

I

Ibiza 63
Icl Raja Mahendra 125
Iersezee 195
Ifigeneia 67
Ikan Bilis 136
Ina 204
Industrial Trader 55
Ingapirca 49
Ioannis A. P. 117
Irenes Blessing 72
Iron Capricorn 72
IRON STURT 176
Isabela B 192
Isidora 68
ISNES (1) 89
ISNES (2) 141
ISNES (3) 172

J

Jade Orient 86
Jade Pacific 90
Jamal 191
Janet C 61
Jeannie III 90
JEBSEN AUCKLAND 193
JEBSEN NAPIER 131
JEBSEN SOUTHLAND 192
JEBSEN TAURANGA 128
JEBSEN TIMARU ... 134
Jeg Fortune 65
JENNES 56
Jin Bin 147
Jing Hai 50
John C. Helmsing. 187
John Hope 47
John P 117
Jovian Liberty 124

K

Kaap Hoorn 195
Kagarlyk 95
Kahlberg 37
Kaliope 204
Kamagong 149
Kampos 62
Kamtin 115
Kanev 88
Kapetan Antonis 57
KAPITAN DROBININ 160
Kappa Power 48
Kaprije 51
Kaptan Yusuf Kalkavan 52
Karadeniz S 143
Karagol 88
KARAMEH 192
KARI ARNHILD 158

Karin S 192	Lord Curzon 116	Mica 43
Karla D 195	**LORD HINTON** 147	Michael S 96
Karosel 96	Lord Jellicoe 116	Midas 82
Karterado 39	LT Verde 193	Midiboy 57
Kathy C 54	Lucillia 80	Midigirl 56
Kian An 44	Lucky Arrow 99	Mighty Michalis 201
Kieldrecht 143	Lucky Star II 39	Mikhail Stelmakh ... 96
Kindly 82	**LUGANO** 125	**MILLENNIUM**
Kingfisher 70	**LUIS ABOITIZ** 165	**DRAGON** 172
Klea 69	Luningning 123	**MILLENNIUM EAGLE**
Koktebel 87	Lux Warrior 201	 171
Korosten 96	Lydia P 42	**MILLENNIUM TIGER**
KORSNES (1) 37		 171
KORSNES (2) 41	**M**	Million Trader 142
KORSNES (3) 47	Maersk Semakau . 106	Milos A 45
KORSNES (4) 102	Maersk Senang 109	Miltiadis M 88
KRISLOCK 106	Maersk Seraya 109	Mina 45
KVITNES 174	Mahogany 150	Minories Luck 54
Kyma 45	**MALMNES** 156	Misan 189
	Mambo 195	Monac 63
L	**MANILA BRAVE** 125	Monach 63
Lady Fox 97	**MANILA HOPE** 118	Monarch 110
Lady Lory 96	**MANILA PACIFIC** ... 109	Montarik 67
Lady V 181	**MANILA PEACE** 118	**MORNES (1)** 63
LAETITIA 55, 187	**MANILA SPIRIT** 130	**MORNES (2)** 153
LAKENES 119	**MANILA SUCCESS** . 136	**MOXNES** 155
LANGENES 167	Manos Save 61	Mufaddal 92
LANGNES 124	Mar Grande 59	Myrrinella 39
LANKA AMILA 151	Marcos M. F 44	
LANKA ARUNA 151	Margherita 38	**N**
LANKA ASITHA 151	Maria Dormio 59	Neva II 65
Lapis 55	Maria Jose 49	**NEW ZEALAND**
LAURA HELENA (1) 195	Maria Lemos 50	**ALLIANCE** 111
LAURA HELENA (2) 202	Marimar 98	Nicolaos G 41
LEKNES (1) 45	Marina Di Alimuri . 67	Nida 201
LEKNES (2) 51	Marina Di Equa 65	**NIDANES** 201
LEKNES (3) 202	Marina I 71	Nikkei Central 143
Leodas 82	Maris 72	Nomadic Dixie 76
LESLIE GAULT 190	**MARMON** 157	**NORDANHAV** 165
Leszek G 191	Maruf 191	Norden 134
Lia 115	**MARY ANDERSON** . 190	Nordheide 39
Liana 38	Marylander 190	Nordlore 43
LIDAN 153	Matumba II 76	**NORDNES** 178
Lidanes 153	Mauranger 41	**NORNES** 163
LIMELOCK 109	Mavroudis 48	**NORSELOCK** 109
Linden 133	Med General 68	**NORTHERN LAKENES**
LINDNES (1) 123	Med Transporter 71	 170
LINDNES (2) 172	Megawave 178	**NORTHERN LANGNES**
LINITO 172	Megoni 97	 168
Linz 195	Meleni 87	**NORTHERN LARSNES**
Livanita 90	Meltem 58	.... 168, 169
LOCKNES 123	Meltem G 58	**NORTHERN LAUNES**
Lofou 195	Merk 81	.... 168, 169
LOFTNES 120	Merkur 81	**NORTHERN LESNES**
Lord Byron 116		 162
LORD CITRINE 146		

NORTHERN LIFTNES 165
NORTHERN LINANES 160
NORTHERN LINDNES 169, 170
NORTHERN LOFTNES 161
NORTHERN LOKNES 168
NORTHERN LURNES 169, 170
Northern Producer 107
Nortroll 106

O

Ocean Baroness 84
Ocean Countess 85
Ocean Giant 180
Ocean Guard 182
Ocean Jay 81
Ocean Land 142
Ocean Leader 179
Ocean Scarlet 159
Ocean Sovereign 48
Ocean Spring 182
Ocean Star 85
Ocean Wood 71
Oceanic Land 123
Odra 199
ODRANES 199
Orastar 198
Osman Mete 76
OSTANHAV 154

P

PACNORSE 1 101
Pandesia 109
Panoria 110
Pantelis P 116
Patria 37
Pax 39
PEARL LUCK 152
PEARL PROSPERITY 151
Penelope 204
Peregrine II 102
Philippine Jay 71
PHILIPPINE KAMIA 124
Pietro 45
Pilion 125
Point Fortune 179
Pointe Du Minou .. 187

Polikos 69
Polydefkis 114
Primosten 66
Protagonist II 143
Proteus 64
Puerto Plata 60
Pyotr Smorodin 95

R

RADNES 82
RAFNES 81
RAKNES (1) 43
RAKNES (2) 50
RAKNES (3) 105
Ramble Cloud 142
RAMNES (1) 74
RAMNES (2) 163
RAMON ABOITIZ 159
Randal 42
Rangelock 135
Red Sky 48
Red Sky Bolivia 48
REFSNES 73, 173
Rega 162
Regal Star 124
REKSNES 90
RENKO 144
Riambel 125
RIKNES 79
RINGNES 76
RISNES (1) 74
RISNES (2) 152
ROCKNES 77
ROCKNES (2) 175
ROGNES 80
Rogoznica 53
ROLLNES 78
Rondane 193
Roniz 46
RONNES 77
RORA HEAD 149
ROSSNES 73

S

SAINT BREVIN 117
SAINT BRICE 117
SAINT JAMES 118
SAINT JEAN 118
Saloos 120
SALTNES (1) 65
SALTNES (2) 130
SALTNES (3) 139
SALTNES (4) 205
Salvador 65
Salvinia 87
Samba 195

SANDNES (1) 136
SANDNES (2) 184
SANDNES (3) 176
Santa Isabela 114
SARINE 112
Sarine 2 110
Satya Padam 52
SATYA PADAM 187
Sauniere 60
SAVA HILL 198
SAVA LAKE 196
SAVA OCEAN 202
SAVA RIVER 196
SAVA STAR 198
Sea Fury 44
Seaboard Chile II .. 184
Seaboard Pioneer . 182
Seaboard Power 184
Seaboard Rover 184
Seaboard Valparaiso 193
SEALNES (1) 68
SEALNES (2) 128
Seas Eiffel 193
Seatrader 42
Seattle 185
SELNES 103
SHARPNES (1) 69
SHARPNES (2) 126
SHEERNES 156
Shun Ying 88
Sider Bay 147
Sider Tide 205
Sider Wind 77
Silver Yang 136
Silverclyde 55
Silverdon 69
Silverforth 52
Silvertweed 58
SINBAD 84
SINBAD SAXON 103
SIR CHARLES PARSONS 146
SIRNES 182
Socofl Star 205
Socofl Tide 205
Socofl Trade 204
Socofl Trust 205
Socofl Wave 205
SOLNES (1) 206
Sotiris 48
SPLITTNES 175
SPRAYNES (1) 66
SPRAYNES (2) 122
SPRAYNES (3) 185
Spyros II 186